THE ILLUSTRATED PRACTICAL GUIDE TO
GARDENING
FOR SENIORS

THE ILLUSTRATED PRACTICAL GUIDE TO
GARDENING
FOR SENIORS

How to maintain a beautiful outside space with ease and safety in later years

ACCESSIBLE STEP-BY-STEP TECHNIQUES AND ADVICE, FROM PLANNING AND EQUIPMENT TO
PLANTING AND MAINTENANCE, WITH OVER 900 INSPIRATIONAL PLANS AND PHOTOGRAPHS

PATTY CASSIDY

With special photography by Mark Winwood

This edition is published by Lorenz Books, an imprint of Anness Publishing Ltd, Blaby Road, Wigston, Leicestershire LE18 4SE

info@anness.com
www.lorenzbooks.com;
www.annesspublishing.com

If you like the images in this book and would like to investigate using them for publishing, promotions or advertising, please visit our website www.practicalpictures.com

Publisher: Joanna Lorenz
Editorial director: Helen Sudell
Project editor: Emma Clegg
Designer: Andrew Barron
Special photography: Mark Winwood
Additional photography: Heather Hawksford and Lynn Keddie
Stylist: Penny Cooke
Illustrator: Liz Pepperell
Production controller: Wendy Lawson

ETHICAL TRADING POLICY

PUBLISHER'S NOTE

AUTHOR'S ACKNOWLEDGEMENTS

I deeply appreciate the many inspiring and gardening senior citizens with whom I have had the privilege to work. Their wisdom, memories and humor have taught me how aging can be full of grace.

I want to thank all of my horticultural therapy colleagues who generously shared their knowledge and creativity with me about working with seniors. Special recognition goes to Teresia Hazen, whose teaching and mentorship opened many new garden pathways for me, and to Melissa Bierman and Shari Katz for sharing their professional expertise.

To the Washington County Master Gardeners and particularly to Jerry Anderson, who had a hand in creating their amazing demonstration garden, for sharing his knowledge of tools that promote accessible and safe gardening for life – all my thanks and admiration.

Many friends and family have encouraged me in writing this book. Special thanks to Heather Hawksford for her wonderful photographs, and to Ann Frazier and Alice Turowski for opening their home gardens for photography.

A very special thanks to Emma Clegg at Anness Publishing for her patience, thoroughness and encouragement during the writing of this book.

Finally, not a page of this book could have been written without the constant support, cheerleading, and careful review that my husband, Gary Miranda, devoted to the project. I will be forever grateful for his steadfast encouragement and belief in me.

DEDICATION

For Michale who opened new garden gates for me, and for Gary, whose love and encouragement keeps me gardening

Though an old man,
I am but a young gardener.
Thomas Jefferson

CONTENTS

INTRODUCTION

I can't remember a time when I didn't garden. One of my earliest memories, in fact, is of planting a row of green bean seeds in a small patch of dirt while my mother hung out the washing. My mother was not much of a gardener, but she was as thrilled as I was when we later discovered the first small sighting of green pushing up through the soil, shaded by the clothes flapping on the line.

ABOVE *Tending a garden is a much-loved pastime and a way to stay healthy, happy and vigorous as we age.*

My current garden, in a residential neighbourhood in Portland, Oregon, is one that I still think of and refer to as "Mrs Marshall's garden", even though my husband and I have been the sole tenders of the plot for over a quarter of a century. I never met Mrs Marshall, who died in her 90s shortly before we bought her house, but over the years many older residents of the neighbourhood have stopped and told me their personal memories of Mrs Marshall and her endless hours working in the garden – always wearing her plaid wool tam atop her white hair. In her younger years she would hike into the nearby Cascade Mountains collecting alpine wildflowers and native plants. While those days of harvesting from the wild are over, every spring I get to witness her heritage of blooming yellow avalanche lilies (*Erythronium grandiflorum*) and several types of trillium. Perhaps when I turn 90 and wean myself from the labours of the garden, my name will be transplanted as a keeper of this garden – though for me, I suspect, it will always be Mrs Marshall's.

The chances are that you, too, have had at least one or two special gardens in your lifetime that you cared for, loved, and derived a great deal of joy from as you spent hours working the soil, growing the plants, and being literally in touch with nature. Whether as humble as the little plot where I first planted beans or as ample as Mrs Marshall's garden, these places keep us connected with the seasons and with the life cycles of all sorts of living things, including ourselves.

From my own experience as a senior gardener and my work as a horticultural therapist with other seniors, I've come to appreciate that these intangible benefits of gardening are not ones that we have to forfeit because of age, though we may indeed have to learn to adapt our spaces, our tools and our techniques to accommodate changing circumstances. I've also noticed, in my work as a volunteer master gardener, that senior gardeners share certain concerns in common and ask similar or identical questions about how to deal with those concerns. Hence this book is written partly to address some of these recurring questions. Mainly, however, it is written in the hope that it will provide an uplifting and positive view of the normal ageing process and encourage all seniors, no matter what environment they find themselves in, to get, or stay, involved with the wonderful and life-giving activity of gardening.

WHO IS A SENIOR GARDENER?

As the title indicates, this book is intended for senior gardeners. I use the term 'seniors' because I prefer it to 'the elderly' or some of the more euphemistic epithets that society has devised to tip-toe around the obvious fact that some of us are not as young as we used to be.

I'm aware that the question of who qualifies as a 'senior' is not so straightforward. It could be defined as someone who is approaching, or beyond, the age at which people retire, though even this is problematic. In the United States, for example, the American Association of Retired Persons allows membership at age 50, while the standard retirement age is 65.

LEFT *Bringing on newly planted seedlings is the start of the gardening journey, but each and every stage has its own pleasures.*

RIGHT *Raised beds and wide, even pathways are two practical approaches for gardens used by older people.*

RIGHT *Energy and motivation are more important than youth when it comes to maintaining a garden.*

Also, many people choose or are compelled by financial reasons to work well beyond this age. Rather than pick an arbitrary number, therefore, I prefer to think of seniors as those of us who have the maturity and wisdom to recognize that we will have to make compromises and adjustments if we want to continue doing the things we love to do – in this case, gardening. If you are reading this book, you have probably self-selected yourself or someone close to you as a member of this group, and that's fine with me.

In keeping with this notion of seniors, the book is designed to address the kinds of compromises and adjustments that ageing often demands, the main ones having to do with our garden

BELOW *Companionship in a garden enhances the experience – and also has the benefit of lessening the work!*

environment and our health or energy level. Retirement often means more time to work in the garden and less energy to do it, and balancing the two is one of the most common challenges that seniors have to deal with. The often heard "I just can't keep up with it" doesn't have to mean that one has to stop gardening, but it may well mean that one has to reduce one's gardening chores, either by getting outside help, or by re-designing one's gardening space or adopting new techniques and tools. For those of you in this group, I'll be suggesting exercises for getting your body ready for garden tasks and ways to moderate your pace so you don't get worn out.

For those moving from a house and garden to some other living situation, continuing gardening will necessarily entail re-thinking possibilities, though this needn't be a negative prospect. Leaving the family home and moving to a smaller set-up such as an apartment, condo or community residence can open up a new world of gardening. I'll be showing you how using containers, growing plants vertically and being more mindful about the seasonal features of plant choices makes gardening an adventure and an on-going learning experience.

Some of you may be mainly concerned with providing gardening opportunities for loved ones or other seniors who are no longer able to actively garden. This group might include children whose parents are living in nursing-care facilities, staff members who care for seniors in such communities or landscape architects charged with designing them. For people helping their senior parents make the transition from the family home to an appropriate residential community, I'll be suggesting questions to ask and features to look for, especially in terms of easy access to the outdoors and the availability of regular and on-going gardening activities.

Finally, changes and transitions to new places, routines and people can be stressful. Understanding strategies that helped you cope with past unsettling events will come into play as you face new beginnings. For many of us, gardening can ease us into meditative states that calm our anxieties and be a physical outlet for pent-up energy. The benefits we derive from gardening – physical, emotional, intellectual and social – tell us that we are engaging in activities that enrich our sense of well-being.

RIGHT *Gardens can provide present delights and trigger pleasant memories.*

FAR RIGHT *Stay creative as you fill old tubs or kettles with your favourite flowers, herbs and cascading plants.*

Finding your way around

There is no single or right way to use this book. If you want to read it chapter by chapter, you should feel free to do so, though I also hope that each chapter can stand alone. While the table of contents may be somewhat self-explanatory, a few words about the book's organization might prove helpful.

In the opening section, called Your Garden Environment, I discuss the broad scope of living situations that senior gardeners might find themselves in, from a house with a garden or an apartment or condo, to various kinds of community residences. Though the content may often overlap, this allows you to literally 'ground' yourself by starting with the environment that relates to your circumstances.

The next section, Making Decisions About Your Garden, is intended as an aid to assessing your options and

ABOVE *Raised beds made from rustic materials create interesting spaces for flowers and vegetables.*

planning your strategies. It includes practical considerations, such as the garden's level of maintenance and your personal level of health, but also aesthetic considerations such as the visual and sensory appeal of the various plants and options available.

Taking care of yourself is a number-one priority, and Staying Safe and Sound provides tips on how to prepare yourself physically for your gardening chores and to execute them in ways that keep you mindful of wise pacing and resting. I describe some simple warm-up and stretching exercises and advise on appropriate clothing.

One of the most efficient ways to ensure that you keep gardening into your later years is to take advantage of the many new and ergonomically improved gardening tools to adapt your tried-and-true favourites to your changing needs. The Equipment and Techniques section is intended to help you make the right tool and technique choices for everything from weeding and transporting to harvesting, watering and tidying up.

The section on Types of Gardens gives you ideas for simple, yet satisfying, projects for different kinds of gardens – those with flowers, vegetables, herbs,

fruits, vertical beds, raised beds and patios, as well as indoor gardens. From creating a herb garden to having a few houseplants on a windowsill, each idea is illustrated and the plants are identified. Mix and match ideas and plants as you reflect on the climate and environment in which you live.

Finally, the Plant Directory categorizes plants by the light exposure they need to survive and thrive. Within each category the plants are listed alphabetically by their Latin name and the focus is on plants that are low-maintenance, offer several seasons of botanical interest and can stimulate several senses. Use this section as a reference for the plants mentioned throughout or simply browse through it to get ideas.

As you progress through the book, let the ideas and illustrations guide, motivate and inspire you, but don't let them limit you. Like your clothes and your living space, your garden should reflect who you are – your distinct personality, your tastes and, yes, your age. "The great thing about getting older", writes Madeleine L'Engle, "is that you don't lose all the other ages you've been". With a little imagination, you can get them all into your garden.

YOUR GARDEN ENVIRONMENT

To some, the word 'garden' brings back memories of a childhood flower plot; to others, grandmother's rose garden or the neighbour's abundant vegetables. While it is useful to have a common understanding of what a garden is, each person's space will be unique.

As we age, many factors determine how our garden takes shape. Gardening may be a form of exercise, a way of engaging with the seasons, or just having fun. Or it may become secondary to travelling, grandchildren and new hobbies. Normal ageing – loss of stamina, arthritis, decreased vision and reduced balance – may limit gardening activities. Most importantly, we need to consider how our physical space defines the way we garden.

This chapter identifies broad living situations and gardening environments that seniors may find themselves in. These include a house with a garden, an apartment with a small garden or patio, and communities for active or frail elders with a shared garden, the latter looking at both independent retirement set-ups and assisted-living communities. A final section looks at the role of gardens in the lives of those who need constant nursing care.

OPPOSITE *Every garden is unique and can be adapted to suit its owner – this one has a raised bed with a wide ledge for seated comfort.*

ABOVE *Every member of the family, including your canine companions, can enjoy the garden and fresh air.*

ABOVE *Appreciating flowers and plants is something gardeners at any age never grow tired of doing.*

ABOVE *Sharing the garden and its produce with grandchildren is one of the most valuable gifts we can give them.*

STAYING PUT: GARDENS FOR INDEPENDENT SENIORS

Seniors today are generally healthier and more robust than their counterparts of even 50 years ago. Thanks to regular exercise, good eating habits, and staying socially active, many independent seniors still live in their family homes and maintain their gardens regularly. Here are some ideas that can help seniors stay connected with gardening, but ease some of the more overwhelming tasks.

ABOVE *Make sure that your water source is close by so that you can easily keep the garden well-irrigated.*

GETTING HELP

One way for home gardeners to increase the likelihood that they continue gardening well into their senior years is to make wise decisions about what tasks others could do for them or with them – like a gardening 'coach'. For example, if you can afford it, a weekly lawn service could relieve you of a time-consuming and less-than-creative activity. During certain times of the year there are other maintenance routines that require much time, energy and risk that an ageing, albeit healthy, gardener could hire out. To cite a fairly obvious example, understanding the risks of getting on ladders as we age, and the devastating injuries that can occur by falling, should encourage the home gardener to hire an arborist or other expert to do the elevated and more risky pruning tasks. Other, less routine, tasks that might call for outside help might include one-off construction of yard or garden features – a tool shed, for example, or a raised bed or a level paving surface – that will contribute to the on-going ease and safety of the home gardener's task.

If hiring professional help is beyond the budget, consider giving friends, relatives or neighbours an opportunity to be generous. A half-day potluck lunch work party can produce wonders in the garden and be a fun social event for families and friends.

MAKING CHANGES

It will come as no surprise, except perhaps to the very young, that ageing means making adjustments. Taking care of how we use our bodies now as we go about our normal gardening routines will go far toward ensuring that we continue gardening well into our 70s, 80s and even 90s.

LEFT *Choose the garden tasks that you like to do and that don't deplete your energy. Gathering dahlias for a bouquet is a pleasant way to start the day.*

Kneeling down to weed the in-ground bed can be hard on both the back and knees, and lugging a heavy hose around to the far corners of the yard can take too much valuable energy and time. Understanding what changes can be made in the home garden's daily work schedule may increase the time spent doing more enjoyable things.

RAISED BEDS

Changing your planting areas to raised beds is one way to ensure that your back and knees get relief and that time spent on weeding and deadheading chores will decrease. This needn't be an elaborate undertaking: merely raking soil in a rectangular shape no higher than 20cm (8in) can create a simple raised bed. A more durable raised bed made of safely preserved wood planks and built at a variety of heights can provide the home gardener with space that is accessible, easy on the joints and muscles and far less demanding to maintain. With help, a more elaborate structure can be constructed with a seating cap all around the perimeter.

This feature gives you a place to sit while weeding as well as a place to rest and to enjoy the fruits of your labours. (*See also* pages 174–181.)

WATERING

Having a water tap (spigot) installed closer to your main gardens or, if possible, getting an irrigation system on a timer to keep the beds watered will make your life easier. A good hose cart that is easily wheeled about is a wise purchase, and will also provide safe and easy storage and reduce the chances of tripping over the hose that didn't get put away. It should attach to your water butt, to make the most of rainwater.

PATHS

Finally, the home gardener may realize that some of the existing garden pathways need improvements, or more significant changes, to allow for easier mobility. Installing lights for evening passage, clearing vegetation off the path, and defining the path edges will make your home safer for both you and your senior guests.

ABOVE *Puttering in the greenhouse or potting shed is a great way to prepare for spring seedlings and vegetable starts.*

The key to making changes in your routine is knowing your strengths and acknowledging your limitations. Just as no two gardens are the same, no two gardeners are the same. More to the point, no one gardener is the same at two different stages of life.

BELOW *A raised bed with a wide seating area makes tending beds easier; the paved floor is flat with no tripping dangers.*

BELOW *A wheeled hose cart takes the awkwardness out of manoeuvring the hose around the garden.*

BELOW *There are many options for flat, stable surfaces – this one uses curved paving that follows the path direction.*

DOWNSIZING TO AN APARTMENT GARDEN

Many seniors may decide to leave the family home, dispose of unused furniture and free themselves from time-consuming garden chores – either because they can no longer cope, or because they want to be ready for future problems. However, their love of gardening will remain undiminished. Downsizing to a smaller set-up such as an apartment needn't mean that gardening is a thing of the past. Here are some things that can be helpful.

ABOVE *Moving to a smaller living space may also reduce your garden area, so use containers to increase your options.*

PATIOS, TERRACES AND BALCONIES

If you are keen to maintain your garden activities, albeit in a smaller context, an apartment or condo that offers a small patio, deck or terrace will be the perfect set-up. When researching an apartment, take note of the sun orientation, since having a sunny or shady location will determine your plant selections and how you use the space.

It's best if the garden is directly connected to your living quarters. This is important for your daily enjoyment of the garden and will allow easy and quick access to get outside and potter about. Some apartments and condos have in-ground spaces for beds and surfaces to place containers.

Determine how many containers you can fit or if there is room for a trellis to allow you to maximize your growing area. Hanging baskets can also give an extra dynamic to a small garden space. Finally, is there a space for a small tree? Adding a slow-growing but richly textured evergreen like a Hinoki cypress can offer you beauty and give you some natural privacy. Alternatively, a small deciduous tree that can add seasons of interest to your terrace is a Japanese maple. A balcony may seem limiting in what you can grow but by placing well-designed boxes and hanging baskets, you can create a lush garden of cascading flowering annuals and perennials.

CHOOSING AND USING CONTAINERS

In a patio, terrace, or balcony garden, containers are going to be essential, not just to hold the plants but as basic design features. Generally speaking, buy the largest container you can accommodate and manage easily, since it will require less watering

LEFT *A small terrace garden can provide all you need to feel at home – lots of plants, comfortable seating and easy access to garden beds.*

ABOVE *A small patio or balcony provides a place for reading the morning paper, sipping coffee or watching the birds.*

and allow you to have a wider variety of plants that make a more interesting garden.

Remember that while colourful, artistic containers are attractive, they can be expensive and heavy – even before you add any soil. Take account of your climate – if you get repeated winter frosts, a ceramic container is likely to crack. Semi-flexible synthetic pots work best in cold regions and these will double up as liners. Plant directly into the plastic pot or liner and then place it in the more decorative container to get the benefits of both.

Also on the market now are terracotta-style resin and fibreglass containers that are more reliable in extreme temperatures. They are also lighter, more durable, less expensive and easier to move. Moving a fully planted container without wheeled support can be dangerous if you don't have the strength and stability. If possible, put your containers on moveable trays since you may want to rearrange your patio area. Techniques for moving containers are explored in more detail on pages 120–123.

CREATING SEASONAL INTEREST

Just because your space is smaller, you don't need to forgo having a garden that is attractive all year round. An important strategy when planning a patio or terrace garden is to think about growing a variety of plants that will give you several seasons of attraction and interest. A careful choice of bulbs, annuals and perennials can give you flowers all year round, and you can add a shrub or two with colourful berries or scented winter flowers. Most of these will need little maintenance other than feeding and watering (if they're in containers) – many bulbs, perennials and shrubs will almost take care of themselves, year after year. If possible, locate the winter containers so they are highly visible from the inside – that way you can enjoy them when it's too cold to spend much time outside.

CREATING HEIGHT VARIATIONS

In a smaller outdoor space you may need to use every part of the area to create interest and to make your own garden statement. One idea is to add a trellis to a large container – this is a good way of giving you more growing space, as well as giving height to your small garden area. By placing the trellis to the back of the container you can add layers of plants in front, thereby creating a mini-garden scene. Climbers such as clematis, honeysuckle and three-leaf akebia can be grown on the trellis, and planting two varieties can provide you with blooms for several months.

A trellis can also be used for growing vegetables such as climbing peas, beans and cucumbers. Certain varieties of tomatoes, squash and melons are also well adapted to grow in small and vertical spaces. With a bit of twine or flexible tape, it's easy to coax these plants on to the trellis and use it during the season for support and stability.

Hanging baskets are another useful feature for patios. Pulley systems are available to assist with the raising and lowering of baskets so that watering and grooming can be done at a safe height. Your planting choices will require a balance of colourful blooms, foliage interest and plants that create the core composition as well as those that cascade over the sides. For easy access, you can use a watering wand with a long handle and angled head (*see also* page 126).

WINDOW BOXES

Not just appropriate to sills, window boxes can also be attached to a terrace or balcony railing. Available in wood, terracotta, synthetic compounds and plastic, they are easily maintained, usually requiring no bending or high stretching. Growing herbs in a sunny window box and in a temperate climate can give you year-round access to fresh culinary treats.

As your garden changes in size and shape, remind yourself that some of the loveliest gardens in the world are grown in small spaces. Think of your garden as an extension of your home – an 'outdoor room' that is inviting and appealing, no matter what the season.

BELOW *The secluded and shady seating area in this garden is created by the house wall and the soft, enclosing foliage.*

COMMUNITY LIVING AND COMMUNITY GARDENS

As the baby boomer generation has aged, the market has responded by creating residential environments to meet the emerging needs of a growing and greying population. These include independent retirement homes, apartments with a community garden, assisted-living communities providing more hands-on backup and, for those needing long-term support and assistance, nursing-home communities.

ABOVE *Keep the joy of gardening in your life wherever you live by making careful choices about your new community.*

RETIREMENT COMMUNITIES FOR ACTIVE SENIORS

These communities are designed for seniors who are independent, physically active, free of the burdens of home ownership and who require little or no staff assistance. Of course, whatever size of plot or garden is available – from a small courtyard to a more spacious garden – it needs to be well maintained. The advantage of many living facilities of this type is that they have a basic level of garden maintenance provided.

NEW OPPORTUNITIES FOR LEARNING

Retirement from the workplace may be disorienting for the energetic senior who thrived on having a schedule, getting things done and working with a team. However, a retirement community can be ideal to channel your competitive drive, still-curious mind and excess energy and leave you more time to devote to individual interests.

One advantage of a retirement community is ready access to others who share your interest in gardening.

Residents are often provided with gardening areas, and may have an organized garden group. This is likely to be composed of like-minded plant people who might have specialist interests to bring. Devising informal competitions, such as who can grow the biggest pumpkin, raise the best rose or produce the most cherry tomatoes, can inspire active gardeners to participate. This interaction and the sharing of fresh food grown locally are meaningful ways to create stronger bonds and a personal sense of well-being.

BELOW *Ensure that there is a private and sheltered place where you can enjoy the garden throughout the seasons and also appreciate the fruits of your efforts.*

BELOW *Sharing a garden creates new friends and a healthy social network.*

ASSISTED-LIVING COMMUNITIES

The goal of assisted-living communities is to help individuals remain as independent as possible, but to offer services that make performing the tasks of daily living easier and safer. While residents have their own self-contained apartments, they can receive a number of services that can include meals, laundry, housekeeping, medication reminders and transportation to and from appointments. These communities often encourage residents to participate in activities programmes, especially gardening groups.

FINDING THE RIGHT PLACE

For gardeners who still want to garden actively, the assisted-living community should provide several things. Smart facility planners and administrators understand that many of their clients will be coming from homes where gardening played an important role. By creating and supporting beautiful grounds, these forward-thinking communities are creating gardens where the residents can have a plot or raised bed to grow plants of their choice. Making sure there are wide, well-lit paths that allow strolling in the gardens will encourage residents to be outdoors. Such gardens will also be designed to accommodate walkers and wheelchairs and will include raised beds, easy and accessible watering options and a supply of adaptive tools.

GETTING YOUR NEEDS MET

A thoughtful assisted-living community will provide a light and airy room where people can gather to discuss their mutual gardening interests and participate in activities. Some homes

RIGHT *Many communities offer plots where flowers and vegetables can be cultivated by a supervised garden group.*

will give the residents an area where they can raise plants and vegetables from seed indoors. This process keeps seniors connected with the cycles of life, and enables the continuation of gardening activities.

Many communities have a horticulture therapist or other specialist who is trained to assist the residents with their gardens, teach horticulture and propagation, and perhaps offer a weekly garden group. When ageing issues limit certain physical chores, the specialist can create an environment in which gardening is still accessible on many levels.

Many such communities will have libraries, or at least a common room with a selection of reading material. If you are lucky, the selection will include many of the books and magazines that have been written about the pleasures of gardening. You probably have your own collection of garden books that you've accumulated over the years. Some of these may be practical how-to books geared to the more active gardener, but others might address

such questions as why we garden, or recount one person's interesting history or journal as a gardener. Reading aloud from these in a group can be a pleasure for all involved. As the Spanish poet Lope de Vega wrote, "With a few flowers in my garden, half a dozen pictures and some books, I live without envy."

OUTINGS AND FIELD TRIPS

Because those who live in assisted-living communities are often able-bodied and mobile, they are able to make trips to local nurseries, arboretums and botanical gardens. Many such locations have naturalists available to give tours and to answer visitors' questions. Choosing these sites so they're accessible to seniors ensures that those with mobility aids such as a wheelchairs or walkers can also participate.

There's no question that assisted-living communities have more limitations than other set-ups, but with imagination and initiative you can turn these limitations into opportunities.

CARING FOR OTHERS

You may be in a situation where you are responsible for a friend or relative who can no longer care for themselves because of their deteriorating physical or cognitive health. In this case a family-care home, a skilled-nursing facility or an Alzheimer's or memory-care community are all options. The goal is to maintain quality of life for residents as their needs change over the course of their disease. In a residential set-up such as this, the garden space can be a defining factor in the quality of life of those who live there.

ABOVE *Well-designed raised beds in communities give residents easy access as well as safe passageways.*

A PROTECTIVE ENVIRONMENT

Adult-care or family-care homes are private residences, staffed and lived in by licensed, trained caregivers who provide their homes for small groups of seniors who need assistance in their daily care. Often, there is a patio or garden where residents can sit in the fresh air and enjoy the sun. When researching adult care homes for your loved ones, ask about the garden facilities to learn what the gardening options are.

A skilled-nursing facility provides a therapeutic and safe environment for an older person. Some residents may be there for a period of rehabilitation; others may be there for long-term care. These nursing facilities offer a range of activities that meet the social, physical and emotional needs of the residents. While the level of involvement in gardening will inevitably change at this stage of life, gardens and the natural world have many benefits and an enlightened facility will provide various gardening and outdoor opportunities. Often a horticultural therapist is available, either in a weekly group or offering one-to-one support to those who are interested.

Increasingly available now are Alzheimer or memory-care communities. These residential homes strive to maintain a rich and appropriate quality of life for those who live there as their physical and psychological needs change over the course of their disease. Many have horticultural therapy programmes, which are very beneficial to this special group of seniors – they help to keep these people engaged with life, connected to others and to the natural world around them.

GROUP ACTIVITIES

Gardening groups have much to offer nursing-care residents. Activities will be seasonally based, designed around residents' requirements. A skilled horticultural therapist will adapt their sessions to meet the needs of the group, or of an individual who may be having a difficult time. For those with memory problems, developing a rapport with each resident and knowing something about their past will help to trigger a memory or relate a story so that they feel respected and connected. Another method is to pass around plants and natural materials that each resident can explore.

While those with dementia can be unpredictable in a group, positive interaction will increase as experiences, gardening stories and memories are shared. With these come laughter, a sense of fun and a mutual respect.

Finding care communities for your loved ones that provide such activities is not always easy, but it will become more so as the benefits of horticultural therapy become better understood and appreciated. Pass the word.

LEFT *Whether you are active or have limited energy, a few quiet moments in the garden can be therapeutic and restorative.*

ABOVE *A garden with a diversity of plants will stimulate the five senses and get people to experience nature in new ways.*

ABOVE *The sweet fragrance of garden flowers keeps you in touch with the addictive pleasure of gardens.*

RESTORATIVE GARDENS

Having an accessible, well-designed, multi-seasonal garden in a nursing-care community allows residents to be in a safe and secure setting while getting fresh air, sunshine and exercise. For many, simply sitting in a chair with a view into the garden can be a comforting and therapeutic experience and provides another connection to the passing of the seasons. Attracting wildlife such as birds and butterflies gives another connection to the natural world. What is more, plantings of old-fashioned flowers with sensory features will stimulate memories.

Research has shown that while many people with Alzheimer's cannot remember what happened only moments earlier, their recollection of events from years ago is unusually strong. The sense of smell may be diminished with Alzheimer's disease, but the sense of touch seems to stay intact. As the actress Helen Hayes wrote in her later years: "I dig my fingers deep into the soft earth. I can feel its energy, and my spirits soar."

These insights are important for planners and staff, but also for those visiting loved ones. Doing something together rather than trying to force a conversation can be a relief to visitor and resident alike. Alzheimer's research has shown that even the simple act of taking your loved one out in a garden creates a focal point for mutual attention and conversation. While most memory-care residents cannot actively garden, they can use small watering cans so that they can irrigate the pots and containers. With one-to-one contact, a horticulture therapist or a visitor can help a resident do some simple weeding or deadheading.

RECEPTIVE GARDENING

The motivation for active gardening, and the opportunity to do so, is minimal when residing in either a skilled-nursing or memory-care community. This is where receptive gardening, or enjoying the fruits of others' labours, comes into play. As we already know, just being around beautiful plants is a great motivator for maintaining people's strength and enthusiasm. What's more, a daily half-hour dose of sunlight on the face and forearms replenishes vitamin D and promotes skeletal health. Even sitting indoors with a view into the garden can be a comforting experience. Contact with plants or flowers will help keep spirits high, and is especially beneficial for bed-ridden patients.

Any good therapeutic garden will track the cycles of life and the passing of the seasons. Spring blooms on tulips, summer sunflowers, colourful foliage in the autumn, and a beautiful evergreen in winter can orientate residents to the pattern of nature's cycles. Simple techniques such as having a peanut feeder near the windows will give a close view of the garden bird life. Another idea is to make dried corncobs and suet available in the winter months – this will attract squirrels and seed-eating birds.

BELOW *If it is difficult to go into the garden, an attractive window view brings the charm of the garden inside.*

MAKING DECISIONS ABOUT YOUR GARDEN

The most enjoyable decisions we make in our garden are likely to be the choice of summer flowers for planting, what vegetable seeds to sow or which new tree to add. However, many other more nuts-and-bolts factors come into play when you are, for example, remodelling an existing bed or getting a feel for a new garden.

The light exposure, the soil type and texture, the amount of rainfall and the climate zone are some of the practical essentials covered here that you need to understand if you're to have a successful garden. Low-maintenance plants and those that appeal to the five senses will involve seniors to the full, both in the management and enjoyment of gardens, and the ideas included here open up possibilities for a beautiful, easy-to-care-for environment full of sensory surprises. As you read this chapter, think about how appropriate your decisions are for your physical potential or limitations – that is, how much gardening are you willing and able to deal with? Being practical and honest about this will keep both you and your garden happy and healthy. In most cases, we don't need to stop all gardening, but rather think about making small adjustments to our routines.

OPPOSITE *Think about what you want – buying small potted plants instead of seeds can save you a lot of effort.*

ABOVE *A salad garden composed of mixed greens and lettuces is both beautiful and practical.*

ABOVE *A cutting garden provides you with flowers of all kinds – to enjoy in place or to bring the delights of the garden indoors.*

ABOVE *Pack a container with tulip bulbs in the autumn and wait for a wonderful spring display.*

PRACTICAL CONSIDERATIONS

Deciding what to plant and where to plant it can be like rearranging the living room furniture. Is the sofa too big for this wall? Will sun fade the new upholstery? Do some of the old pieces need replacing? Often the process shifts as you see how the space looks as a permanent fixture. Planting a garden is a similar process. However, given that plants are dynamic, living organisms, creating and maintaining a garden involves even more factors.

ABOVE *You may decide to remove those floppy tall flowers that require staking and replace them with more 'obedient' plants.*

INITIAL ANALYSIS

All gardeners have successes and failures in the planting decisions that they make. Even an experienced gardener sometimes loses a plant, in spite of careful planning.

For senior gardeners, the chances of losing plants and therefore of having disappointments in the garden need to be minimized. The plain fact is that every failed planting means that extra time and energy needs to be spent organizing a replacement. There are, simply, better ways to spend your time. So for those with limited energy, how can you minimize your failures?

The answer is to choose plants that are reliable, and make sure you can give them the right conditions. The material in this book is designed with this in mind, to offer plant suggestions that will give you the best chance of being successful and feeling rewarded for your labours.

FACTORS TO CONSIDER BEFORE MAKING PLANTING DECISIONS

What is the climate?
For many seniors who may relocate in their retirement, perhaps escaping from a harsh winter climate to a warmer, dry environment, a whole new gardening world awaits. Look at the gardens in the area and see which plants are thriving to get reliable planting ideas.

How much space is there?
Downsizing to a small patio or terrace from a family home with trees, beds and a lawn will alter your options.

What is the light exposure?
Knowing if your garden is in full sun, full shade or a combination of both will guide your plant choices.

What is the soil quality?
Learn about the soil composition (clay, sand or loam) as well as its pH value (the balance of acid and alkaline). This will help you select appropriate plants or encourage you to begin the amendment process to improve the quality of your soil.

Watering options?
If the soil is dry and watering is a problem, try to choose plants that can tolerate drought conditions. This also creates a low-maintenance garden – lugging around awkward hoses or heavy watering cans is unsafe and can add stress to joints and muscles.

SOIL CARE
Protect the soil structure by covering it with green manure crops or an organic mulch. This also protects the creatures who live beneath the soil.

FAR LEFT *A rotavator is a labour-reducing method of breaking up the soil to prepare it for planting. They can often be hired.*

LEFT *A well-conditioned soil will pay dividends in terms of enhanced plant growth and development.*

DETERMINING YOUR SOIL TYPE: THE SQUEEZE TEST

You need to know the soil characteristics of your garden so that you can choose the best cultivation technique. Each type of soil – clay, sand and loam – has a specific visual and handling quality. Loam is the easiest soil to manage, but you can work on both clay and sandy soils to make them as productive. Remember that some plants actually prefer sand or clay. Take a handful of your soil and gently squeeze it to a ball shape to establish which you have. (See *also* pages 73–79 for more information on amending the soil in your garden.)

Clay soil = a sticky ball

Soil with this quality can easily be formed into a ball. Your soil will be clay if water pools on the soil surface, or it sticks to your boots in winter and dries hard in summer. Clay soil is the most fertile, but can have drainage problems. To improve poorly drained clay, dig in grit and bulky organic matter, such as well-rotted manure or spent mushroom compost (soil mix).

Sandy soil = a hard-to-make ball

This soil will disintegrate when you try to form it into a shape. A light-coloured, free-draining soil, it is constantly thirsty in summer and is the poorest quality soil. It is best to mulch sandy soil like this with manure to make it more moisture retentive and fertile. Do this by covering the surface of the damp soil with a thick mulch of well-rotted manure.

Loam or silt = a crumbly ball

You can form loam into a ball that crumbles under pressure. A mixture of sand and clay, this is the best balanced soil for the gardener and poses few cultivation problems. Loams are usually dark because of their high humus (decayed organic matter) content, but lighter soils can be significantly improved by digging in manure.

ABOVE *If you need to work on wet soil, stand on a plank of wood to ensure it is not compacted and its structure destroyed.*

ABOVE *Dry weather causes clay soils to crack, which can be a benefit as it develops their 'crumb structure'.*

ABOVE *Some plants prefer either clay or sandy soils – the sea holly (*Eryngium maritimum*) thrives in sand or shingle.*

DETERMINING YOUR SOIL pH

This is a measurement of your soil's acidity (sourness, a measure of below 7.0) or alkalinity (sweetness, a measure higher than 7.0). It will help you decide which plants will thrive in your garden. Most plants prefer a specific pH range – acid, alkaline, or near neutral. Soils with a pH of around 6.5 generally have the most

RIGHT *In order to reduce the acidity of the soil add some lime a few weeks before planting.*

nutrients available and are suitable for the widest range of plants. Purchase soil test kits from nurseries or send soil samples to your local agriculture or horticulture agency.

MEASURING YOUR SOIL pH WITH AN ELECTRONIC METER

1 *After loosening several different areas of soil, moisten using rainwater (tap water could give false readings) and allow to soak through the ground.*

2 *Take a sample of the wet soil from the first patch only and place in a clean, dry jar, adding more rainwater if necessary, ready for the reading.*

3 *Always clean and dry the probe on the pH meter first to eliminate the risk of an incorrect reading. Do this between each soil reading.*

4 *Push the probe into the moist soil sample and wait until the needle stops moving. The readout will show how acidic or alkaline each sample is.*

UNDERSTANDING THE LIGHT IN YOUR GARDEN

All plants (with the exception of fungi), from the small fern to the towering maple tree, depend on light. To understand how it affects our plants we need to consider three key features of light – quantity, quality and duration.

You need to understand how much sunlight your garden receives each day and where the bright and dark spots are, especially during the growing season. For most gardens, the sunshine is more intense during the summer and particularly from mid-morning to mid-afternoon than during the rest of the day.

RIGHT *In this garden the morning sun glances off the top of the arbour and lights up the border garden of dahlias and flowering shrubs.*

For many plants, the length of time that light shines on them regulates their rate of flowering and fruit ripening. During the growing season, most fruit, vegetables and herbs require at least 6–8 hours of full sunlight a day. Root crops like beets and carrots will do well with 3–6 hours of partial sun.

Some plants deal well with the cool morning sun while others thrive in warm south-facing rock gardens (Northern Hemisphere) or in north-facing rockeries (Southern Hemisphere). Beware of early morning sun striking plants that are prone to frost damage, such as camellias with their early spring buds – warming up more slowly will reduce the risk of harm.

Because most plants can thrive in partial sun or shade, there are many varieties to choose from. Reputable nurseries label plants with essential information, including light requirements.

ABOVE RIGHT *At midday the patio is in full overhead sunlight and, in the summer, pretty warm. The arbour now has a welcoming patch of noontime shade.*

RIGHT *Another day in the summer garden passes. In the evening the patio and bench are in shade and coolness. The setting sun sends down its last warm rays.*

EXPOSURE TABLE

This will give you a quick and easy reference when diagnosing your garden's exposure and what plants will thrive where.

Exposure	Description	Details	Suggestions
6 or more hours of direct sun	Full sun	Late morning through to late afternoon provides the most intense sunlight	Vegetables, most herbs, stonecrops, succulents, cactus
3–6 hours of direct sun	Partial sun or partial shade	In the morning or early afternoon the sun will be diffused through high canopies of shading trees	Most woodland and understorey plants
2 hours or less of direct sunlight	Full shade	The sun is blocked by or heavily filtered through evergreens	Ferns, hostas, camellias, rhododendrons

WORKING AROUND INDIVIDUAL DISABILITIES

Modern medicine and healthier life choices allow today's retirees a greater range of activities and interests. Eventually, however, the physical conditions associated with normal ageing will necessitate some changes in the way that we garden. However, take heart – by knowing our new limitations and adapting our activities accordingly, we can extend the potential of those pleasurable days in the garden.

ABOVE *Arthritis doesn't have to keep you from gardening; discover the tools and plants that will help you stay active.*

ARTHRITIS

Despite medical advances, there are chronic physical conditions that older adults will develop and will need to cope with. Arthritis is the most common of these. It can reduce one's strength, endurance and flexibility. But with adaptive gardening tools, devices and procedures, the senior gardener can stay involved. A wide array of ergonomically designed tools are available to assist you with most garden chores. Cushioned hand grips, adjustable handles, smaller to larger sizing options – all of these can help arthritic gardeners continue their gardening activities.

HYPERTENSION

To prevent or control high blood pressure, one of the most important things we can do is to be physically active. Research shows that gardening is an activity that can help with hypertension as well as reduce our risk of heart disease. To help reduce blood pressure, improve heart health and control diabetes it is suggested that 30 minutes of moderate-level physical activity is advisable almost every day of the week. Power mowing the lawn and raking leaves are both good forms of exercise. With the support of your doctor, gardening can provide you with your own custom-made exercise programme. Think of your garden as your very own private health club!

VISUAL IMPAIRMENTS

Sight is likely to be the first sense that provides us with information about the garden. It is also often the first sense to deteriorate with increasing age. In fact many people notice their sight becoming less acute in their mid- to late forties, and sometimes earlier. Visual impairments usually develop quite slowly and so it's important to pay attention when we feel uncertain about what we're seeing, how we're processing the light or darkness, and how safe we feel negotiating the few steps from the porch.

At first these changes may seem inconsequential, but as time goes on they can be distressing and discouraging. We may begin to have trouble with focus and clarity, become sensitive to glare or lose the ability to discern colours.

In addition, our depth perception can become compromised and we can become confused by changes in levels

FAR LEFT *Stay active by walking in the garden. Your cane can serve as a support as well as a way to explore a flower bed.*

LEFT *Wheelchair-accessible gardens are increasingly common and are popular in retirement communities.*

or surface materials – for example at the back doorstep. Falling or tripping is an undeniable risk, so it is important to think about fine-tuning the garden to ensure maximum safety and security. Installing a small ramp, adding handrails to steps or painting the stairs a contrasting colour are all ways to reduce the risk of falling.

Cataracts can inhibit gardening, but surgery can correct this condition and allow one to resume most activities. For other low-vision issues, such as macular degeneration (compromising the ability to see details), tasks will need to be refined so they're safe as well as satisfying. Storing hoses off pathways in easy and practical carts and always stowing tools away neatly eliminates the danger of tripping and therefore reduces potential accidents. Painting or taping tool handles in a contrasting colour to the ground will make it easier to find them in the garden bed.

SAFETY NOTE

If you notice any changes in your health, you should always consult a physician, particularly concerning your ability to garden.

LEFT *If you are unsteady on your feet, use a flat and stable surface such as these pavers and tiles to avoid tripping hazards.*

BALANCE

As we age, our sense of balance is often compromised. There are, however, various ways of making conditions safer where balance is an issue.

Make sure that walking surfaces are smooth and level with good traction, and install a hand rail along main walkways. Grass can be an uneven surface and might throw you off balance, so replace lawns or grassy areas with level paving materials to make movement easier within the garden.

Raising the garden bed will reduce the need to bend over while tending the bed and will also provide a place to sit as you go about your chores. Providing seating in the most frequented spots will allow you to take regular rests. Chairs positioned in shady areas will offer an escape from the sun and a place to sit to enjoy your work – and if they are lightweight they can be moved around easily as the light changes.

ABOVE *This raised bed is designed to accommodate a gardener in a wheelchair.*

BELOW *Failing eyesight is likely to affect us all – this partially sighted man investigates garden scents with his guide dog.*

WHAT TO PLANT: PERSONAL PREFERENCES

Often, we choose to create a garden based on our early childhood experiences. Helping grandma to plant her sweet peas may forever make you want a few of these growing in your garden. Don't fight it. Apart from evocative garden memories, however, there are contemporary trends, such as growing organic produce or being kind to the environment, that may also influence what we decide to plant.

ABOVE *Grow vegetables that you love to eat, especially those that can be sampled as you harvest them.*

FLOWERS

Because they are showy and attractive, flowers are an essential component of most gardens and often the one that we take the most pride in. They are also valuable in attracting pollinators. Growing plants that have a variety of shapes and heights – the tubular types like fuchsias, the flat-headed varieties like Queen Ann's lace or the open-face disc of tall sunflowers – will provide an accessible entry and landing platform for a variety of bees, flies, butterflies and other beneficial insects.

If you make the right choices you can have flowering plants blooming from the early spring right into the late autumn. Bulbs and tubers, such as daffodils and anemones, can start the early spring garden. Asters and chrysanthemums are great closers to the floral season. And all the flowers in between will grace your garden with their colourful petals.

VEGETABLES

As we learn more about the importance of organic foods in keeping us healthy, creating a vegetable garden becomes ever more appealing. Rule number one when making a vegetable garden is to choose vegetables you really like to eat! While it's fun to look for interesting varieties, make sure you grow the things you're most likely to maintain and harvest. Also, be sure that you make the garden accessible for your particular needs and living situation. Growing beans up a trellis is likely to allow you to harvest more than if you are growing a bush-type bean. Or perhaps a large container with a variety of lettuces and a few potted cherry tomatoes will satisfy your need for fresh salad ingredients.

While vegetable gardening in any form can be incredibly rewarding, remember that there is a considerable amount to plan and to do. Knowing your energy level, ease of access and ability to maintain the crops will help you determine the ideal type and size of your vegetable garden. Plan the work and then work the plan!

LEFT *This garden is full of scented plants including* Lavandula stoechas *and* Rosa *'Gertrude Jekyll'.*

FRUITS

Depending on where you live, fruit growing can be a satisfying adventure if you choose the appropriate variety for your climate conditions. In some warm and temperate climates several types of fruit will give you a continuous supply during the spring, summer and autumn months. Strawberries can be harvested in the spring, followed by raspberries, blueberries, peaches and apricots during the summer. Grapes ripen in early autumn and then the apple orchards reward us with their bounty.

You can produce many types of fruit in your home garden or retirement community – in the ground, in special pots, trained up a wall and climbing on an arbour. Something that has only recently become an option, thanks to recent research and development in horticulture, is the availability of 'designer' fruit trees that are smaller and more productive. Columnar apple trees serve several roles in the senior's garden – they take up little space and produce great fruit that is very accessible for harvest.

BELOW Grow climbing vegetables such as green beans for weeks of convenient harvesting and satisfying eating.

ABOVE *Dwarf fruit trees can produce a plentiful crop of apples that can be harvested easily.*

TREES AND SHRUBS

No garden, however small, should be without its complement of trees or shrubs. They are the bones of any garden: they give scale and contrast to other plants and are a year-round presence when the flowers and vegetables die back. For the senior gardener, choosing these wisely will enhance the garden for many years. Choose trees or shrubs that provide multi-seasonal features, including in the winter months, are tolerant of your particular soil and climate type and require little or no maintenance. Unlike annuals or vegetables that need to be planted each year, a tree or shrub will be permanent, so make sure it is in the right place and give it the recommended care, especially in the first year. (*See also* fruit trees on pages 164–165.)

WILDLIFE

Creating a wildlife habitat in your garden can be one of the most enjoyable by-products of gardening. A healthy garden is one that has a balance of trees and shrubs – both deciduous and evergreen – as well as a diversity of plant material. These leafed and needled plants provide habitat for animals that may want to nest or roost in your garden. Try to include plants that produce nectar, berries, nuts and cones – food for all kinds of animals. Your garden will attract birds and butterflies that will you give you hours of enjoyment and wonder as you watch them in action.

BELOW *Greenfinches enjoy a meal from the feeder as they delight both indoor and outdoor observers.*

WHAT TO PLANT: LOW-MAINTENANCE GARDENS

Besides being familiar with the climatic features of your garden space – sun, shade, wind, soil and moisture – you also need to gauge how much time and energy you are willing or able to commit to your garden. It is sensible to plan your garden as an adaptable feature where the maintenance demands can be changed according to personal preference or your own emerging needs.

ABOVE *Select potted seedlings in preference to sowing seeds to jump-start your spring garden.*

ESTABLISH YOUR MOTIVES

For seniors who spend all their spare time gardening, having a low-maintenance garden might not be a priority. For others who love to garden but also enjoy activities away from home, such as hiking, bird watching and canoeing, finding ways to reduce gardening tasks is highly desirable. If your stamina and strength aren't sufficient to keep up a complex and high-maintenance garden, finding ways to reduce the garden care is a necessity. Finally, some people just want to have more time to sit and relax in their garden rather than working in it. Whatever your situation, here are some options for simplifying your garden space without detracting from its aesthetic appeal.

When making decisions about how to maintain your garden easily you will obviously focus on plants that are 'low-maintenance'. However, you may still choose to grow a few favourite 'difficult' plants, if you are prepared to give extra thought to their care. Here are some of the ongoing maintenance activities that will need to be considered as part of this equation.

EASY PLANTING

The work involved varies depending on the combination of what, where and how much you decide to plant. Making planting easy and accessible probably has as much to do with ensuring ease of access by using raised beds, containers and appropriate positioning in the garden, as with choosing plants that will inspire you to maintain and care for them.

You also need to make sure the seasonal requirements of your choices suit you. Bulbs, for example, need to be put in the ground in most climates in the autumn before the temperatures dip and when you can still work the soil. Similarly, autumn is the best time to plant trees or shrubs, although any time up to late winter is an option, except in very cold areas. For a vegetable garden, late spring or summer is the best time to plant.

Window boxes and containers work on all levels for ease of maintenance. Ensure interest from one season to another by using plants that mature in the early spring, such as lettuces which are cool-weather vegetables, right through to pansies or cyclamen that can be planted in the autumn wherever the winters are milder. Buy seedlings from nurseries and garden supply stores for convenience, or sow and tend your favourite seeds indoors until they are ready for transplanting.

LEFT *A high-rise terrace offers the feel of a garden with its comfortable seating and variety of container plants.*

RIGHT *A patio garden full of rich planting textures can become your outdoor living room for several months in the summer.*

WEEDING

It is advisable to find ways of discouraging weeds because weeding is time-consuming and weeds will affect the health of your plants. By suppressing weeds you will help your soil retain its moisture and nutrients for the 'good' plants, giving you time to do more satisfying things.

You can use chemical or organic herbicides to control weeds. However, avoid using chemicals, as these toxic compounds can affect the flora and fauna in your garden as well as your own health. The exception would be where highly persistent weeds cannot be effectively controlled by hand weeding or mulches.

DEADHEADING

When you deadhead flowers, you channel energy away from the production of seeds and into the creation of more flowers. For many plants, particularly annuals, this garden task promotes repeated flowering on

BELOW *Combine a variety of containers with different heights of plants for an interesting 'garden' on your patio.*

plants that would otherwise stop early on. Deadheading can be done by hand or with scissors or pruners, depending on the nature of the plant. Some senior gardeners will tolerate a garden that loses its bloom early because deadheading does take time and could involve more maintenance than they may want to undertake, but many varieties of plants will perform well without it, so try different ones.

WATERING

A healthy plant is made up of 75 to 90 per cent water, so adequate water is critical during the first few weeks of growth when the plants are building their root systems and getting established. While well-established plants in the ground can take advantage of the seasonal rains, there will be times when most gardens will need watering. For most gardens the optimal amount of water from rain or watering is two and a half centimetres (an inch) every week, but many established plants could easily tolerate short periods of dryness. If heat and drought are prolonged, water your most vulnerable plants, especially newly planted ones.

If you use containers and window boxes, you should assess where they are situated. If eaves or overhead structures block natural rainfall, then watering will be one of your regular garden routines. (*See also* Watering on pages 124–129.)

LEFT *Ground elder (Aegopodium podagraria 'Variegatum') is a colourful ground cover, but it can be invasive!*

RIGHT *This colourful perennial border hugs and intertwines around the fence and brings dazzling colour to your boundary.*

LOW-MAINTENANCE PLANTS

Unsurprisingly, the plants to choose for a low-maintenance garden are those that don't require a lot of time and fussing. Invariably they won't need staking, which is a big advantage for senior gardeners since this process can be fiddly. A low-maintenance plant will continue to look stunning without frequent deadheading and will also not need frequent dividing or heavy fertilizing.

All growing plants make demands, but these are reduced when you choose the right plants for the local climate and soil conditions, and those that will work with the character of your outdoor space. For example, planting a perennial, evergreen ground cover instead of annual flowers around a tree or in a garden bed will eliminate the annual (and expensive) process of purchase and planting. Plants that suppress weeds, such as bergenia and hosta, or can cope with dry conditions, such as agapanthus and lavender, also have low-maintenance advantages.

DO YOU REALLY WANT A LAWN?

Lawns are a high-maintenance area with yearly schedules of fertilizing, watering and mowing. Another low-maintenance option is to reduce the grass areas in your space by replacing some of it with a thick-growing ground cover such as pachysandra or wild ginger. Other lush and green ground covers will provide the visual impact of a 'green carpet', but need less maintenance than grass requires (*see also* below).

HARD LANDSCAPING

Decks, balconies and front porches can become your low-maintenance garden oases with a few well-chosen plants growing in beautiful and unusual pots. Container gardening can provide you with a way to have a variety of plants and still be able to control their care. Adding a drip system to the pots can even reduce your need to be vigilant about watering. With all the wonderful prepared soil mixtures available you are also free from dealing with poor garden soil.

LEFT *Use less lawn and more low-maintenance plants for a lush garden without all the labour.*

Gaultheria procumbens

Cornus kousa

Coreopsis verticillata

Euonymus alatus 'Fireball'

Sarcococca confusa

LOW-MAINTENANCE OPTIONS

Each plant included in the directory on pages 208–249 has a maintenance categorization, indicating either low, moderate or high care. If you are planning a low-maintenance garden here are some of the least demanding planting options from this selection.

Ground covers

• Wintergreen (*Gaultheria procumbens*) (page 224)
• Allegheny spurge (*Pachysandra procumbens*) (page 226)
• Shuttleworth's ginger (*Asarum shuttleworthii*) (page 220)
• Christmas fern (*Polystichum acrostichoides*) (page 227)

Perennials

• Sedum (*Sedum* 'Herbstfreude') (page 218)
• Moonbeam coreopsis (*Coreopsis verticillata*) (page 215)
• Black-eyed Susan (*Rudbeckia fulgida* var. *sullivantii* 'Goldsturm') (page 218)
• Stella d'oro daylily (*Hemerocallis* 'Stella de Oro') (page 217)
• Purple coneflower (*Echinacea purpurea*) (page 216)

Shrubs

• Abelia (*Abelia* x *grandiflora* 'Little Richard') (page 228)
• Burning bush (*Euonymus alatus* 'Fireball') (page 229)
• Sweet box (*Sarcococca confusa*) (page 233)
• Oak-leaf hydrangea (*Hydrangea quercifolia* 'Snow Queen' or 'Pee Wee') (page 232)

Small trees

• Kousa dogwood (*Cornus kousa*) (page 229)
• Serviceberry (*Amelanchier arborea*) (page 228)
• Crape myrtle (*Lagerstroemia indica*) (page 230)
• Sourwood (*Oxydendron arboreum*) (page 230)

Hydrangea quercifolia

Rudbeckia fulgida var. *sullivantii*

Sedum 'Herbstfreude'

Pachysandra procumbens

Echinacea purpurea

EASY ORNAMENTALS AND THOSE TO AVOID

We all want to have some flowers in our spaces and there are plenty of reliable blooms that don't require constant care. A self-sustaining garden bed full of perennials is a great option that looks great without much effort. Black-eyed Susan, shasta daisies, coneflowers and coreopsis are some suggestions that will provide colour in garden beds, and cheerful bouquets when cut and combined. Beds of ornamental grasses give long-lasting interest and need very little care, but some varieties may self-seed too freely, so check before you buy them – or be prepared to cut off the seed-heads before they ripen.

There are some perennials which, while they are definitely worth growing because they are so easy and reliable, can prove invasive in some gardens. These may include (depending on your climate zone) yarrow (*Achillea millefolium*), montbretia (*Crocosmia*), Japanese anemone (*Anemone* x *hybrida*),

ABOVE *Conifers shelter the boundary of a windy garden and provide privacy. Mix in a few perennials or small trees nearby to balance the weight of the evergreens.*

yellow loosestrife (*Lysimachia punctata*) and gooseneck loosestrife (*Lysimachia clethroides*). An alternative might be to opt for easy-to-grow, compact evergreen shrubs such as azaleas, heathers and abelias. These ensure that you have colourful blooms and interesting foliage and texture all year, while the growth is kept under control.

While spectacular in bloom, you might want to avoid tall plants such as delphiniums, which need the extra care of staking. For height, opt for sturdier flowers such as hollyhocks (*Alcea rosea*), red hot pokers (*Kniphofia uvaria*) or monkshood (*Aconitum*) (but note that the latter is poisonous). Breeders have developed compact and disease-resistant cultivars, so if you would like some of these plants look for these low-maintenance traits.

LEFT *Echinacea is a sturdy, reliable and lovely flowering plant to add to a sunny spot in your garden.*

RIGHT *Daylilies brighten any garden and, other than thinning every few years, require little care.*

EVERGREENS

Evergreen trees and shrubs, both coniferous and broadleaf, will add privacy to a garden or porch. They are easy to care for and don't shed leaves that require raking. While you're researching these, do look at varieties that are slow-growing and small in stature, such as dwarf Chinese holly (*Ilex cornuta* 'Rotunda') and dwarf nandina (*Nandina domestica*), since they eliminate the need for regular pruning and shaping, but of course they will give considerably less privacy than large, fast growers.

WHEN CHOOSING LOW-MAINTENANCE PLANTS:

• Look for drought/wet tolerance that matches your soil type

• Add perennials because they usually require only one planting

• Choose plants that will give you multiple seasonal value

• Look for plants that have a long blooming duration, such as bellflower (*Campanula*), tickseed (*Coreopsis*), coneflower (*Echinacea*), daylily (*Hemerocallis*), red hot poker (*Kniphofia*) or perennial flax (*Linum perenne*)

WHAT TO PLANT: SENSORY OPTIONS

Garden plants and trees that appeal to the senses can be particularly pleasurable for older gardeners, because they stimulate responses that may have become less acute. Moreover, sensuous choices that offer strong visual, audible, fragrant, tactile and tasty characteristics in a garden bring the environment dramatically to life. The following pages show ideas to stimulate each of the five senses in your garden.

ABOVE *Flowers and plants are not just for viewing – feel the feathery blossoms and touch the succulent leaves of sedums.*

SENSORY PLEASURES

Gardens are special and unique places that connect people to nature. As we age and perhaps work less and sit more, we may become more interested in how our senses are activated in the garden.

Using grasses or bamboos that rustle in the wind is a good start. Or introduce an accessible patch of fuzzy leaves that feel just like the soft fur of a lamb's ear to remind you that gardens can be for touching – and not just watching. The overpowering perfume of roses and other fragrant blooms are another strong motivator. Spending time alone in the garden can also make you more aware of the birds, bees and butterflies that visit.

As we age, it's important to keep our senses as keen as possible, as they tell us about the world we live in. Creating a sensory garden can help us re-engage with senses that may have been underused. This is likely to animate your interaction with your garden, and make it a more pleasurable place to be.

RIGHT *The soft lavender colours of this ornamental cabbage are a stimulating complement to the stacked slate wall.*

RIGHT *The red oak (*Quercus rubra*) will dazzle you in the autumn with its brilliant foliage and small clusters of acorns.*
.

BELOW *No old-fashioned garden is complete without a crop of sweet-smelling and colourful sweet peas.*

Gardens to stimulate sight

For most of us, our sense of sight gives us the initial information about a garden. The colours of the flowers, the textures of the leaves and the shapes of the plants all contribute to the picture. The importance of this is unlikely to change, but the sorts of colours and colour combinations that we like may shift as we get older, and any deterioration in our eyesight may require us to change the way our gardens work visually.

ABOVE *Majestic and tall, a bright yellow sunflower will stop people in their tracks as they gaze into the seed-studded disc.*

COLOUR AND CONTRAST

As we age we are likely to have more trouble detecting pale and pastel colours. Having contrasting colours in a garden compensates for this and provides important visual stimuli.

Purple flowers next to yellow, white against green foliage, or orange adjacent to blue will boost the garden experience for ageing eyes. So, to enhance the visual impact in your own garden, plant yellow daffodils

(*Narcissus* spp.) in front of a dark green hedge, or red and orange crocosmia next to white daisies. Both black-eyed Susans (*Rudbeckia fulgida*) and dwarf sunflowers (*Helianthus* spp.) offer this contrast within a single flower.

Vegetables are not just for eating, because they also offer some exciting colours. Consider the humble vegetable Swiss chard (*Beta vulgaris*) that adds a fun splash of colour with the variety 'Bright Lights'. The brightly coloured stems and foliage are as tasty as they are beautiful and look stunning among perennials. Another common vegetable that can serve double duty in your garden is the beetroot (beet) cultivar 'Bull's Blood' (*Beta vulgaris*). This has bright burgundy leaves that are highly attractive in the border.

Matching plants with complementary colours allows you to 'paint' a beautiful garden and these choices will add colour contrast and drama to the garden experience.

CHANGING EYESIGHT

To stay involved in gardening and being outdoors it helps to understand that our eyes adjust more slowly to light levels as we age. They have trouble compensating with abrupt changes in illumination, such as suddenly stepping

LEFT *Red hot pokers (*Kniphofia uvaria) *catch the eye as they stand like brilliant burning candles in front of dark foliage.*

into bright sunlight or entering deep shade. So take care when entering or leaving the garden by sitting a while to get used to the different light levels.

An eye condition such as glaucoma can reduce seniors' ability to distinguish fine details, instead focusing on form and shape. An evergreen tree has a consistent year-round form that orientates the observer well. So we become familiar with the shape of the tall stately fir or the drooping limbs of the weeping cedar.

Mobile elements are another feature that can appeal to those with compromised vision. A gentle breeze means that strands of spiny grasses and tall flowers will catch the wind and start bobbing and weaving.

For those with reduced eyesight, the key to staying active in the garden is learning adaptive techniques that will build competency and confidence.

You can space vegetables or annuals equally in rows using a notched wooden board as your planting template. If you enjoy hand

BELOW *Autumn brings many colours to our attention. Maple trees are especially famous for their brilliant shows.*

ABOVE *A selection of chrysanthemums make a big impact in this bed because of their rich, velvety purple and pinks.*

sowing, use large seeds such as peas, beans and sunflowers, which are easier to handle. Similarly, using seed tapes makes planting tiny seeds such as carrots and radishes easy and reliable (*see also* pages 88–89). Grouping plants with similar watering requirements will help with irrigation tasks. Labels or tags with large lettering or Braille will help you identify special plants or the locations of seeds.

BEAUTIFUL FOLIAGE

When we think of leaves we tend to think of green shades, but foliage can be found in many colours and patterns. A member of the coleus family, for example, will introduce a rainbow of leaf colours into your garden that will mix and match together and with their companions. Another great foliage choice is the chartreuse-coloured ornamental sweet potato, *Solanum tuberosum* 'Margarita'. Finally, caladiums are excellent for those shady or partly shady areas in your garden as they enliven the garden with foliage of

green, white, pink, rose, red and chartreuse. If you can plant them so that the setting sun beams through the leaves, you'll achieve additional visual impact.

MAINTAINING ANNUAL INTEREST

Aim to have a selection of plants that will ensure year-round enjoyment. So you might have green fiddlehead ferns (*Pteridium aquilinum*) that will uncurl in the spring, tomatoes (*Lycopersicon esculentum*) that will ripen deep red on the vines as summer passes, and the opportunity to collect lovely yellow ginkgo (*Ginkgo biloba*) leaves in the autumn. Some seasons will expose structural elements such as interesting branches and colourful bark. A Japanese maple, for example, offers a graceful network of flowing twigs and branches that has considerable presence during its winter dormancy. Winter is also the time that we appreciate how much shape and height contribute to the garden picture.

BELOW *Think contrasting colours when choosing flowers – pair oranges and blues or purples and yellows for a striking effect.*

Gardens to stimulate sound

The ability to hear may deteriorate as we age. However, finding ways of tuning into the sounds in our garden, both naturally occurring ones such as bees collecting pollen and man-made features such as wind chimes, will awaken our auditory sense and enhance our garden experience. With a little practice on our part and the addition of some new features, our gardens can be 'wired' for sound.

ABOVE *Birdfeeders with a variety of seeds will attract many different kinds of birds who will animate your garden with sound.*

RUSTLING GRASSES

Here are a selection of grasses that rustle in the breeze.

- Greater quaking grass (*Briza maxima*)
- Jose select tall wheatgrass (*Elytrigia elongota* 'Jose Select')
- Miscanthus (*Miscanthus sinensis* 'Morning Light') – upright, arching foliage and bronze plumes.
- Miscanthus (*Miscanthus sinensis* 'Silberfeder') – sturdy green foliage and white seed plumes.
- Prairie sky switch grass (*Panicum virgatum* 'Prairie Sky') – tight-growing sky-blue foliage and airy, sand-coloured flower spikes.
- Silver grass (*Miscanthus oligostachyus* 'Nanus Variegatus') – has a pretty bamboo-like foliage.
- Bamboo (*Phyllostachys*) – lovely foliage that appears to whisper in the wind. Their tall and erect stems produce a hollow sound when knocked together.

Panicum virgatum   *Phyllostachys*

RIGHT Briza maxima, *a quaking grass, sounds like a small ripple of water as it catches the wind and quakes in its roots.*

ABOVE *Clinking threaded limpet shells are merely one kind of chime that will add sound and melody to your garden.*

ORIENTATION WITH SOUND

The sounds of nature tell us so much about the habitat in which we are gardening and relaxing. Listening to the low buzz of a bumblebee or the sweet trill from the blackbird will be, quite literally, music to your ears. What's more, sounds in the garden orientate us to what season we are entering or leaving. From the dripping of water droplets from icicles on the eaves to the honking of geese overhead, these simple natural sounds tell us in gentle ways where we are in time.

There are many natural ways to add sounds to your garden. Attracting wildlife such as birds, insects and mammals is one way. Adding plants, such as bamboo, grasses and palms, and flowers that form interesting seed pods can also introduce new auditory

experiences. If you let an area of lawn go unraked in the autumn then you will hear the crunching and crackling of dried leaves underfoot.

Adding man-made features such as wind chimes, bird and squirrel feeders and bird houses will bring many musical and wildlife sounds into your garden. Water channelled through a water feature can create a sense of peace and calm, and have healing benefits. A simple water feature, especially one that flows, bubbles, sprays or drips, will also attract more wildlife. Even if you can only manage a shallow birdbath, you will still enjoy hearing birds splashing about the pool as they flap their wings. For feathered and furry visitors, water features offer a reliable drink and a place to clean themselves.

REDUCING NOISE POLLUTION

Having moving water in the garden can be a creative way to mask offensive sounds such as traffic or machine noise that can disturb the peace. Often referred to as 'white noise', water movement helps drown out traffic and other noise pollution, allowing you to relax undisturbed by the world beyond.

RIGHT *The bright orange pods of the Chinese lantern are an autumn favourite. Plant it in a big pot, as it can be invasive.*

BELOW *Crisp, colourful autumnal leaves carpeting a path will crackle and rustle under your feet.*

PLANTS WITH SEED PODS
Here are some of the seed pods that make attractive sounds:

• Poppies (*Papaver*) have showy blooms, require little care, and form geometric seed pods. Full of seeds for next year's garden, the pods make an attractive rattling sound when shaken.
• The Chinese lantern plant (*Physalis alkekengi*) produces rows of inflated papery, orange-red lantern-like seed pods that can be heard moving in the wind.
• Honesty (*Lunaria annua*) forms disc-like seed pods that change to purple and then brown – rub them to reveal the silver discs that hold the seeds.

• Columbine (*Aquilegia*) is an early summer flowering plant, and one of the easiest perennials. Once the seed heads form and a hint of brown emerges, deadhead them and create a rattle bouquet from the pods.
• Love-in-a-mist (*Nigella damascena*) is a delicate plant, showy in the spring with bright blue, white or rose-coloured flowers, but the fun starts when it forms paper-textured puffy seed heads which rattle when shaken. The minute black seeds will ensure next year's growth.
• The money plant (*Lunaria biennis*) has lightly scented purple or white flowers in the spring and translucent, silver-dollar seed pods that flutter gently in the wind.

Nigella damascena   *Lunaria annua*   *Aquilegia*   *Papaver*

Gardens to stimulate smell

Our sense of smell brings alive our experience of gardens. The perfume of a rose can capture a special memory, and the garden after rainfall is filled with the aroma of moist earth and greenery. However, this sense does deteriorate as we age. It might also be compromised by certain medications or being a smoker. Whatever our nasal ability, there are plants – and not just flowers – that are sure to stimulate and delight.

ABOVE *The sweet fragrances of old-fashioned climbing roses fill the air and say, "Come in for a closer look".*

SEASONAL PERFUMES

Fragrances can elevate our mood and increase our feelings of well-being and overall happiness. Whether from sweet-smelling blooms, pungent leaves or strong herbal essences, olfactory stimulation is undoubtedly one of the joys of gardening.

Each season brings its own unique scents that can remind us of our past history in gardens. Even if you are tending just a large container, you can still grow fragrant plants.

In the springtime, sweet-smelling shrubs sited near your entranceway will welcome visitors to your garden. Low-maintenance daphnes, lilacs (*Syringa* spp.) and many deciduous azaleas can dazzle you and your visitors with their charming perfumes. Think about the subtle scents created by spring bloomers such as violets (*Viola* spp.), lily of the valley (*Convallaria majalis*), stocks (*Malcolmia maritima*), pinks (*Dianthus* spp.) and sweet alyssum (*Lobularia maritima*). Summertime mock oranges (*Philadelphus coronarius*) and roses (*Rosa* spp.) will stop you in your tracks as you are greeted by their wafting aromas. In the autumn, flowers on Chinese holly (*Osmarea* x *burkwoodii*) or osmanthus offer fabulously sweet smells.

In the winter, sweet box (*Sarcococca*) packs such a scent in its tiny, inconspicuous flowers that people have been known to think that someone has been using too much perfume. This can be uplifting for those of us who can feel down in the short, dark days of winter.

LEFT *Plants including mountain pine (*Pinus mugo*), lavender (*Lavandula stoechas*), Rosa 'Gertrude Jekyll', bronze fennel (*Foeniculum vulgare purpureum*) and iris create an experience that will linger all day.*

WHERE TO SITE SCENTED PLANTS AND SHRUBS

Planting fragrant plants near the entrance to your garden will perfume the area as you enter. Another idea is to add plants with aromatic leaves to places with a narrow span where you will be brushing against the plant, for example as you walk under an archway. Scents are stronger and easier to detect when the sun is shining and the temperature is warm, so an arbour covered with honeysuckle or fragrant clematis needs only a sunny day to create a perfumed experience. Sweet peas trained on wires against a sunny wall will also create sweet aromas.

If you don't have room for scented shrubs, then create a fragrant container or raised bed with various scented geraniums (*Pelargonium* spp.). These come in perfumes that include apple, lime, nutmeg, pine, lemon and rose. They are powerhouses of fragrance and bloom all through the summer and into the autumn.

USING HERBS

Herbs are great way to keep fragrances alive in a garden space, whether they are planted at ground level, in a raised

BELOW *A path under a covered archway of blooming sweet peas may be one of the sweetest walks you ever take.*

bed or in a container. Planting some scented thymes (*Thymus subphylum*) and other herbs between pavers or stones offers an effortless way to activate fragrance. Walking on them will crush the leaves, causing them to emit their aroma into the air.

Familiar favourites, such as rosemary, lavender and mint, will provide you with months of classic scents that might motivate you to use them in other ways – for teas, seasoning or crafts. Or, if you're feeling more adventurous, try unfamiliar herbs such as the curry plant (*Helichrysum italicum*). In addition to having a heightened aroma – on sunny days its yellow flowers fill the air with a spicy fragrance – this evergreen plant has other attractive features. The foliage is a variegated silver-grey in colour and has a wonderfully attractive fuzzy texture.

ABOVE *Fragrant thyme is a great herb to grow among walking pavers where it is hot and dry. A slight foot pressure will release the thyme's lovely aroma.*

BELOW *Grow lily of the valley (*Convallaria majalis*) in a pot and site it in an area where you can benefit from its perfume.*

Gardens to stimulate touch

Unlike the other senses, the sense of touch seems to be retained no matter what our age. Certainly, few things are more satisfying for gardeners than digging their fingers into the soft earth. Reassuringly, the sense of touch is always there to fall back on, providing a way of connecting with the world around us if other senses are less reliable. Here we look at the possibilities for stimulating this grounding sense in the garden.

ABOVE *Sempervivum tectorum has sculpted leaf forms, tight rosettes that appear waxed and polished.*

SMOOTH AND SOFT TEXTURES

Adding smooth and soft textures to your garden can have a calming effect if they are close enough to allow touching and rubbing. A good example is lamb's ear (*Stachys byzantina*), an old-fashioned favourite with gardeners. Each elongated leaf feels like a swatch of silky velvet or soft felt. Then there are the springtime pussy willows (*Salix caprea*) with their small grey bundles of softness that are a delight to handle for old and young alike.

BELOW *These soft, tall grasses create a sense of place for this partially sighted man.*

WAXY AND LEATHERY TEXTURES

Plants that grow in the desert or in alpine zones often have a waterproof coating that feels as if they have been rubbed with wax. Many of these are popular houseplants, such as the Christmas cactus (*Schlumbergera* spp.). Sedums growing in a rock garden have many forms, all interesting to feel. Another that appeals in this category is *Bergenia cordifolia* – not only are the leaves leathery and waxy, they also squeak like a pig when rubbed together!

BELOW *Scirpus grass produces small fluffy flowers at the stem tips.*

ROUGH AND SPIKY TEXTURES

The idea of 'tree-hugging' is often associated with environmentalism, but this expression is inspired by the sturdy power of trees and of their textured bark. Many barks feel rough and have deep grooves for fingers to explore the nooks and crannies.

The purple coneflower (*Echinacea purpurea*) is an ideal choice for a sensory garden since its stems and foliage have stiff hairs that give the plants a rasping, sandpapery quality when rubbed. The seed pods of the

BELOW *The Chinese snowball (*Viburnum macrocephalum*) forms soft flower clusters.*

ABOVE *The exquisite bark of the Himalayan cherry (*Prunus rufa*) has attractive peeling, reddish-brown and amber bark.*

coneflower resemble a pincushion but won't pierce your fingers as you feel the pointy hardness of the seeds.

PAPERY TEXTURES

Some flowers provide us with interesting seed pods, some of which have been mentioned in the 'gardens to stimulate sound' section on pages 38–39. The money plant (*Lunaria biennis*) is one that will give many seasons of interest. When the flower dies it forms round, silvery seed pods. It's fun to feel the papery outer layers as you peel them off to reveal a translucent membrane that resembles a silver dollar. You can use these to create dried flower arrangements to enjoy all year round.

Pearly everlasting (*Anaphalis margaritacea*) produces white, papery bracts with yellow-to-red flowers in the centre in tight clusters at the top of the stem. The flower bracts dry and in late autumn they can be cut for a dry flower arrangement. When moved, they sound just like paper rustling.

OTHER DELIGHTS

While our hands are our primary tool for touching and feeling, let's not forget our feet. Digging our toes into lush, cool grass can refresh and relax us. A small water feature with a place to cool your feet would be an excellent addition to a sensory garden. Adding aquatic plants, such as water lilies, water lettuce, water grasses and bulrushes will provide other interesting tactile experiences.

Those smooth rocks or collection of shells you found on the seashore can be added to your sensory garden. The coolness and contours of the rock and the smooth edges of the shells will stimulate your sense of touch and bring back vivid memories of that day on the beach. A bowl of nuts, seeds and pods is also fun to have nearby so you can easily pick one up and enjoy the shapes and textures. Another option is to get a fine outdoor misting machine for your garden – this will cool and refresh your skin on a hot day.

ABOVE *The Devon green hosta has heart-shaped leaves that are leathery in texture with prominent veining.*

BELOW Pennisetum villosum*, aptly called 'feather top', produces cascades of graceful creamy white, plume-like inflorescences that are hard to resist.*

Gardens to stimulate taste

Admiring the colourful produce in a vegetable or fruit garden is a small step away from knowing how the ripe green cucumber or the plump red strawberries taste. Other garden elements to enliven our taste buds might be a bed of edible flowers, a container of herbs or a vine of sweet honeysuckle. Because the sense of taste becomes less acute as we age, let's take measures in our gardens to keep it alive and well.

ABOVE *Harvesting fruit that you have grown is one of the most satisfying experiences for a gardener.*

THE VEGETABLE GARDEN

There is nothing more rewarding than the harvesting of sweet cherry tomatoes growing in pots in your patio, and they can be eaten freshly picked, just like fruit. Other delicious vegetables you can grow include greens, such as spring greens (collards) and kale (*Brassica oleracea* var. *acephala*), mustard greens (*Brassica* spp.), rocket (arugula), chard (*Beta vulgaris* subsp. *cicla*) and lettuce (*Lactuca sativa*), with tasty leaves that are full of vitamins and antioxidants. Then there are pole or bush beans, which come in all sizes and many colours and are one of the most reliable and tasty crops to grow.

Potatoes (*Solanum tuberosum*) can be cultivated in a 45-litre (12-gallon) bucket or in a raised bed. These vegetables are easy to plant and maintain, and are fun to harvest and prepare. Small, fingerling types taste especially buttery. Squash (*Cucurbita pepo*) is another option – you can grow summer varieties, such as courgettes (zucchini), as well as winter ones. Cucumbers (*Cucumis sativus*) can be grown on a trellis to save space – there are many varieties to choose from, including the lemon cucumber. (*See also* pages 146–153 for other options.)

FRUIT CROPS

The possibilities for fruit growing are extensive, even within a small garden. If you like apples but do not have room for full-sized trees, use small columnar of dwarf apple trees, but remember you will need two or three different ones to ensure pollination. Grapes can be grown almost anywhere – with a careful selection of cultivated varieties in warm areas you can have them ripening over a long season.

Strawberries are a must-have crop for a small garden, so find a variety that will do well in your climate and conditions. Blueberries are a small shrub that can serve as both an ornamental plant and a fruit bearer.

LEFT *On a warm evening, there is nothing better than spreading the table for an outdoor supper with garden produce.*

A good approach is to plant several varieties to maximize pollination and then you will have berries over a longer period. A few raspberry canes are an attractive addition that will reward you with their sweet, delicately perfumed berries – they are easy to harvest with proper staking and are prolific over a long season. (*See also* pages 154–165 for other fruit options.)

HERBAL TASTES

Flavouring food with herbs makes cooking and eating a more exciting experience. Using herbs is also a healthier option than adding flavour with salt or sugar in our cooking. We tend to use the leafy part of herbs, so the ideal time for picking them is in the morning before the sun gets hot and the leaves wilt. You can store them in an open bag or perforated plastic bag in your refrigerator crisper for several days. When using fresh herbs in a recipe you will need almost three times the amount you'd use with dried herbs.

Many herbal flowers and leaves make lovely teas. These include lemon verbena (*Aloysia triphylla*) which has tiny creamy-coloured, citrus-scented blossoms that can be steeped as a

ABOVE *Autumn-fruiting varieties of raspberries produce their delicious berries over a long period, starting in summer.*

herb tea. Others are raspberry and blackberry leaves, hibiscus flowers, which have a cranberry flavour with citrus overtones, and hibiscus petals that can be dried to make an aromatic and tasty tea. *Camellia sinensis* will give you an ample supply of traditional tea leaves and if you have rose hips, don't forget to save them for tea next winter.

EDIBLE FLOWERS

Both herbs and some plants normally seen as ornamental produce flowers that can be eaten. Floral edibles are currently going through a revival as chefs and creative home cooks are using flowers to create colourful garnishes and delicate tastes.

Nasturtiums, marigolds (*Calendula officinalis*), roses (*Rosa*), scented geraniums (*Pelargonium*) and dandelions (*Taraxacum officinale*) are all easy to grow. If you like spicy and savoury flavours, use fresh nasturtiums, young dandelions or marigold petals in salads or sprinkled on the top of rice. Rose and carnation petals are sweet and attractive additions to

desserts. Scented geranium flowers offer many flavours, including citrus. Sprinkle the blossoms over desserts, add them to refreshing drinks or freeze them in ice cubes as a floating garnish.

Light purple chive blooms can be tossed on salads to add an onion scent and flavour, and lavender flowers can be added to cookies. Sweet basil flowers sprinkled over a salad or pasta add strong flavour and a spark of colour. Yellow dill flowers are a great seasoning for soups, seafood and salad dressings.

SAFETY NOTE
When using edible flowers in your diet, observe these guidelines.

• For those who are on restrictive diets or who are taking medication, it's wise to consult with your doctor when using a new food such as edible flowers.
• Be sure that the flowers you are selecting are safe to eat. Consult a good reference book.
• Eat only flowers that were grown organically – with no pesticides!
• To begin with, eat small amounts to track any adverse reactions.

BELOW *Many flowers are edible and good for you – add nasturtium flowers to your salads for colour and a peppery taste.*

BELOW *Growing fruit and vegetables that you can eat in the garden provides the perfect, healthy afternoon nibble.*

STAYING SAFE AND SOUND

Shakespeare wrote, "Out of this nettle, danger, we pluck this flower, safety". The Bard's garden is a metaphorical one, but in our real gardens we need to create a safe and healthy environment so we can spend time there happily and comfortably. Considered here are two broad areas of garden safety – our bodies and our environment.

Gardening is rated as one of the most popular leisure activities for people over the age of 50. Because we choose to interact and work with plants, soil and tools, as seniors we need to take more precautions and care in our gardening work habits and routines. Our body is our most valuable 'tool', so it's important to know how to take care of it and protect it. Just as you might pamper a favourite, expensive piece of equipment, your body also needs good maintenance. As our reflexes lose their acuity and our other senses become less alert, understanding our limitations and relearning how to use our bodies in order to stay healthy and safe in the garden will allow us to continue our gardening for many more decades.

OPPOSITE *A sheltered bench is ideal to take time out from the summer sun – or for a leisurely chat while enjoying the garden.*

ABOVE *A wide brimmed hat and long sleeves will keep your skin from getting too much sun.*

ABOVE *Cover the tips of garden support stakes with small flowerpots to avoid uncomfortable collisions.*

ABOVE *Kneelers or cushions will keep your knees protected and comfortable as you dig in the garden bed.*

ASSESSMENT AND PREPARATION

Gardening and working with plants should be an enjoyable leisure activity as well as a therapeutic one. It not only relaxes your mind and nourishes your spirit, but also can give your body a pretty good workout. So in order to stay capable and well as a gardener, aim to do a personal assessment of how you feel on a particular day and think about anything additional you can do to prepare yourself.

ABOVE *Use your garden for relaxation as well as garden maintenance – and enjoy the fruits of your labour close-up.*

PACING YOURSELF

It's good to assess how you are feeling before you venture into the garden. How rested do you feel? If you had a poor night's sleep and feel unusually tired, you'd probably be wise to postpone gardening, or at least modify your planned activity. Are your aches and pains distracting you? If you are feeling soreness or stress in parts of your body, maybe just sitting in the garden and enjoying the scene is all the 'gardening' you should do that day.

How much time do you have? If you're anxious to get a particular task done, give yourself enough time to finish it, or instead do a smaller project that you know you can resolve easily. Rushing, and perhaps cutting corners, to accomplish a job may result in anxiety, or even an injury that could put you out of commission for several days. Plus rushing takes the fun out of gardening and makes it a chore!

STRATEGIES

There are other ways to make gardening more efficient. Make a realistic to-do list of the projects you wish to get done in any given day or session. It's best to do the more strenuous tasks first when you have more energy.

If the weather is hot, use the coolest part of the day, usually early in the morning or late in the day, to do your gardening. If you can, try and plan your work area to be in, or near, the shade. Another idea is to collect the tools you will need and store them so they are accessible. Keeping the essential tools close to hand – in a bucket, say, or in your garden apron – will reduce unnecessary walks to the shed.

Similarly, plan on doing particular tasks when the conditions are most suited to them. For example, cultivating or weeding in soil that is slightly moist is much easier than handling dry, compacted earth. Conversely, clay soils that have become soggy from spring rains will be too heavy for you to lift – and you can actually ruin your soil by moving it when it is in such a sodden state. Try to transplant or sow seeds close to predicted rainfall. Aligning such gardening activities with the weather takes advantage of the natural conditions and saves you time watering. However, if the timing is not optimal, assess how much water you will need to irrigate your plantings and ensure that you have an appropriate hose or suitable water containers nearby.

LEFT *A greenhouse expands the range of plants you can grow and means you can keep warm during the winter.*

ABOVE *Plan the day's garden projects so you can pace yourself and feel a sense of accomplishment.*

ABOVE *Choose a cool day or a sheltered spot to do your transplanting and repotting so the plants are less stressed.*

PREPARING FOR GARDENING

If you live in a climate where tending your garden is possible in all four seasons, your gardening activity can become a regular form of exercise. If your climate is more variable, you may have another exercise regime to use when you can't garden. For those who don't have a regular regime, just like animals emerging from their winter hibernation, starting a new routine of physical exercise takes more time. However ready you are, here are some suggestions as you look forward to getting your hands in the soil again.

It's always advisable to consult your physician if you are going to increase or change your exercise habits. If you've recently started or changed your medication, your doctor may have advice about how these will affect your time and exposure in the garden.

Consider how new optical prescriptions or glasses – particularly those with bi- and tri-focal lenses – can affect your physical exercise. While these all-purpose glasses are convenient, be aware that they can cause some distortion of depth perception before the user becomes accustomed to them. So it can be wise to ease into some gardening tasks until you get used to your new glasses.

Another important factor is to anticipate the parts of your body that you'll be using most. Take time to warm up in the same way you would before doing any other exercise. Just walking around the garden will achieve this and also allows you to assess what projects you might enjoy doing. Even marching in place for a few minutes, stretching and flexing your muscles, will give your body that initial warm-up so it is ready for some more physical exertion.

The following pages describe appropriate warm-up exercises for gardening in more detail. The challenge is to anticipate how much time you need to spend warming up to maximize your flexibility without compromising the amount of time you want to spend gardening.

WARM-UP EXERCISES

Mark Twain once quipped, "I'm pushing sixty. That's enough exercise for me". Witticisms aside, however, gardening is a physical activity and, for many of us who are getting older, this may be our primary form of exercise. Whether you're a regular gardener or have not gardened for a while, it's worth spending time gently loosening up, warming up and stretching before you start. This means you will reduce any muscle aches and the risk of injury.

ABOVE *Exercising with a partner is an effective and fun way to get your body ready for gardening.*

THE EXERCISE OF GARDENING

Gardening helps us maintain muscle tone, joint flexibility, bone strength, range of motion and general physical stamina. In addition, research shows that gardening for 30–45 minutes five or six days a week has other significant health benefits, such as decreasing the risk of high blood pressure and the occurrence of diabetes.

As we age, we all lose some physical ability and we may develop arthritis and other conditions that limit our movements. Always talk to your health care provider about starting a new physical routine. Having a partner or an exercise group helps you stay motivated to keep limber and strong so you can do the physical activities you love without injuring yourself.

Get yourself ready by knowing what activities you will be doing. Will you be digging, kneeling, bending, lifting or pruning? Being aware of the parts of your body you will be using most and getting them prepared using the suggestions in this chapter will help you limber up for whatever lifts, bends, pulls and lunges are required to accomplish your garden goals.

LOOSENING UP WITH GENTLE HEAD TILTS

This exercise is great for getting some of the 'kinks' out of your neck.

LOOSENING UP WITH SHOULDER SHRUGS

This exercise helps to strengthen and build the muscle mass at the area of the shoulder joints.

1 *Stand comfortably with your feet about shoulder distance apart from each other. Without moving your upper torso, tilt your head to the right, directing your ear towards the top of your shoulder. Count to 5. Then bring your head back to the upright position.*

2 *Repeat the same head tilt to your left side, again directing your ear towards the top of your shoulder for a count of 5. Repeat 3 times on each side. If you prefer, you can also do this exercise sitting down.*

1 *Stand comfortably with your shoulders relaxed and your feet at a shoulder distance apart from each other.*

2 *Elevate your shoulders towards your neck. Hold this position for a count of 5. Relax and repeat the exercise 5 times. If you prefer, you can also do this exercise sitting down.*

UPPER BODY TWIST

Spine twists increase the range of motion in the upper body by training the trunk to spiral on the central vertical axis. Make sure that you twist both sides equally, trying not to favour one side, and be gentle at first as you ease into deeper twists.

1 *Stand comfortably with your feet about shoulder distance apart from each other and with your hands on your hips.*

2 *Slowly turn your upper body, including your neck and head, from your waist as far as possible. Hold for the count of 5 and return to the centre position.*

3 *Repeat the exercise on the left for a count of 5. Repeat 5 times.*

WRIST CIRCLES

Wrist exercises are a good way to prevent stiff joints and carpal tunnel syndrome, which causes tingling and numbness of the thumb, index and middle finger. Increased wrist strength will make many tasks easier.

1 *With hands in front of your body and elbows held at a comfortable angle, gently rotate your wrists in a circular motion. This shows the downward pointing direction.*

2 *This shows the man bringing up his hands towards him.*

3 *This shows the man's hands in an upwards pointing direction. Do 5 repetitions in each direction.*

WALKING OR CYCLING

Walking and cycling are great ways to warm up and can be done on the spot.

LOWER BACK STRETCHES

This exercise stretches the lower back muscles that are activated while gardening. Balance on one leg, holding the lifted knee. Do this near a wall if you need support.

1 *Walk in place for a few minutes or for the time that suits you. You could also use a stationary bike or treadmill.*

1 *Bring your right knee as high as you can to your chest and clasp your knee with your hands. Hold for a count of 5.*

2 *Place your foot on the ground and repeat these movements with the other leg. Do 5 repetitions with each leg.*

ARM SWINGS

These movements do for your arms what walking does for your legs, and you are more likely to use your arms as you garden. Always do the first couple of swings gently and then increase the stretching if the movements feel comfortable.

1 *Stand with your feet comfortably apart, knees slightly bent, and start with your arms at shoulder level. Stretch your arms straight out to the side so you make a T-shape with your body.*

2 *Slowly bring your arms back behind you, pulling your shoulder blades together.*

3 *With a slow and steady movement, gradually bring your arms around to the front of your torso, and hug your shoulders or upper arms. Repeat these steps, gradually speeding up the movements. Increase the range of motion until your muscles feel warm.*

STRETCHING

Don't start any stretching exercises until your muscles have been adequately warmed up with low-impact exercises, such as those shown on pages 50–52.They should be done gently and holding the stretch is important – here we advise holding for a count of 5.

The exercises on this page will stretch the lower back and the calf muscles, the upper arm and shoulders, and the upper leg. All these muscle groups need to work quite hard as we garden and so giving them a stretch before gardening starts will make you feel more comfortable and should safely avoid any strains.

These stretching exercises are also recommended to use once your gardening session is over because they work the body parts that you are most likely to have used. So build them into your gardening routine.

CALF STRETCHES

This exercise is the perfect way to stretch your calf. It can also be done seated.

1 *Place one foot about 45cm (18in) in front of the other. Keep your back leg straight with your heel on the floor. Push against a wall to increase the stretch in the calf. Hold to the count of 5 and repeat with the other leg. Do 5 repetitions with each leg.*

UPPER ARM STRETCHES

This will help to loosen up your upper arms and shoulders.

1 *Raise your right elbow alongside your right ear and with your left hand put a gentle pressure on the raised upper arm until you feel a stretch in the arm. Count to 5 and release. Repeat on the left side. Do 5 repetitions.*

UPPER LEG STRETCH

This exercise involves balancing on one leg. If you need support, do this near a wall or hold on to the back of a chair. The front part of your thighs should feel a stretch.

1 *While standing, move your right heel toward your right buttock and clasp your foot with your right hand. Hold your foot until the stretch is felt in the front of your thigh. Count to 5.*

2 *Repeat step 1 on your left side. Do 5 repetitions with each leg. As much as you can, keep your knees together and your hips level.*

SOME FINAL WORDS ABOUT EXERCISING

Some of us come to gardening with years of experience; others prefer to 'putter' gently, which may not include digging or moving mulch, but still activates and utilizes parts of the body. Whatever your degree of endurance, you should stay engaged in gardening at your personal comfort level.

If you're not already active, begin slowly. Start with exercises that you are comfortable doing – then you're less likely to injure yourself, and being cautious will help prevent soreness. Remember that you do not have to exercise at a high intensity to get the maximum health benefit.

If you're not feeling well, it is advisable to postpone your routine and wait until you feel better before you resume your exercises. If you miss your routine for more than two weeks, be sure to start slowly again.

MAXIMIZING COMFORT

No matter what physical activity you are engaged in, you are more likely to stick with it if you're feeling relatively strong, balanced and safe. We need to feel comfortable as we engage in activities and hobbies. 'Comfort' is a broad term, so let us narrow it down to how it comes into play in several areas of gardening, clothing, preparation and choosing the right tools and equipment – all these need to support us in the job we are doing.

ABOVE *No gardener should be without a pair of practical and comfortable wellington boots.*

CLOTHING

Before starting any gardening, check the weather conditions so you can dress appropriately for the temperature and the local conditions. If gardening is one of your primary means of getting exercise, then it is worth investing in good-quality clothes for all weathers to keep you warm and dry. Thanks to the

BELOW *A sturdy, wide-brimmed hat is an essential for gardeners. It prevents sunburn and keeps the whole body cool.*

availability of lightweight, yet warm and waterproof, fabrics you can move about easily in the garden without heavy, bulky clothes in your way. Comfortable and sturdy shoes, appropriate gloves for the task at hand and a good hat can all add to your comfort in the garden.

We all have our favourite gardening clothes. The author's preference is for Japanese gardening trousers with little pockets in the knees for stuff-in knee pads. But as we age, we need to put

safety and comfort first, as well as wearing seasonally appropriate clothes. Did you know that light colours in the summer keep you cooler and that dark colours in winter absorb heat and help you stay warm? Let's look at some common-sense features to consider when choosing a gardening outfit.

THE HEAD

A hat with a good brim keeps the top of the head shaded from the sun, and shelters our eyes from glare that can be

RIGHT *A garden apron and a pair of protective gloves is a versatile outfit for most gardening jobs.*

disorienting. Many gardeners have fair- and foul-weather hats. It is advisable to wear a hat with a warm liner (and maybe earflaps) when it's cool. Most body heat is lost through our heads so it is good to retain that heat to maintain the rest of your body warmth. A waterproof hat is a must in wet weather and a hat with a chin tie will stay on your head if a gust of wind comes along.

THE NECK

Necks have a role in regulating the loss and retention of body heat. In warmer weather, a bandana with a moisture-absorbing polymer will keep you cool and comfortable for hours. Alternatively, a lightweight wool or fleece scarf around the neck can help retain your body heat.

THE TORSO

Your clothing will depend on the weather. A rule of thumb is to use light, loose-fitting clothes that cover your skin. Even

BELOW *Wheelchairs have add-on accessories to improve comfort – this parasol will keep this gardener out of the sun.*

RIGHT *A garden apron and a pair of protective gloves is a versatile outfit for most gardening jobs.*

though we seniors should have at least 20 minutes of sun exposure on our faces and forearms several times a week, we also need to protect ourselves from over-exposure. Some clothing comes with UV protection embedded in the fabric. A lightweight, long-sleeved shirt can provide protection in the summer from the sun, bugs and scratchy twigs. On cooler days, wear several layers of lightweight fabrics, enough to keep you warm but easy to remove if you get too hot. Front-fastening shirts and jackets are good as they are easier to put on than pullover styles.

Garden aprons keep your tools organized and near you while you work. Aprons come with many features and in many styles. Some are made of sturdy denim, canvas, and synthetic materials with several kinds of quick-release buckles, an important feature when wearing gloves. Consider how the pockets are sized and placed. Can they hold a water bottle, snacks, a mobile phone (you can miss a lot of calls trying to get those gloves off so

you can find your mobile)? Most importantly, test the apron with the pockets filled; the last thing you want is a garden apron that puts too much stress on your neck.

BELOW *This apron has useful pockets for storing the handy tools that you want to have by your side.*

ABOVE *For most garden tasks there is the perfect glove to protect your hands from the cold, wet and prickly thorns.*

ABOVE *Wear comfortable, solid shoes to protect your feet from the sharp edge of a spade.*

ABOVE *Well-fitting gloves that are breathable and water-resistant give you dexterity when digging or weeding.*

THE HANDS

Your hands are your most important tool, so take good care of them. Find gloves that are well constructed and fit comfortably. Be aware too of any special needs in your hands, wrists or fingers. For arthritic hands there are special gloves with strategically placed padding to help reduce blisters, calluses and fatigue.

At the simplest level, wearing comfortable, padded gloves, such as fingerless bicycle gloves, is an easy way to provide a good grip, and gives you comfort, ease and protection.

Choose gloves to fit the job. Those made of cotton or jersey are good for light jobs, with rubber or nitrite palms to help grip pots and handles. Rubber gloves protect hands from dirt, chemicals, water and thorns. Leather gloves are best for heavy-duty tasks and will also protect from prickly plants.

Gloves come with options, such as reinforced fingertips, snug wrist bands, and webbing at the base of the fingers to allow for maximum comfort and breathability. Look for the features you need, and choose gloves that can be machine washed and air-dried quickly.

THE LEGS

As well as being appropriate to the weather, leg wear should also be lightweight and loose-fitting. If a gardening task takes you into wet bushes or tall grasses, waterproof trousers will keep you both comfortable and clean. Some senior gardeners may decide to avoid growing thorny or prickly plants, but if you do grow any, or have to tackle thorny weeds, you need a material on your legs (and arms) that is heavy enough to protect you. Finally, good coverage on arms and legs keeps you from coming into contact with stinging or irritant plants, or biting insects.

THE FEET

Wear protective shoes that are comfortable and easy to get on and off. Shoes that are fastened with Velcro are a great option. Usually, the nature of the garden task will determine if you need a sturdy pair of work boots for digging, or lighter shoes for less strenuous chores. Garden clogs are popular since they are easy to wear and clean, but they

don't give much support. A good walking shoe for gardeners should be more sturdy than clogs. Seek out those with non-slip soles and waterproof uppers. Studies on the incidence of falls suggest that athletic shoes, canvas shoes or sneakers are the safest choice for footwear since they have a low heel and a large area of contact between the shoe sole and the walking surface.

Keeping your shoes clean is important, so look for those made of rubber or another waterproof material that is easy to wash. Once you have finished gardening you can just slip them off and quickly hose them down, leaving them to dry until your next visit to the garden.

WARMING UP

Warming up and stretching will add to your comfort while gardening, especially with ageing muscles and frail joints. (*See also* pages 50–53.)

OPPOSITE *Comfortable, non-binding clothes allow easy movements, and sturdy shoes keep you steady whatever the surface.*

SUPPORTIVE EQUIPMENT

Changing the ways in which we garden is the key to keeping us all gardening in good health and for longer. This requires mental adjustment and entails a knowledge of the new accessories and tools that can help us garden efficiently. Below are basic gardening devices that senior gardeners should consider. They are grouped according to the three stances most commonly assumed when gardening: kneeling, sitting and standing.

ABOVE *Knee protectors come in all shapes and sizes, so find those that work with the way that you garden.*

KNEELERS

A garden kneeler keeps you safe, comfortable and clean. If some of your garden beds are at ground level, a kneeler can keep you close to your plants without having to stand and stoop.

The most basic garden kneeler is a foam pad designed to cushion the knees and keep you from getting dirty. Such kneelers, however, can crush foliage and flowers and therefore should only be used carefully or just on garden paths or grass.

A more useful kneeler is one that holds you slightly above the ground, avoiding crushing plants. This design, shown opposite, usually has arms at the sides, to steady you as you raise and lower yourself, and has a second function as a seat. You simply flip the kneeling pad over and the arms become two sturdy legs supporting a raised seat with a good weight capacity. You can place an adjustable kneeler-seat at the perfect height and work at a raised bed or container while you are comfortably seated, without worrying about crushing foliage and plants. Make sure they're comfortable and suit your build.

Such kneelers should come with a strong steel frame and sturdy handles so use your arms to help raise and lower your body. Look for those made of durable steel with catches that lock in place. Foam cushions are important, and if they are waterproof all the better.

There are also knee pads that attach to your knee with straps, doing away with the need to adjust the position of the kneeler as you move along a bed.

For more convenience, many models supply pouches, storage aprons or containers to add to the kneeler/seat – these hold your tools so you don't have to make unnecessary trips to the shed.

Make sure your kneeler is easy to clean – at the end of the day a good hosing will remove dirt and garden debris. Finally, check out how easily it folds up both for carrying and storage. Always try a kneeler in your garden space – if it doesn't meet your needs, return it and try another; there are many designs available. Some gardeners like to save money by making their own kneeler from scratch or recycling other household objects to make a garden kneeler.

BELOW *Gardeners who like to get close to the plants enjoy the comfort and convenience of kneelers.*

RIGHT *This tool caddy and garden stool provides a raised seat from which to garden, as well as easy access to a varied range of tools.*

BELOW *Rubber kneelers come in moulded styles to cradle your knees and are convenient to carry around the garden.*

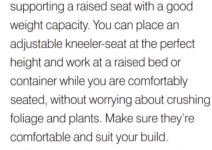

ABOVE *A combination kneeler can be used for kneeling mode (as shown here) and gives useful side grips for leverage.*

ABOVE *When turned the other way, the combination kneeler can be used as a mobile seat to use as you garden.*

ABOVE *The lightweight combination kneeler folds down neatly for easy transport and storage.*

ABOVE *Prune shrubs without reaching or bending by sitting comfortably on the seat of this inverted kneeler.*

STOOLS

A garden stool will give you a simple and safe place to sit in the garden. If you need to carry your stool to other areas of the garden, make sure it is fairly lightweight and has convenient handles for easy transport. Some can be folded for carrying and storing, and some not. Several stools on the market come with smooth, rolling wheels for easy mobility on grass and walkways. They're often designed with plenty of storage for tools and refreshments. As with all purchases, give the stool a try. Is the seat big enough? Is the storage compartment easy to reach and easy to open? Check out the weight limit and any assemblage that may be too complex.

WHEELCHAIRS

Being in a wheelchair shouldn't discourage anyone from gardening. Almost anything that can be grown in the ground can be grown in a raised bed or various sorts of container, window box and hanging basket. Vertical frames and trellises can be tended while sitting in a wheelchair.

If you garden from a wheelchair, use a lapboard, tray or simple shallow box to transport your supplies or tools. A bag hanging on the back will serve as your 'tool shed'. Wheelchair gardening can be simply achieved by placing a plywood box on a table. The space underneath the table allows the wheelchair to get close to the bed so you can plant and groom easily and comfortably.

WALKERS

Don't let the instability that can accompany ageing interfere with your gardening. With a little help from a metal frame and some wheels, you can stand on your own two legs, get to your garden spaces and keep up with the activities. Walkers provide wonderful stability if you're at risk of falling or have difficulty with balance. Walkers range from the very basic to 'fully loaded'. The most common types have two or four legs. The important thing is to correctly match the walker to your needs, abilities and limitations, as well as the environment.

BELOW *Well-designed motorized carts are easy to steer and allow you to get close to maintain raised bed planting.*

ROLLATORS

A rollator is a walker with tyres. It is ideal for those who want to go into the garden on their own, because it provides more ease in movement, stability, support and independence. If this is an option, you need to make sure that the surface area and texture of your garden environment will accommodate rollators.

PATHS, STEPS AND RAMPS

When planning a new garden, or adapting an established one, consider the following factors to improve access.

LEFT *Wheeled walkers help you access your outside space easily and safely so you can experience the garden close-up.*

RIGHT *A small transitional ramp addition allows wheeled devices safe passage over shallow steps or risers.*

BELOW RIGHT *Uneven patches of land can be made accessible for wheelchairs with telescoping ramps such as these.*

Pathways should be no less than 1.2m (4ft) wide – this will allow for a single wheelchair or walker or for a couple walking side by side.

Getting to areas that are on a slope or different level can present challenges for those with impaired mobility or low vision. If you use steps, the risers should be no higher than 10cm (4in). Painting the edges a contrasting colour reduces the risk of missing a step.

A ramp creates a smooth transition from one level to another. Ramps should be solidly constructed and have high-traction surfaces. They need a gradient of no more than 30cm (1ft) for every 50cm (20in) of length (1:20); a shallower slope is better.

Stairs or ramps should have solid handrails at a comfortable height. For those with low vision, mark the beginning and end of the ramp or stairs with high-visibility white or yellow paint to orientate the user. Another idea is a strategically placed wind chime or water feature at the entrance and exit, which gives an audible signal to those with failing sight.

LEFT *Adding a ramp to the entrance of your home or garage smooths the entry over the threshold.*

LEFT *This decking ramp connects the entrance of the house to the garden, making it accessible for wheelchair users. Adding a handrail would give extra stability to those with unsteady feet.*

FAR LEFT *Wind chimes animate a garden and can also be appropriately positioned so that owners with low vision can orientate themselves.*

OTHER SAFETY MEASURES

Safety considerations should never be ignored, but particularly for older gardeners who may have compromised balance and mobility and therefore are more vulnerable to accidents. You will know what you are capable of and what you are nervous doing. Generally, your instincts are the best guide. However, there are a number of precautionary things you can do to make the environment safer and make you feel more comfortable and confident in the garden.

ABOVE *To avoid slipping hazards for uncertain feet, use non-slip surfaces such as wood covered with chicken wire.*

A SAFE ENVIRONMENT

Using strong chemicals to deal with pests or weeds can be very toxic to a senior and to the garden environment. As a rule of thumb – green thumb, that is – it is advisable to avoid using pesticides and herbicides. Not only are they toxic but they can be complicated to use and store.

If you use a diversity of plants in your garden and keep them well maintained you can keep a chemical-free garden, which eliminates your exposure to toxins. There are also safe and non-toxic ways of getting rid of unwanted insects, animals and plants. These include traps, companion plants that deter harmful insects, beneficial organisms and insects, natural botanical pesticides and repellents and mulches to suppress weeds.

If memory loss is an issue for visitors, make sure you can secure the gates or fences to keep everyone safely inside.

AVOIDING ACCIDENTS

Paths and walkways should be made of a material that is sturdy and level. To keep the surface skid-free add some texture lines or grit material. Surfaces should also be kept clear.

As we age, our pupils respond more slowly to darkness or bright light. By tinting concrete or using an off-white colour, you decrease the incidence of high glare which can temporarily dazzle you when you step on to a bright, sunlit surface from a more dimly lit area.

Choose surfaces without a sheen that will reflect light, such as non-slip paving materials made with an exposed aggregate or sandstone finish.

In rainy climates, paths can become slippery and cause falls. One way of avoiding this is to ensure that wet leaves and plant debris are kept off paths. In shady areas, paths and patios can develop slippery moss that is invisible to the eye. To remedy this, use a misting bottle and dilute a third of a cup of household bleach with two-thirds of a cup of water and use this to spray the area. Let it stand for one hour and then

ABOVE *A tight, low hedge creates a decisive, controlled walkway by keeping users out of the garden and on the path.*

RIGHT *A flat, stable pathway is ideal for unsteady feet, with a slight texture to avoid the danger of slippiness in wet weather.*

rinse off with a hose. Repeat this in a few days depending on the level of damp and the amount of sun on the area.

Borders and hedges should be regularly trimmed back from paths so that sharp leaves or thorns don't scratch you. For this reason, try to avoid planting prickly or thorny shrubs in areas where people frequently walk.

Keep your garden tidy and make sure that there are no garden stakes or sharp objects or abandoned equipment to fall over or trip on. Stow hoses away from pathways and, when using them, keep them away from the traffic areas.

PACE YOURSELF

Prepare yourself gradually for a new season of gardening, especially when you are used to being indoors for the majority of the winter. When you get outside start with a low level of activity and work in shorter sessions than you would later in the summer. Don't exert yourself to a point of fatigue.

Once you've acclimatized to a regular routine, continue to pace yourself – gardening should not be a job but a relaxing pastime. On hot, sunny days try to garden in the early morning or whenever it is cooler, and keep an umbrella handy to give you quick, instant shade. Keep water at your side so you can stay well-hydrated. Take regular rest breaks, either sitting down, or walking around. If you feel pain, stop; this is your body warning you that something isn't right.

RIGHT Place identification markers at the head of newly seeded rows to mark what you have planted and where to water.

BELOW Define the edges of your garden beds and pathways by using a contrasting colour edging material.

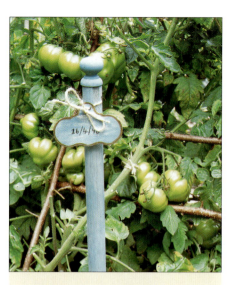

SIGHT AND SAFETY

Even though our vision decreases with age, gardening can still provide a viable form of recreation and exercise. However, safety in the garden becomes more of a priority as our ability to focus and see details is reduced. Here are some practical things you can do to make your garden secure.

• Pathways need to have a clear beginning and a clear end. To help guide those with less than perfect sight you can paint a brightly coloured stripe down the centre of a pathway.
• Orientate yourself in the garden with auditory cues from wind chimes or water features.
• Have an easily accessible water source near the garden or patio. Alternatively, install a permanent irrigation system or soaker hoses that can be turned on at the garden tap. This will also reduce any danger of tripping over trailing hoses.
• Wear a multi-pocket tool apron or a utility belt to keep your tools close by and safely stored.
• Spray tool handles in a bright colour so they can be easily found if left in the garden.
• For vegetable gardening, use a raised bed that has clearly defined rows with row markers.

AVOID STRAINING YOUR BODY

Try to maintain good posture to reduce the chance of putting pressure on joints and muscles. Try not to slouch over or put your weight on one leg or one arm. Correct your stance when you are slouching or if your weight isn't well balanced, perhaps resulting in too much pressure on one leg or arm. Change positions often and switch tasks. Repetitive movements can lead to injury, so use different parts of the body throughout your garden session – for example, go from raking leaves to sitting down, back to raking and then sitting to do some deadheading.

USE APPROPRIATE TOOLS

Senior gardeners need to be efficient in conserving their energy and health, so use the right tool for every job. The next chapter on Equipment and Techniques looks at this subject in detail. Some of the most helpful advice is to use lightweight tools and to add padded

ABOVE *For jobs such as pruning trees it is advisable get someone who is fit and active and has the right equipment to help you.*

grips to handles for increased comfort. If you have problems with your grip, strength or balance avoid using power tools and instead ask for help. If you are still fairly active and steady and you are using power tools, wear goggles

and ear plugs in addition to other safety precautions. Have someone assist you or make sure that someone else is near in case of a mishap.

AVOID RISKS

In our hurry to get that last plant in or a final branch pruned, it is easy to become careless and push ourselves too hard. Fatigue and weariness are among the chief causes of accidents, so stop before you reach that point.

You should also take care when folding or putting away sharp objects such as pruners and saws and avoid using ladders – it is a simple fact that people at retirement age or older have a much higher risk of accidents involving ladders. Get someone younger to give you a hand when appropriate. Finally, take care of any cuts, bruises or insect bites immediately to avoid complications. In conclusion, think of tomorrow as your reward for working safely today.

LIFTING OBJECTS

Don't attempt to lift or move objects that are too heavy. Instead, wait until you can ask for some help. Attempting to carry heavy things can lead to hand and wrist or back injuries. If you can, roll, push or drag rather than lift heavy loads. For loads that you can manage, this shows the best technique to keep your body safe and sound.

1 *Face the object and keep your back straight.*

2 *Bend your knees, minimizing back movement, until you can hold the object.*

3 *Finally, straighten your knees and lift up the object.*

EQUIPMENT AND TECHNIQUES

They say you can't teach an old dog new tricks, but some of us 'old dogs' would be wise to learn new gardening techniques so we can prolong our long days of summer in the garden. Fortunately, in response to the large wave of 'baby boomers', garden centres and nurseries carry a huge array of innovative and adaptive equipment, including ergonomically designed tools for almost every garden task, helping you to carry on gardening no matter what your age or health restrictions.

We start by looking at the tools themselves, with a focus on those that suit the older gardener, or existing tools that can be modified to fit your precise requirements. Then we look at individual techniques: making soil amendments; digging; cultivation, planting and fertilizing; cutting, trimming and pruning; weeding and hoeing; transporting; watering; harvesting; and tidying up. These are presented with a full range of equipment ideas and techniques for using them that will make gardening less arduous. Whenever possible, suggestions are included about how those with mobility aids, such as walkers and wheelchairs, can take advantage of the tools and have their own active place in the garden.

OPPOSITE *Having the right tool for each job keeps you involved in most gardening tasks, especially where it reduces the effort required.*

ABOVE *You can use watering wands attached to a garden hose to ensure access to hard-to-reach areas.*

ABOVE *Tools for garden tidying up such as this four-wheel trolley are important items to have in your collection.*

ABOVE *Tools help at every stage, from digging, cultivating, raking and weeding to making the perfect hole for spring bulbs.*

TOOLS AND THEIR ADAPTIVE FEATURES

You may still be using the favourite tools that have been at your side for years. However, if some of the normal ageing problems such as arthritis or failing eyesight have become part of your life, there are new tools that can assist you. Here, we'll discuss the general principles of tools designed to make gardening a more satisfying, safe and successful experience. We'll also review basic ways to adapt existing tools so they are more useful.

ABOVE *Keep sharp pruners, protective gloves and an all-purpose knife handy whenever you are working in the garden.*

BASIC TOOLS

Before we move to special tool requirements for senior gardeners, let's first consider what core selection of hand tools is required. Most essential garden jobs can be done with a small tool kit that includes a spade, a fork, a trowel, a hand fork, a pruning saw, secateurs, shears, a hoe, a cultivator and a rake. Spades, forks and trowels are often made in stainless steel, a material that is long-lasting and strong. However, stainless-steel tools can be heavy and therefore hard to manage for those with restricted movement, a weak grip, stiffness or arthritis. We will address these requirements in the sections that follow, covering the tools and techniques for individual jobs. You will probably want to add gloves, a knife, a soil test meter, a dibber, some twine and some plant pots, labels and ties to this essential selection. These are useful tools for all gardeners, whatever their age or ability. If you have grass you will also need a lawn mower, even if this is for the use of a helpful and sprightly person who agrees to do the job for you.

ERGONOMIC TOOLS

The current buzzword for various products and devices is 'ergonomic', meaning 'the technology to do with the design, manufacture, and arrangement of products and environments to be safe, healthy and comfortable for human beings'. Ergonomically designed digging and other garden tools are abundant in the marketplace, many of them using modern alloy metals such as carbon, aluminium, polypropylene and thin steel so that they are lightweight and easier to use. Unfortunately, any tool can be labelled 'ergonomic', so you may find a confusing array of tools that make this claim. The answer is to do your research carefully – see the panel on the opposite page summarizing specific points to consider before purchasing tools.

LEFT *Basic tools for any garden include a garden fork, a trowel, secateurs, a hoe, plant pots and identification labels.*

ABOVE *The long-handled fork enables this gardener to stay more upright as he weeds and cultivates.*

ABOVE *A gardener tending to his garden from a mobility cart gets the job done using a long-handled trowel.*

LONG-HANDLED TOOLS

You can garden longer and with far less stress on your body if you keep your back as straight as possible. Having garden tools with long handles makes this easy to achieve. In fact, gardeners of all ages use long-shafted spades and forks because the extra leverage saves backache. These long-handled tools become more and more essential as we age because we become less able to cope with stresses to our backs and legs.

Digging, raking and hoeing are all activities that you can do in a standing position since there are long-handled tools available for each of these garden activities. You can also use hand tools that do these tasks by removing their handles and fitting longer ones. Weeding is more tricky, and you sometimes need to be close to the ground, but many weeds can be loosened using a small, long-handled fork.

Using long-handled tools that are lightweight and suit your height should prevent any body strain. They also give a sense of enablement to those with physical restrictions or those who need to garden from a wheelchair or a seated position.

A number of long-handled tools will be introduced in the sections that follow on specific garden activities, from soil cultivation to harvesting. *See also* extending handles on page 72.

ERGONOMIC TOOLS

The design of all tools should aim to improve the user's efficiency and reduce discomfort, fatigue and the risk of injury. An ergonomic tool is not automatically going to fulfil your needs and some adaptation may still be required. Here are some practical considerations to bear in mind:

- Look for lightweight tools constructed from state-of-the-art metal alloys and strong plastics. This is important for tools designed to extend a person's reach.
- Use long-handled tools, which decrease the body's need to extend or bend beyond a comfortable reach. Extended handles also encourage a two-handed use that distributes force over more muscles and joints and improves leverage.
- Tools with a depression or ridge in the handle for your thumb to rest on will keep your hand in the proper alignment.
- Use gardening gloves that pad the joints of the hand and protect sensitive skin.
- Consider using good-quality children's garden tools – they weigh less, have shorter handles, smaller blades, and require less strength to use. These can be helpful to the wheelchair user and seated gardener.
- Keep cutting edges on digging tools and pruners sharp to reduce the force needed to use them.
- Modify a grip area by adding soft padding to increase gripping ability and enhance comfort. Make a circle with your index finger and thumb to indicate the size of grip your tools should have.

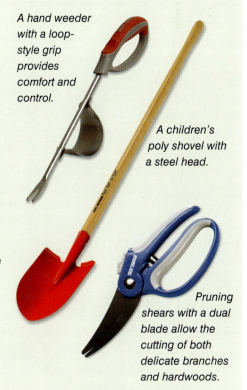

A hand weeder with a loop-style grip provides comfort and control.

A children's poly shovel with a steel head.

Pruning shears with a dual blade allow the cutting of both delicate branches and hardwoods.

SHORT-HANDLED TOOLS

In general, short-handled tools are ideal for working in raised beds or when gardening from a seated or kneeling position. The standard short-handled tools familiar to us continue to have a valid place. But if you have problems with your hand mobility, you should also consider those with specially designed easy grip handles. These are angled to minimize strain, keeping the hand and wrist at a natural angle.

An easy grip fork and trowel

CUSHIONED HANDLES AND COMFORT GRIPS

If you can improve your grip when using any tool, you will work more comfortably, which will enable you to sustain a task for a longer period.

Many ergonomically designed tools are fitted with cushioned handles, giving you extra comfort and grip while also reducing stress on your joints and muscles. Tools with larger hand grips and with indentations for placing your fingers are more comfortable and easier to hold on to.

Many tools are lightweight with curved and angled handles that are designed to keep the gardener more upright while they are scooping soil or compost (soil mix) – or even snow! Make a point of testing these specialized tools, rather than blindly investing in them, so you can establish whether or not the design is to your comfort and liking.

Some tools come with large, comfortable, curved or 'O'-shaped handles that allow a greater range of natural hand positions, avoiding wrist strain and making gardening easier and healthier. If you have wrist issues such as carpal tunnel or arthritis, you may find this a great asset to gardening. Even with ergonomic tools, sustain an activity for 20 minutes (or less) and then rest and change tasks.

ABOVE *Easy grip short-handled tools are here used for maximum convenience and comfort to tend plants in a raised bed.*

LEFT AND BELOW *Short-handled tools with easy-to-grip, curved handles give extra stability to close-up planting and garden maintenance work.*

'O'-shaped handle on a garden spade

ADAPTING HANDLES

While there are specially designed ergonomic tools for those with specific physical requirements, it is often possible to adapt standard tools yourself to make them more comfortable to hold (see technique below) and to improve the grip. You can find specially designed handle wraps or bicycle grips, or you can add gripping or baseball tape to your handles. There is also a special handle adaptor that helps distribute the weight of buckets across the width of the gripping area.

Bucket handle helper

ABOVE *Create a cushioned grip to your favourite tools by adding bicycle handle foam to the grips – and using a bright colour will make it more visible.*

ABOVE *Handle cushions distribute the weight of buckets or other hand-held objects more evenly and take the pinch pressure you would feel in your knuckles.*

MAKING YOUR OWN FOAM HANDLE

Adding a home-made foam handle to a wooden or metal handle can help those with a weak grip. If you need more cushioning to fit your hand size, polystyrene (Styrofoam) pipe insulation is an inexpensive method that adds comfort.

1 *To modify the grip area of existing tools add soft padding, such as foam, to increase gripping ability and enhance comfort. Here a piece of soft foam is used.*

2 *Roll the foam around the handle and secure with duct tape or any strong general-purpose tape. You could also add a bright tape to highlight the tool.*

3 *Larger grips are easier to hold on to, so use the full handle length with a short-handled tool, and an adequate length to allow an easy grip with a long-handled tool.*

ADD-ON ASSISTIVE DEVICES

People suffering from arthritis or reduced grip strength can take advantage of add-on equipment options, such as arm cuffs and interchangeable D-grip and T-clamp handles that slip on to your own tools and allow you to hoe or rake without bending over. Designed to keep our hands and wrists at a natural angle, these tools eliminate the strains and blisters that can be caused by conventional garden tools and can keep us working in the garden no matter what our limitations. Such helpful adaptations are available for all garden tools and from a number of companies (*see* useful addresses on page 250).

Arm support cuffs

These aids are designed for use with long- and short-reach tools and are available in a number of lengths.

Using one makes full use of forearm and upper arm strength and improves overall control, enabling one-handed control for certain tasks. They can be used in a standing or seated position.

BELOW *A long-handled hoe is made more useful and safer by using an add-on D-grip device.*

A D-grip attachment used with a spade

RIGHT AND BELOW
Each of these holding devices gives extra control to garden tasks, benefitting those with compromised strength.

D-grips

An adjustable D-grip is attached at a distance down the tool handle. Adding this to a long-handled tool improves your wrist angle when you grasp. This grip option helps motions that involve lifting, pushing and pulling, such as shovelling, raking, weeding and hoeing. It also reduces awkward bending, increases your leverage and makes lifting easier.

These grips can be used with any long-handled tool. They may create minor adjustments to the function of a tool, but they can have major benefits by preventing lower-back injuries, from repetitive tasks and from the single execution of a task.

BELOW *Used here with a rake, the double hold created with a D-clamp distributes the weight of the tool evenly.*

D-grip handle

T-clamp handle

T-clamp handle

Arm support cuff

T-clamps

The T-clamp is attached at the upper end of the handle and is designed to give pushing and pulling control to the back hand. Choose a clamp material such as foam or a moulded plastic – this enables you to grip the handle with comfort and support.

The hand-grip keeps the angle of the wrist in an almost neutral position, which reduces the chances of blisters or tendinitis, puts less pressure on the lower back and reduces the energy required to complete the task.

Adding a T-clamp to the handle of a traditional tool also lets you work in the garden from a wheelchair or motorized cart. The placement of the clamp can be easily adjusted according to your height and whether you are left- or right-handed.

USING AN ARM CUFF

Well-designed adaptations to our tools help us to continue gardening. When our hands and wrists feel weak or tired, adding a lightweight arm cuff with a sturdy grip enables us to use our forearm strength for leverage and control.

Arm cuff used with long-handled tool
A cuff added to a long-handled weeder lets you weed and cultivate without bending.

Arm cuff adaptability *These cuffs are adjustable and can be lengthened or shortened to suit your working position.*

Arm cuff used with short-handled tool
A hand trowel adapted with a cuff keeps this gardener active in his garden.

USING A T-CLAMP

For weakened hand grips and wrist power, adding a T-shaped attachment to your favourite tool enables you to grasp more easily as you weed the beds.

T-clamp used with long-handled tool
Modify a tool with a T-clamp or another gripping device to give more control.

T-clamp close-up view *T-clamps are easy to add to handles and come in cushioned, moulded and foam designs.*

SOURCING TOOLS: RESEARCH THE MARKET

In a marketplace where many options are available, all claiming to be the latest wonder tool or the one that no gardener can be without, consider the following points:

• Know your physical strengths and weaknesses and choose your tools accordingly.
• Consult with a health professional to help you plan the tools and motions you need to adopt.
• Talk to other gardeners who have used new tools and can vouch that they do make gardening easier and more comfortable.
• When researching tool stores or garden centres, ask if you can try the tool in your garden and return it if it doesn't satisfy your comfort needs.
• Handle a tool before you buy to test the weight and balance.

USING A MULTI-PURPOSE TOOL

With a little ingenuity and research about the use of adaptive tools, you can avoid carrying many different tools around with you. Look for an option where the handles are easy to change. The one below has a push-button mechanism.

1 *This hand fork weeder can be attached to a long or a short handle.*

2 *The short handle is useful when working in a raised bed, or sitting in an adjacent bed.*

3 *Add a long handle to get the length you need to remain standing to do the weeding.*

4 *The extended handle lets you get into hard-to-reach places to dig out those weeds.*

INTERCHANGEABLE HANDLES

As we age and change some of our gardening habits and work styles, we are likely to realize that we need fewer tools but those we do have need to be more versatile and multi-purposed. Options for adaptable tools include those with a customized handle where a tool head can be changed as the requirements of the job change.

Some tool systems on the market offer one handle that fits many tool heads with easy-release snap-lock devices. Some of these are similar to the attachments that connect your tap (faucet) to a hose and your hose to different devices such as a sprayer or sprinkler.

These products provide a versatile range of heads and handles that clip together quickly and easily as they equip you with the perfect tool for the task at hand, and make it much easier to reach difficult places. They also give you more power, leverage and control, which helps prevent injury to back, legs, wrists and hands.

Such tools will not replace heavy-duty tools for bigger jobs, but they offer a useful alternative for the senior gardener. They also conserve space in the garage and – no small matter – reduce the number of things you can trip on!

EXTENDING HANDLES

Telescoping handles greatly enhance the abilities of those who have limited hand strength, reach and dexterity.

The handles on the tools can be adjusted to fit the length you need for a job. A typical set of tools attaching to a telescoping handle includes a trowel, a 3-tine cultivator, a 5-tine rake, a shrub rake and a hoe. The telescopic handle adjusts from about 68cm to 1m (27 to 40in). This handle reduces pressure on your back and enables you to work from a wheelchair. Adjust the handle before you buy to make sure it is easy.

BATTERY TOOLS

Battery-operated tools are generally recommended for older people over electric or petrol-driven tools because

A long interchangeable handle comes with connectable attachments.

they're safer (there's no cord to trip over or accidentally cut, no starter to pull and no need to store fuel in your garage). Such tools remove the hazard of electric cords for those whose mobility or eyesight is not as good as it once was.

Some battery-operated tools have a non-removable battery and need to be plugged into a charger, while some have removable batteries. The latter are probably more convenient for tools you use a lot: you can always have one battery charging while using the tool and then, when the one you are using gives out, you simply take it out and pop in the newly-charged one. See also battery-operated cutting tools and equipment on pages 108–109.

There's a proverb that goes, "A man too busy to take care of his health is like a mechanic too busy to take care of his tools." With a little research, you can take care of your tools and your health at the same time.

SOIL AMENDMENTS, COMPOST AND MULCH

For most of us, what grows on top of the soil is our first measure of a successful garden. But without what lies below, the garden above may look very different. Any materials added to a soil to improve its physical properties are classed as soil amendments, and will have a significant part in improving its water retention, drainage, aeration and structure. Let's spend some time here demystifying the process of being a soil steward.

ABOVE *Organic soil amendments include fruit and vegetable remnants, straw, grass clippings and other garden waste.*

THE IMPORTANCE OF SOIL QUALITY

Very simply put, healthy soils produce healthy plants – they'll look better, produce more abundantly, be less stressed and, therefore, will have fewer pest problems. This is because good, living soil is the foundation for successful gardening. Just remember, feed your soil and let your soil feed your plants. There are two broad categories of soil amendments, inorganic and organic.

INORGANIC AMENDMENTS

Any additions to your soil that are either man-made or mined are called inorganic amendments. These include vermiculite, perlite, pea gravel, rock, sand and recycled tyres, to name a few.

ABOVE *Successful composting will create rich, organic matter that teems with valuable earthworms.*

ORGANIC AMENDMENTS

Additions to the soil that are derived from something that is or was alive are organic amendments. Examples include composted bark, peat, wood chips, grass clippings, garden compost, coffee grounds, manure, rotting hay, straw, moss, bonemeal and, yes, shredded newspaper. (Peat is best avoided as its harvesting causes serious damage to the environment.) Organic amendments not only improve the structure of the soil that is so important for healthy root growth but they also act as an organic fertilizer (*see also* Using Fertilizers on pages 98–99). Organic matter is an important energy source for beneficial bacteria and the fungi that live in and nourish the soil. Finally, if you see earthworms in your soil, be cheered, as they are doing their part in aerating and enriching the soil.

IMPROVING SOIL STRUCTURE

One of the best ways to improve the structure of the soil is to add as much organic material as you can, preferably when the soil is dug. For heavy soils, this is best done in the autumn. If the soil has already been dug, work into the soil surface about 5–7.5cm (2–3in) of well-rotted organic material with a garden fork. This will increase the fertility and volume of the soil and improve the water-retaining ability of dry, sandy soils, while improving the drainage on heavy ones.

Perlite

Vermiculite

Sharp grit

Sharp sand

COMPOSTING

The black and crumbly earthy material created by the decomposition of organic matter by microorganisms (and the human activity that makes it happen) is called compost. This adds an abundance of nutrients to our soil and boosts its overall health.

It's easy to make your own compost by collecting materials and mixing them together and then letting nature take its course. Compost wants to happen. Taking advantage of the variety of plant material waste from your own garden and kitchen will always reward you with nutritious

soil amendments for your containers and beds, as well as for the environment in general.

On the following pages you will find various ways of composting that might appeal to older gardeners, selective approaches that are designed to meet your space and energy requirements.

COMPOSTING MATERIALS

Soil needs many nutrients but the three major ingredients are nitrogen, phosphorus and potassium. You can give your soil all of these without using commercial fertilizers by composting organic materials and adding them to your soil as natural fertilizers. These fertilizers work more quickly on the soil, have a more powerful effect and will save you money.

Grass clippings – *rich in nitrogen and other nutrients, use grass clippings in small amounts, well mixed with other materials.*

Rotten fruit – *a good nitrogen source, add to compost with dry and more substantial browns to avoid compaction.*

Decaying leaves – *a good carbon source. Compost these separately to make leaf mould.*

Kitchen scraps *are full of nutrients when broken down, but avoid dog and cat waste, meat and chicken protein, grease and dairy.*

Animal manure *is rich in nitrogen, phosphorus and potassium. Use well-aged manure to prepare beds in the spring.*

Straw mulch *breaks down quickly, contains a range of balanced minerals and also insulates and protects the soil.*

HEAP COMPOSTING

There are various ways of having a compost heap. For casual gardeners, an easy method of creating compost is to make a heap of your garden debris, leaves and kitchen scraps directly on the ground. Pick a site that is as concealed as possible but near the garden so getting the compost to the site is convenient. A site near the kitchen is ideal but not always possible. If your site is farther away, you can collect any scraps in a small bin in the kitchen and carry it to the pile. Access to water for those times when the heap needs extra moisture is helpful but not essential, as you will not usually need large amounts.

To begin the heap, start with a 7.5cm (3in) layer of dry, brown material and then add 2.5–15cm (1–6in) of green ingredients, followed by another 4.5cm (3in) layer of browns, and then more green matter. Loose material such as green bean vines and tomato stems can be applied in a thicker layer. Grass clippings and kitchen scraps are denser materials that can mat together, so layer these thinly (2.5–5cm/1–2in). As you build

the heap, alternate layers of brown materials with green matter. Carbon-rich browns add the necessary bulk to a pile; green materials, rich in nitrogen and high in moisture, decompose quickly. Without the greens, decomposition will come to a halt. Turning of the materials once a month will give bacteria the oxygen to keep breaking down the matter.

ABOVE *A basic holding enclosure is enough to keep the open compost pile in bounds as it slowly decomposes.*

COMPOSTING: HOLDING UNITS

Units for compost can be holding units or turning units. Holding units include bins constructed from masonry, plastic, wood, wire, or combinations of these. Add the material as described for open heaps, and turn regularly with a compost turning tool or garden fork (*see* page 77). Many gardeners have two or three bins, enabling them to transfer decomposed material into the next bin. This movement provides the necessary aeration and mixing.

Wire-mesh holding units, using simple galvanized chicken wire or hardware cloth, are inexpensive and easy to build or purchase. These units provide good ventilation and allow the easy turning of organic materials. The bigger the bin, the hotter the heap will become, which will make the process quicker and more efficient. A plastic bin, with a lid, will also be warmer than a more open one. (Any container without a lid can be covered, for example with a piece of carpet, for insulation and to keep the rain off.)

BELOW *A simple heap of leaves, grass and other debris is a fine start to your garden compost.*

BELOW *The results of your composting efforts are full of nutrients and can be used to revive tired soil in all parts of the garden.*

FILLING A COMPOST BIN

Every garden should have a compost heap where organic materials are recycled to create a highly nutritious soil conditioner. Use any vegetable matter or fruit that is disease free and will decompose easily.

1 *Place the bin on the soil, lightly water the brown area and add up to 15cm (6in) of twigs along with other drier 'brown' materials such as dry plant stems. Water the brown layer.*

2 *Add a similar depth of fresher 'green' material, such as grass cuttings and raw fruit and vegetables. Dense material such as grass clippings should be in thinner layers.*

3 *Every couple of layers add decomposing microbes with a little compost from another heap or garden soil. Leaves of nettle or comfrey are also effective activators.*

4 *Finish with a final layer of 'brown' material. You should then cover the bin, in this case with a carpet or a plastic sheet, to conserve the heat and moisture.*

COMPOSTABLE GREENS AND BROWNS

Potential ingredients for your compost heap will be either 'brown' or 'green'. Browns are dry and dead plant materials. Because they tend to be dry, browns often need to be moistened before they are put into a compost system. Greens are fresh plant materials. They contain more nitrogen than browns and are are a protein source for the billions of multiplying microbes. A good mix of browns and greens is the best nutritional balance for microbes.

• Carbon-rich drier 'brown' materials include coffee grounds, dry plant stems and twigs (preferably shredded), scrunched-up paper, egg shells, straw, hay and torn-up cardboard.

• Nitrogen-rich 'greens' include grass cuttings, raw fruit and vegetables, seaweed and garden pond clearings, tea leaves, manure, non-seeding annual weeds and soft hedge clippings.

TRENCH COMPOSTING

The technique of trench composting is a great low-effort option for those of you who have small gardens and don't want to have a visible bin, pile or tumbler. Simply dig a shallow trench or hole and gradually fill it with organic matter as described above and on pages 74–75. Each time, cover the debris thinly with soil. With the decomposing material buried, little nutrient content leaches away and earthworms reap the benefits from this underground feast as they begin their processes of nourishing the soil. Also, there's no problem with odour, insects or animals disturbing the 'cooking' compost. As with all composting methods, never add dog or cat wastes, proteins such as meat or chicken, grease or dairy products.

RIGHT *Trench composting is simple – dig a hole, put the material inside and cover.*

AERATING AND COMPOST TURNING

We add many tangible things to our compost piles – twigs, spent flowers, grass clippings and kitchen scraps, to name a few. But the one thing we don't physically add when creating compost is oxygen.

Any bin with plenty of ventilation holes can produce good compost in time, even without turning. (If there are not enough holes, the pile may not decompost properly, and could produce an unpleasant odour.) However, turning the heap regularly will bring in more oxygen and the decomposition process will be much quicker. (A heap that is left completely open will not suffer from lack of oxygen, but it will not decompose as quickly because it will lose more heat, which slows down the process.)

There are a number of tools that can be used to turn the heap. A pitchfork or a shovel may work, but these can be awkward and difficult to handle,

especially if you have arthritis or weakness in your arms and hands. A special tool has been designed for the task of aerating. This consists of a T-handle atop a long pole that has an ingenious set of 'wings' that open up after you pierce the tool into the compost. The wings spread open to a span of about 18cm (7in) and, as the pole is withdrawn, they move everything around in the pile. Just a few of these movements in the pile over a few minutes will be adequate to keep your compost effectively aerated.

Wings are not the only options with aerating tools – other compost aerators have a total of four useful functions, where a flanged steel blade can be used to chop, mix, turn and aerate waste inside the composter.

Whatever your method for making compost, the goal is to achieve a fast and effective decomposition that does not smell bad and results in a soft and crumbly end product.

4-way compost turner

Compost aerator with metal flanges that close in as you push down

spike aerator for lawn and turf

ABOVE *If used regularly, a compost aerator introduces air to the compost pile so the bacteria will thrive, resulting in a speedy breakdown of the compost.*

AERATING TECHNIQUES

To make your compost heap as nutritious as possible you need to mix and aerate your compost regularly. An aerating tool means that you can mix and aerate the waste in your bin very easily for faster composting. Alternatively, for the more energetic gardener, turning the compost pile with a garden fork can be a regular and relaxing task.

1 *Using an aeration tool with metal flanges, simply push it into the compost heap as far as you can. This shows the metal flanges closing in as it pushes down.*

2 *As you pull the aerator out, twist it around to maximize the movement of the compost. The metal flanges at the bottom will expand as you pull out the tool.*

Garden fork method *Pick up small loads and move the debris around to allow air to penetrate and circulate. Add a leverage device to the handle for easier movement.*

COMPOST TURNING UNIT

Turning units, tumblers, or drums are barrel-like tubs mounted on stands to hold your garden debris and kitchen waste. There are many models to consider – some are designed for gardeners in wheelchairs. With hand cranks or handles, these manually rotated drums make turning or aerating your organic refuse easy and efficient. Instead of having to dig into a dense heap or pile, rotating bins promote air circulation that accelerates the decomposition process.

Compost materials need to be saved until there are enough to fill a bin. Food waste can be collected in a container such as a plastic bucket. Add sawdust to each day's scraps to reduce odour.

A drawback is that these units are less effective if you add woody or tough fibre, but they are effective with a mixture of vegetative kitchen wastes, soft garden cuttings, dead plants and shredded paper. Some people add compost activators, comfrey leaves or nettles, and a few trowel fulls of rotted compost to give the process a jump-start. And you need to rotate only 3–4 times a week.

In 3–6 months, you will have your own compost. Sieve the compost with a riddle to sift out any large lumps and leave a fine material suitable for seed sowing and potting mixes.

ABOVE *Use a metal riddle as a sieve to remove stones, twigs and large clumps and produce a fine-textured compost.*

USING A ROTATING COMPOST TUMBLER

There are many models of compost bins. While some are stationary and require mixing by hand, others, such as this one, can rotate, thereby regularly and more easily turning the compost. Deciding to use a rotating bin will relieve back stress as it takes away the bending and shovel maintenance that a traditional compost heap requires. Choose a rotating composter that fits your physical and space needs. Make sure it is easy for you to operate, is the right size for your space, and has convenient loading and unloading openings.

1 *Find a tumbler that is easy for you to fill and put it in a convenient place where you can access it with your wheelbarrow or cart.*

2 *Many of these tumbler bins have convenient handles. The turning sequence is shown in the next three pictures. Start by tipping over the bin.*

3 *The weight of the compost gives momentum to the turning. One full rotation will be enough if you are turning regularly.*

4 *The bin then returns to its original position. Open the bin door every few days to check on the composting process.*

MULCHING

Not strictly a soil amendment, mulch is rather an organic or inorganic material that is spread on top of existing soil to protect it from erosion and diseases, to reduce weed growth and to help keep the soil cool and moist. Think of it as a protective blanket for your garden.

Mulches come in all styles, sizes and materials, such as lava rock, crushed brick, river rock – even recycled tyres can be used as inorganic mulches. Organic mulches include shredded bark, wood chips, cocoa bean hulls and filbert shells. Home-made compost and well-rotten manure are excellent, and will improve the soil as worms carry them down, especially if applied in a thick layer. Compost can also be dug in whenever you plant anything in the garden.

Each type of mulch has strengths and weaknesses. Decide on the look you want – dark wood chips around the tree or white stones on top of the flowerbed. Bear in mind that light, loose materials may become scattered over paths and could be a nuisance.

A good rule for the active gardener is to add 7.5cm (3in) of nutrient-rich, organic mulch every year to perennial borders, around trees and in vegetable

HOW TO MULCH

Choose your site for mulching. Do a good job of weeding and generally preparing the surface or garden bed where you will be laying the mulch.

1 *Bring mulch material to the site either in a wheelbarrow or bags (get help with this if you need it).*

2 *Before spreading the mulch you should water all the plants in the area. Then apply the mulch around the plants.*

beds to maintain a healthy population of soil organisms. Heavier mulches can be applied in a thin layer and lighter mulches in a heavy layer. It's best to apply mulches either in late spring when the soil has warmed or in mid-autumn before the winter chill has set in.

You can use a weed barrier before mulching. Do this with newspaper (*see* method on page 113). Then shovel small piles of mulch in the area. Using a rake, spread the small piles to cover the soil with at least 5cm (2in) of mulch material. Do not let mulch touch trunks or stems, as this may induce rotting.

ABOVE *A rich mulch benefits fruit trees. Keep it from touching the trunk but spread a depth of 7.5cm (3in) around the trunk to reduce weeds and retain moisture.*

ABOVE *Bark chippings make an excellent organic mulch and can also be used for paths. These are not appropriate, however, for those using walkers or wheelchairs.*

ABOVE *Dried bracken makes a good autumn mulch that breaks down after winter. Cut up the bracken in 7.5–10cm (3–4in) pieces so it decomposes quickly.*

DIGGING

British socialite and garden writer Beverly Nichols once said, "To dig in one's own earth, with one's own spade, does life hold anything better?". Perhaps not everyone would agree with this. But it is nonetheless a therapeutic activity. It can be a rewarding experience to run your hands in the dark earth and feel its coolness and texture. Pushing a shovel blade into soft earth and turning it over as you prepare a bed can have the same effect. It can help you to feel connected to the earth and to nature.

ABOVE *A garden fork is an essential and versatile tool as it allows you to aerate, cultivate and loosen your soil.*

AN ESSENTIAL TASK

While many gardeners thrive on digging, some consider it a chore. It is certainly one of the inescapable tasks of gardening; you're not going to get that soil ready for planting by turning it over in your mind. Whether you're breaking up the soil to make it ready for planting or removing soil to level an area for a new bed or pathway, you're going to have to do some digging.

Ground-breaking, however, needn't be back-breaking. Raised beds and containers such as large whisky barrels reduce both the amount of digging and the amount of energy required. Ergonomically designed shovels and spades can also take much of the strain out of digging.

APPROACHES TO DIGGING

Whether or not you enjoy digging, it needs to be done safely so you stay healthy. Using a sensible technique makes it much easier and less strenuous on muscles and joints. There are various things you can do to make digging easier, firstly assessing the task before you start. You need to consider what type of soil you'll be working with. In the earlier section about soils we learned how to determine the consistency of our garden medium.

Next, be aware of the moisture content of the soil, and never work it when it is too soggy or you'll ruin its structure for a long time to come. When you know what conditions you have, you can plan accordingly. Soil that is compacted, mostly clay, or very rocky, for example, can present problems for seniors because the work is difficult and can cause stress and strain on muscles and joints. Having considered the soil and

LEFT *A floral shovel has a small scoop-shaped head that will keep the load light and manageable.*

weather conditions, make sure you have the physical stamina to do the work and that you have appropriate, safe and well-maintained tools.

BASIC DIGGING TOOLS

Our main job as senior gardeners is to minimize effort and maximize pleasure. Here are some basic tools that will help you along the way. Some of the tools here will also be relevant to later sections on cultivation and weeding.

Shovels

The best-known hand-digging tool, the shovel, is used to dig holes, clear debris or move large amounts of soil or mulch. A pointed shovel is best for digging holes, while a shovel with a large, flat head is best for clearing debris or moving earth or other materials. The traditional round-point shovel allows us to penetrate the soil, loosen it, and then scoop it, adding it to a pile. This is the tool you want when planting dahlia tubers or digging holes for your blueberry bushes.

As we age, we need tools that are smaller and lightweight. A popular garden shovel for seniors is called a 'border' or 'floral' shovel. It's typically a half to two-thirds the size of a standard shovel, offers a shorter handle and is lighter in weight, but provides a blade that has a deeper dish. Some shovels have a folding option for easy mobility and include a canvas sheath that attaches to a belt loop or hook.

Spades

A spade is a digging tool with a flat metal blade and a long handle that is often made of wood. Some spades have treads near the top of the blade so you can use your feet to help push them into the ground. This centralizes the downward pressure of the foot, minimizing the strain on the lower back and making the digging process balanced and easier, even in the hardest of soils. These allow you to keep your balance and achieve more with less effort. It also stops your foot from slipping off the side of the tool. With their sharp, squared-off blade, spades are designed for cutting straight edges for a bed at the edge of a lawn or digging a trench for a row of raspberry canes. Spades with extra-long handles give you greater leverage and reduce the need to bend.

When buying any new tool, seniors need to consider its weight. A heavy spade, for example, can be a challenge for a gardener who is limited in arm and hand strength. Look for tools that are made with lighter components such as aluminium alloy, carbon fibre or plastic.

Some types of spade are designed to reduce back strain and effort. A back-saving spade allows you to dig from a standing position, eliminating the need to bend over to lift and turn the soil. The system involves pulling back on the handle and a large spring at the base of the shaft throws the soil forward.

ABOVE *This autospade allows you to dig from a standing position, which eliminates the strain of bending.*

Long-handled floral shovel

Folding shovel

Border spade

Edging spade with a stirrup tread

Edging spade with a centralized tread and an ergonomic, forward-tilting handle

Backsaver autospade

LEFT *Shovels and spades come in all shapes and sizes, focusing on both suitability for purpose and the physical needs of the user. Choose those that combine these needs most effectively.*

Garden fork

This is a versatile tool, also called a spading fork, that can be used for digging and aerating the soil. It is especially useful in dense, compacted or rocky soil. To many gardeners, this is a garden essential since it can be used as a spade, a shovel or a cultivator.

Gardeners often have emotional attachments to tools that they use frequently and that have important associations. This is especially true of such an indispensable tool as the garden fork. It is fine to employ traditional equipment such as this – but select examples carefully and be aware of alternatives if such tools become less straightforward to use.

While there are many styles and sizes of garden fork in the marketplace, for the elder gardener a flexible option is one that is called a 'border fork'. This is smaller in scale – smaller than the size of the traditional English garden fork – and yet is well-suited to prepare beds and borders and even containers. With a standard D-grip and a compact size the fork is easy to use.

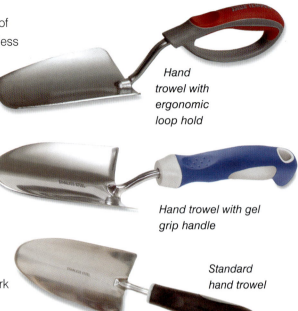

Hand trowel with ergonomic loop hold

Hand trowel with gel grip handle

Standard hand trowel

Hand trowel

One of the most popular and versatile tools is the hand trowel, used to pick up small amounts of soil, dig up weeds and agitate the earth to dig small holes. These are available with long handles to reduce kneeling when digging or enable access to awkward places. In this way a gardener can stay upright when weeding and cultivating, or tend the garden from a seated position.

Post-hole digging bar

If you have to sink a post in the ground for a fence or raised bed you'll need a digging bar, which adds leverage for clearing rocks and roots from holes and ditches. While a useful tool, it can weigh up to 9kg (20lb) so this may be a job that you ask someone to help with.

DIGGING PREPARATION

Before you start, warm up by doing some simple exercises (*see* pages 50–53). You should also wear strong garden footwear if you need to push the blade into the soil with your foot. Use clean, sharp tools – the blade of a spade can be sharpened slightly if necessary (*see* page 134).

Garden fork

Border fork

Border fork with centralized tread

Long-handled trowel

Post-hole digging bar

LEFT *With tools for every imaginable digging purpose, think about your needs and choose the one that suits you best.*

DIGGING TECHNIQUES

If you're prepping your garden bed for vegetables, 'simple digging' is what you need. You just lift the soil, invert it and drop it back in its original place. This also cleans the soil surface of any debris and non-persistent weeds. This method works best when working with irregularly shaped beds or moving around existing plants. Limit your digging to around 20–30 minutes at a time.

Other types of digging require more exertion. Single digging involves loosening and creating an even soil texture to a depth of 30cm (1ft), and double digging is used when drainage needs improving or if the ground needs recultivation. These techniques are not covered in detail here as they require harder physical exertion. If you want a new bed or want to reconstitute your soil then ask for help or hire a professional. To paraphrase an old saying, "Pride comes before a back sprain."

SIMPLE DIGGING

This technique demonstrates the basic method of turning the soil. It should also be applied when you're amending your soil with organic matter.

1 *Drive the blade firmly into the ground with one foot (never jump on the spade). Rock the blade back and forth, and only insert the blade to three-quarters of its length. Bend at the knees to lift and slide one hand down the shaft.*

2 *Take small amounts of soil on to the spade. Keep your back straight and bend your knees when lifting. After a few minutes, straighten up and with your hands on your lower back, bend gently backwards and from side to side.*

SIMPLE DIGGING WITH A D-GRIP

A D-grip attachment can be helpful when digging, giving a double-handed grip to help support the weight of the spade and control your movements. Work slowly and carefully, making sure that you are not overloading the spade.

1 *Attach the D-grip about halfway down the spade handle. Drive the blade firmly into the ground with one foot.*

2 *Rock the blade back and forth, if necessary, and only insert the blade to three-quarters of its length. Bend at the knees to lift and hold the D-grip with your other hand to act as a fulcrum.*

3 *Take small amounts of soil on to the spade. Keep your back straight and bend your knees when lifting. Straighten up, and with your hands on your lower back, bend gently backwards and from side to side.*

CULTIVATING THE SOIL

Getting any garden bed ready, whether it is established or new, needs to start with concentrating on the soil as we prepare it for whatever we are planning to plant. We've already looked at the importance of having good soil and using the right equipment for doing this effectively. The next step is to consider our contribution – that is, the mechanical and physical tasks that are required to keep the soil healthy. These tasks should not be demanding – just divide the work up into accessible stages.

ABOVE *When breaking up surface soil with a Dutch hoe you should stand holding the hoe as you would a broom.*

WHAT IS CULTIVATION?

A broad term used in gardening, cultivation means the preparation, improvement and care of the soil, and the growth and tending of plants. Here we're focusing on the shallow stirring or digging of the soil to keep it fluffy and porous and to keep down the weeds.

As older gardeners we need to plan cultivation activities in a timely manner without over-exertion. Cultivation will often take place at a time of year when our muscles and joints haven't been engaged in this way for a few months. So we need to pace ourselves to enjoy the process and stay in good shape for planting and maintenance throughout the growing season.

BELOW *A long-handled cultivator enables an experienced gardener to get the garden bed ready for spring planting.*

Weeder cultivator

Classic 3-pronged cultivator

Dutch hoe

ABOVE *Three popular cultivation tools are the double action weeder-cultivator, the three-pronged cultivator and the Dutch hoe.*

CULTIVATION TOOLS

The role of tools used to cultivate the soil is to help break up the soil surface around plants, which allows air to circulate and helps to retain water. Some of the tools appropriate for breaking up and aeration, such as garden forks, have already been covered in the digging section. Some hoes and other weeding tools are also useful for cultivation, because the removal of moisture-competing weeds helps the growth of the plant. Tools specifically for weeding, including winged weeders and oscillating hoes, are covered in detail on pages 114–117. Here we introduce a selection of tools that are more specifically useful for the gentle, ongoing cultivation of the soil.

Dutch hoe

The most common and historically used tool for cultivating is the Dutch hoe, a long-handled tool with a rectangular steel blade that has sharp edges and corners to slice into the surface of the soil or, with some energy, go deeper. Keeping the hoe's edge sharp will make cultivating much easier, and it can become blunt very quickly. So every time you use it – or even more than once in a session – touch up the edge with a file to create a good, sharp blade.

The Dutch hoe is used both for cultivation and for general weeding – it is controlled in a push-pull motion while walking backwards with the blade just below the surface of the soil. Don't overlook the short-handled hoes that are perfect for the raised bed or container garden.

Senior gardeners need to find a hoe that 'fits' our bodies and hands. Checking the length of the shaft to find out if you have to bend uncomfortably is a great way to 'size' the tool to your body. Consider adding foam or cushioning to the grip so your hands are at ease as much as possible (*see* page 69).

Weeder cultivator

As the name suggests, this tool weeds/hoes and cultivates, but it also rakes and digs. Its cultivating tines will catch roots and rocks. Turned over, it becomes a scuffle hoe which moves smoothly through the soil, cutting weeds below the surface.

Three-pronged cultivator

Also called a claw fork or a garden claw, this tool does several things in one motion. It cultivates around shrubs, bushes and trees, loosens all types of soil, aerates your garden and disturbs weeds. The cultivated soil will absorb

Hand cultivator with a loop-style handle

Hand cultivator with a foam grip handle

ABOVE *A three-pronged cultivator is used with a chop and pull motion so that the curved prongs remove weeds or break up clods.*

USING A SOIL MILLER

The soil miller works in a simple push-pull action. It can be used for crumbling soil to a fine tilth for sowing seeds or planting, or for combining peat, manure and fertilizers.

1 *This soil miller is interchangeable, so can be used with a short handle for raised beds or containers, or with a long handle to work at ground level.*

2 *The gardener has a longer reach with the long-handled soil miller. This is easier on your posture as you stand rather than bend over as you work.*

water better and help prevent waste by runoff. By using it you provide much-needed air to the roots of plants and increase the porosity of the soil.

Soil miller

A truly multi-talented tool, a soil miller has one or several wheels with long spikes that, when in motion, break down the soil into fine particles as you move it backwards and forwards in an easy push-pull action. It is suitable for preparing a seed bed and will incorporate rotted manure, compost or fertilizer into your soil. It's available with short and long handles. The short version allows you to work in a raised bed or container, and a long handle significantly reduces the risk of back strain when working on the ground.

Single-wheel miller

LEFT *The tools shown here have a rotating cutting blade (or blades) at the back, which digs into the soil, breaking it up and aerating it, when it is pushed backwards and forwards.*

Soil miller/ garden cultivator

Soil miller head that fits into an interchangeable handle

SEED SOWING

"Convince me you have a seed there," wrote Henry David Thoreau, "and I am prepared to expect wonders." One of the true wonders of gardening is the range of things you can grow from seed. Sometimes your options are limited by your physical abilities, your climate or the space you have. When the growing season is a few months away and you're itching to start gardening, there are many fun and important decisions to make. Do you want to sow seeds? Do you want to sow directly outdoors or start inside?

ABOVE *Whether flower, vegetable or herb seeds, each packet has the tantalizing promise of the gardening season to come.*

SEED-SOWING EQUIPMENT

When planting seeds you will need a commercial sowing medium, sterile planting containers (such as seed trays or flats, degradable or plastic pots and plastic cells), a hole maker called a dibber, a widger and a water mister. The seed packet will give some indication of sowing times and experimentation will also help you to fine tune when to start. A soil thermometer is useful, though not essential, to help you decide when to sow outdoors.

The dibber is used for pricking out and transplanting seedlings, breaking up the top of the soil if it hardens over in the

ABOVE *It's critical to know the correct soil temperature when planting many vegetable crops.*

BELOW *Here is the basic selection of tools and equipment that you will need for seed sowing.*

trays and making planting holes for the small seedlings in their new pots. The widger helps to remove new seedlings when you are potting on.

INDOOR SEED SOWING

Vegetables and flowers are often started indoors. The growing season in many areas is shorter than the time the plant needs to produce flowers or fruit, and many flowers and vegetables will produce weeks earlier if started in the shelter of the interior. This also allows many gardeners to grow plants and varieties that are not native to their area.

The general rule is to begin sowing indoors six to eight weeks before the last frost date for your area. Some tender plants such as peppers, tomatoes, courgettes (zucchini) and petunias require more time. Hardier plants such as cabbages, chard, kales and lettuce require less. Some people will do a series of sowings, especially for lettuces and cabbages, to spread the harvest over a longer period.

When sowing seeds, always read the information on the back of the seed packets. Most seed packets will include advice on how and when to sow, spacing recommendations and the number of days until seed germination, as well as the height and spread of the plant at maturity. It is a good idea to save the packet as reference during the growing season or as a reminder to get that variety the following year.

Dibber

Widger

Seedling tray

Row planter with lid

Water mister

PLANTING SEEDS

Cultivating seeds adds another stage to the gardening process, but it is a way of reducing the cost of buying established seedlings and being in control of the whole planting and flowering cycle. The easiest seed-growing options are annuals that need to be sown in the spring and result in summer flowers. Here is the basic technique for sowing seeds indoors, although you will need to adapt this around the instructions on the seed packet.

1 *You will need to fill your containers with moistened sowing medium to within 5mm (¼in) from the top, and level off the surface. Then use a dibber or a similar device for making the appropriate size hole for the seeds.*

2 *Plant the seeds to the desired depth, generally about twice their diameter, except for very fine seeds. The packet instructions will guide you. The seeds here are small so they are scattered on the surface and then covered thinly with soil.*

3 *Be sure to label each seeded container with the seeds that you planted and the expected date of germination since newly sprouted seedlings tend to look alike.*

4 *Cover the containers with clear plastic covers or slip them into clear plastic bags. Keep the plastic off the soil and away from the shoots once they emerge. No additional watering should be necessary until after the seeds have germinated.*

5 *Place the seeds in a warm location for germination (18–24°C/65–75°F is ideal) and remove the plastic covers once the seeds have germinated to prevent damping off (stem rotting).*

6 *When seedlings develop their second set of leaves, transplant them to a more permanent position. Hold one of the second leaves, remove the seedling and move it to its new home, using a dibber to settle the soil. Keep them moist and well lit.*

ABOVE *To sow flowers using a seed mat, fill the pot with potting soil, place the seed mat on top, cover with more soil and water.*

CUSTOMIZED TECHNIQUES

Planting small seeds can be frustrating as they are difficult to see and handle and therefore fiddly and laborious to sow. Carrot seeds are one of the smallest seeds – a teaspoon holds in the region of 2,000!

A simple solution is to fold a piece of paper, pour the packet contents into the fold and tap the end lightly so that the contents slide down into your furrow. Sprinkling the seeds with a little talcum powder will prevent them from sticking.

Another way to deal with small seeds is to use seed tapes (see technique shown below). These are designed especially for sowing small seeds that need thinning after germination, such as carrots, beetroot (beet) and lettuce. Many companies manufacture these seed tapes, simply made from a strip of paper with seeds glued on it at the proper spacing for the particular seed variety. The tape eventually decomposes, leaving the seed to grow and prosper.

HOW TO MAKE YOUR OWN SEED TAPE

Here is a home-made solution for the fiddly process of planting small seeds. Make the seed tapes and at planting time place the tapes in planting beds and cover with a layer of soil and water. The paper strips will rot within a few days.

MATERIALS
- Toilet paper or white copy paper
- Scissors
- Cornflour (cornstarch) and water
- Wooden spoon
- Paintbrush (medium)
- Paintbrush (fine) or chopstick
- Plastic bag with labels
- Small seeds such as carrots, beetroot (beet) and radishes

1 *Cut toilet paper or white copy paper into 5cm (2in) wide strips at the length you want.*

2 *Blend 1 tablespoon of cornflour in 250ml/8fl oz cold water. Place over medium heat.*

3 *Cook the mixture, stirring, until it is like a gel. Allow it to cool and collect on a brush.*

4 *Paint the paper strips with the paste. Alternatively, place dots of paste at the correct spacing (consult seed packet).*

5 *Wet a smaller paintbrush or chopstick with the paste, pick up one seed at a time and place it on the strip.*

6 *After the tapes have air-dried on a flat surface, roll or fold them up and store in a plastic bag. Date and label it.*

7 *At planting time, prepare the row, roll out the strip and cover with soil. Water and wait for your seed tape to sprout.*

Precision seeders

There are various other devices for seed sowing that are helpful if you find small seeds fiddly to handle or difficult to see. Carrots, lettuce, radishes and parsnip seeds, to name a few that are tiny, can be facilitated by using seed dispensers that distribute the correct number of seeds per square centimetre or inch. These include mouth-operated sowers, push-button sowers and plastic ball seed sowers.

Mouth-operated precision seedsower

Push-button seeder

Proseeder with plastic ball dispenser

THINNING SPROUTS AS THEY APPEAR

No matter how careful you are in the sowing technique, be prepared to do some thinning when sprouts come through. Simply use little scissors to snip off crowding sprouts at the soil line. Thinning this way lessens the danger of accidentally damaging the nearby sprouts that you want to grow.

PRECISION SEED TECHNIQUES

Sowing small seeds can be challenging but with new devices on the market there are plenty of options for staying connected to this favourite garden activity.

Option 1 Mouth-operated seed sower
A long straw-like flexible tube is connected to a mouthpiece that allows you to use suction to pick up seeds and put them in the soil. A filter at the mouthpiece ensures that you don't inhale dust or seeds.

Option 2 Push-button seed sower
This syringe-type device allows you to accurately place small seeds into your sowing medium. This works well for most seeds up to 2mm (⅛in).

Option 3 Plastic ball dispenser
This device uses suction to collect and then dispense seeds in three simple steps – squeeze, hold and release. The tool comes with interchangeable heads and is able to plant a variety of seed sizes, one seed at a time.

Option 4 Compost blocks
Compost blocks encourage rapid plant development and involve less root disturbance when seedlings are transplanted. Make a single hole so you can keep track of what you have planted. Buy the blocks or get a compost block maker.

PLANTING SEEDS OUTDOORS

Sow seeds directly outdoors and you will create a row of vegetables or a drift of flowers. Generally, outdoor sowing is used for fast-growing seeds, those that are large and difficult to transplant from indoors. It avoids the root disturbance caused by transplanting outdoors, but also makes it harder to protect the seedlings from slugs and other pests. Adequate water, light, oxygen and heat are important for successful germination, along with knowing when to sow them. Spring and summer offer ideal conditions in which to sow the seeds of vegetables, perennials, biennials and annuals.

Preparation

The first step to sowing seeds outdoors is to prepare the soil. Get rid of all weeds and dirt clods. Work in plenty of compost to a depth of 25–30cm (10–12in). The soil should be loose, crumbly and moist. Rake the top to a fine texture. Leave it to settle for a few weeks. Any weed seeds you disturbed will then have a chance to germinate, and you can remove them easily before saving.

ABOVE *When sowing seeds outdoors, create designs by marking the areas with light coloured sand poured out of a bottle.*

Outdoor sowing technique

Plant your seeds when the time is right, your beds are ready and the seeds are selected. The packet recommendations will give the sowing depth, based on the rule that the larger the seed the deeper it must be planted.

For some crops, you need to make a furrow, space the seeds according to the instructions and then cover them with soil. For others, such as squashes, you need to make a 25cm (10in) circular mound that is raised about 2.5–5cm (1–2in). Firm the soil over the seeds. If you choose to sow tiny seeds such as carrots, they can be scattered on top of the soil barely covered, if at all.

Some of us may question the generous spacing directions on the seed packets, but not following these can result in overplanting, thereby crowding the newly germinated plants.

Water the entire bed with a gentle yet penetrating flow to damp the soil down to a depth greater than the planted seeds. Be careful not to wash soil off the seeds. Check daily to ensure the soil is moist.

Sometimes it will be necessary to cover newly planted seeds with a mulch such as straw or sheer fabric row covers to dissuade birds and other creatures from damaging the new leaves and shoots when they emerge.

SOWING HARDY ANNUALS

Hardy annuals such as nasturtiums are among the easiest plants to grow, as they demand little from the soil and are sown where they grow. If you thin overcrowded seedlings and give them a sunny position, the results will be bright and pleasing.

1 *Wait until the last frost in your area. Then clear the bed where you are planting the seeds, removing any weeds and debris.*

2 *Distribute the seeds on the surface. Then cover with soil so they are planted about 2.5cm (1in) below the surface.*

3 *Nasturtiums are fast growing and will usually start to sprout within a week to ten days of being planted.*

SOWING IN DRILLS

Straight drills are the most common way to sow vegetable seeds and can also be useful for flower seeds to help you distinguish seedlings from weeds. On heavy clay soil, it helps to sprinkle a layer of sand or grit along the drill before sowing the seed. Outdoor seeds need regular weeding and protection from slugs, snails, birds and rodents. A covering of fleece or cloches discourages creatures from digging up seeds, and a form of slug control should see your seedlings past the vulnerable stage.

1 *Use a hoe or a length of wood to make a drill of a depth to suit the seed being sown. If the soil is dry, water the drill lightly and sprinkle the seeds evenly along it.*

2 *For planting larger seeds, use a dibber to prepare the holes at even intervals along the drill.*

3 *Gently cover the seed with the soil that you removed. If the soil is dry and rain is not forecast, water thoroughly. Continue to water until the seedlings emerge.*

Typically, no more than 65–80 per cent of seeds germinate, so don't become discouraged with irregular sprouting. Some of the more successful seeds are cosmos, nasturtiums (*Tropaeolum*), zinnias, Mexican sunflowers (*Tithonia rotundifolia*) and sunflowers (*Helianthus* spp.). A favourite cottage garden flower is the sweet pea (*Lathyrus odoratus*), whose seeds can be planted in early spring. These gems of assorted pastel colours twist their delicate curly tendrils up trellis or arbour poles as they fill the air with perfume.

Make a label for each seed type using a clear marker – soft, black pencil usually lasts better than pen – and place it near the planted area. Dating lets you track the germination time and might encourage you to keep a sowing journal.

With proper timing, good soil preparation and realistic plant choices, the seeds should germinate and will suffer none of the checks in growth that transplanting would cause.

Broadcasting seeds

This method is typically used to spread grass seed on lawns or cast wildflower seeds into gravel areas, open spaces or fields. In small garden spaces where seeds are very small, we may broadcast them into our beds knowing

that thinning will be necessary later on. Do not broadcast seeds on a windy day or on to hot, dry or sodden soil.

You will need to prepare the bed, removing all the weeds, as described on the previous page. Slightly mist the soil if it is dry. One method that is used for broadcasting is to put the seeds in a covered can with white sand, which makes the broadcasting come out more evenly. Then scatter the seed-sand mixture over the planting areas by walking in one direction and them walking back in the opposite direction. Finally rake the area lightly, barely covering the seeds with soil – you don't want to bury them. Water with a fine spray, keeping the soil surface just damp until the seeds sprout. When the seedlings shoot up, gradually decrease watering.

LEFT *Seeds planted in gravel need enough underlying soil for their roots to settle in. Seeds that grow well in a gravel area include aubretia and blue fescue (*Festuca glauca*).*

TRANSPLANTING

Whether you started your plants from seeds growing on a sunny windowsill or purchased a six-pack of seedlings from the local nursery, there's a process to get these youngsters in your garden or container. Inevitably, the first sunny, warm day of spring gets our gardening juices flowing and we can become over-zealous in our desire to get things planted in permanent growing spots. With patience and by following a few routines, you will increase the chances of your 'little ones' surviving and thriving.

ABOVE *Newly planted pelargonium cuttings can remain in their pots for several months as they grow more leaves and sturdier stems.*

ABOVE *When transplanting a plant from one pot to another, the common rule is to go only one size larger.*

CHOOSE THE BEST EXAMPLES

When selecting annual vegetable and flower seedlings ensure they are healthy, free from disease, and have established roots before transplanting them permanently. You want the plants to have a set of 'true' leaves, those that have grown at least three or four pairs of new leaves but are not too mature or yellow. Avoid plants that have flowers or fruit since these often fall off after planting.

RIGHT *Choose healthy, well-watered corn seedlings that have mostly green leaves as you begin to plan your vegetable garden.*

FAR RIGHT *Blocks of sweet corn will thrive outdoors with enough sun, moisture and organic matter mixed in the soil.*

HARDENING OFF

The first step when transplanting is to introduce the seedlings outdoors gradually by taking them outside periodically before they settle there for good. This is called 'hardening off' your seedlings. By leaving them outdoors for longer and longer periods each day they will smoothly acclimatize to the climate, sun and natural elements.

Start by sheltering them under a bench or deck during the day and then bring them indoors by night or during inclement weather. After three days, you can safely keep them in the sun for half a day, but bring them in at night. By the end of a week, they'll be tough enough to soak up the rays all day and stay outdoors in the night.

WHEN TO TRANSPLANT

Transplant your seedlings to your garden on a day that is overcast and, ideally, still and damp, to minimize water loss during the transplanting process. Always water both the outside ground and the seedlings an hour or two before you move them.

If you're planting in the ground or a raised bed, you can make a guide for straight rows using a piece of twine that is tied between wooden stakes. Then on the soil, under the guide twine, lay a yardstick or some other length guide that has spacing intervals marked. Another idea is to mark an area for each plant with a stick in the soil. These will indicate where you should dig your holes for each transplant (seed packets will indicate spacing requirements for individual seeds).

PREPARING PLANT CUTTINGS

Very often we may admire a neighbour's interesting plants or be asked about one of our own specimens. Fortunately, we can, with a bit of care, technique and patience, make a 'clone' of these coveted plants by taking cuttings. It is a cost-efficient way of creating new plants to use and to share.

1 *Take 2–4 healthy cuttings from the host plant – here a penstemon is used. Ideally the cuttings should be taken in the morning and then placed in water for an hour. Cut the stems at an angle to give the cuttings more surface area to produce roots. Most cuttings root best if the cut is made 1cm (½in) below the leaf node.*

2 *Remove all but 1 or 2 leaves, and cut large leaves in half, to reduce water loss by transpiration, while the roots are not yet established. Add sterile planting medium to your pot and make a hole. If you like to use a rooting hormone (to stimulate growth), dip the stem in the powder and tap off the excess before planting. Otherwise, just plant the stem.*

ABOVE *Using seedlings or 'plugs' as a start for your container garden can give you a feeling of enormous satisfaction as the plants start to thrive.*

3 *Make a label that shows the name of the plant and its variety and the date you made the cutting transplant. Cuttings root more quickly and reliably in a warm rooting mix, so try to keep your cuttings at a temperature of 18–24°C (65°F–75°F). A heating mat can help if your area is cold.*

4 *Place the planted container in a plastic bag and close it lightly. The bag keeps the humidity high around the plants while they are forming. Open the bag up for about 10 minutes each day to let fresh air circulate. Feel the soil to test the moisture content – add water if necessary and mist lightly.*

USING ROOT HORMONES

As a general rule, avoid using chemicals if the job can be done without them. Most cuttings are successful without hormones, but they may help with difficult varieties, and the powders usually also contain fungicide to help prevent rotting.

A natural technique is to use willow stems, which have a mild form of root stimulating hormone called IBA (indolebutyric acid), a natural plant growth regulator. Cut up 2 cups of willow twig clippings, boil these in 3.75 litres (1 gallon) of water for 3 minutes, cool, label and store. Stand plant tip cuttings in this overnight prior to planting.

PLANTING ESTABLISHED CUTTINGS

Established cuttings will have already been transferred to a small pot and will have a good root system before they can be transplanted permanently. You should keep all plants in their pots and remove them just prior to planting. Water the plants many hours before in order to hydrate the entire plant, and do not let the roots be exposed to sun, heat or wind.

MATERIALS

- Established cuttings in pots
- Spade
- Soil amendments and fertilizer: 1 part well-rotted manure or garden compost and 1 part bonemeal
- Long-handled trowel or spade
- Hoe
- Watering can or watering wand

GARDENER'S NOTE

When removing plants, loosen and separate them gently from their pots. Always handle plants by their individual leaves or by the roots and avoid grasping the stem. As much as possible, leave the root ball intact by not disturbing the soil surrounding the plant's roots.

1 *Always groom plants before settling them in the ground by trimming off dead or dying foliage or flowers. Then prepare the space by digging it twice the width of the pot and the same depth as the root ball.*

2 *Dig all the holes at regular intervals before removing the transplants from their container. This reduces the time the roots are exposed. If you have difficulty bending and can't reach the ground, ask for help digging the holes.*

3 *Add the soil amendments and fertilizer to the hole and water the hole. Remove the plants from their pots and put each one into the hole at the same level that they were growing in the pot.*

4 *Place the transplant into the hole and fill in and firm the soil around the transplant with a hoe. Fill the hole halfway with water, then back-fill with soil and tamp lightly. This is called 'puddling'; it supplies moisture to the plant's root rather than to the soil's surface where it quickly evaporates.*

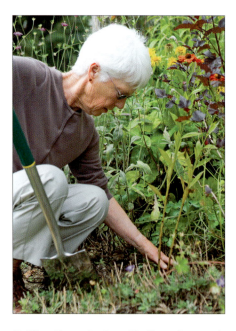

5 *Allow the water to settle the soil around the roots and then finish filling the hole. The final stage is to lightly firm the soil around the transplant.*

ABOVE *Transplant tomato plants deep and at an angle so that much of the stem is in contact with the soil.*

ABOVE *A simple protection tent will shelter a new transplant from the wind and the harsh sun.*

ABOVE *If frost threatens your tender plants, enclose them in plastic or paper domes to keep them safe.*

TRANSPLANTING TOMATOES

While the transplanting sequence shown opposite works for most plants, tomato plants are an exception. They should be planted much deeper than the depth they had in their growing container. In fact, a leggy tomato plant can be buried at an angle to keep more of its stem up in the warmer soil levels. Tomato seedlings treated in this way will develop a stronger root system by growing roots all along the underground portion of the stem.

Another tip for successful tomato transplanting is to achieve a minimal soil temperature of 10–13°C (50–55°F). Use a soil thermometer and, if necessary, cover the soil with black polythene (plastic) or cloches to warm it up.

FOLLOW-ON CARE

Keep an eye on the new transplants and protect them from wind and hot sun with cardboard or newspaper. Alternatively, cover them with a cloche, basket or flowerpot. Cloches can also be used to protect plants through the winter or as temporary cover in the spring when frost threatens.

RESCUING A ROOT-BOUND PLANT

A 'root-bound' plant is one that has outgrown its container and has created a thick mat of roots growing in these confined quarters. This condition stresses plants as their roots can't take in enough nutrients and water nor grow outwardly.

1 *Remove the plant from the pot by either squeezing around all parts of a plastic pot or by giving the bottom several firm raps with a small hammer.*

2 *Hold the matted root ball and remove old soil. Tease out the roots by unwinding them so they no longer hold a tight circle. Pull out any matted strands at the base.*

3 *Cut off any strands that look decayed. Then plant in a well-watered hole that has some compost (soil mix) forked into the bottom.*

BULB PLANTING

Planting bulbs, corms, tubers and rhizomes (all loosely classed as bulbs) is a great idea for those who want quicker, easier and more reliable results than can be achieved from seeds. Bulbs are a modified stem and bud, swollen to form a storage organ, that goes dormant at certain times of year. Most bulbs should be planted in the autumn so they can put down roots before producing their leaves and flowers in spring when the new season's warmth spurs the bulbs into growth.

ABOVE *The bulb is one of nature's greatest miracles – with soil, moisture and warm temperatures they grow into flowers.*

AN INSTANT TRANSFORMATION

The transformation from bulb to flower is one of nature's miracles. When our spring garden erupts with bright purple crocus, radiant yellow daffodils and a rainbow of tulips, our winter-weary hearts soar. Our last autumn activities in the garden when we planted those unassuming bulbs now pays us back abundantly. By choosing the right spot for bulbs, planting at correct depths, providing food and taking into account where the spring sun will deliver its warm rays, you can increase your success in achieving a colourful blooming border.

Getting bulbs in the ground is a seasonal and fun garden activity for seniors; planting them doesn't take a lot of strength and often it's a pleasure to be out on a crisp autumn day sowing next spring's flowers. For some seniors who are planting their bulbs in a new patio garden or raised bed, a cushioned kneeler and hand-trowel or dibber may be all that is needed to get the job done.

BULB-PLANTING TOOLS

Some gardeners use tools designed for planting bulbs, which come in various diameters to allow for different bulb sizes. Shaped like metal cans with no bottom, the edges are serrated to allow easier penetration in the soil. They come with long and short handles, which are easy to adapt if you need to add more cushioning or other grips to assist your hands and wrists. Many styles come with a depth gauge printed on the outside, which can help you plant bulbs at the correct depth.

BELOW *Available in long- and short-handled forms, bulb planters reserve the soil that then covers the planted bulb.*

Short-handled bulb planter

Long-handled bulb planter

Short-handled bulb planter

GARDENER'S NOTE

Use PVC pipe to make a less costly tool for planting bulbs. Cut one end at an angle to make a sharp point, making the shaft the length you need. The sharp end acts as the hole digger and the tubing is the conduit for the bulbs. The pipe diameter must be large enough to fit the bulbs you are planting. Add an adaptive handle or foam padding for a comfortable grip.

ABOVE *A drift of blooming spring bulbs with a show of colour and texture makes the labours of the autumn worthwhile.*

To use a bulb planter, push it straight into the ground and, if the soil is hard, use a twisting action. When you pull the planter back up, it should bring up a cylinder of soil, making a hole suitable for planting.

Younger, more energetic home gardeners developing their gardens and planting hundreds of bulbs will like the long-handled auger that can save their backs. There is also an auger tool that attaches to a cordless drill for even more efficiency and speed.

Planting small, early-blooming bulbs such as snowdrops, crocus, muscari and trout lilies in random places in your turf is called 'naturalizing', and will brighten up a space as winter turns to spring. Take a handful of these mixed bulbs and scatter them over the lawn or garden bed. Where they land is where you plant them (with your bulb planter). The resulting growth pattern that comes up in the spring will then look fresh and unrehearsed.

PLANTING BORDER BULBS

Don't plant a border bulb garden in a perfectly neat row but rather try to cluster a few bulbs together to get a more natural growth pattern.

1 *Turn over the soil along the edge of the garden bed. Loosen the dirt and dig a row as wide as the size of your bulbs require and as long as you want the border to be. Make the soil light and fluffy and free of weeds. Sprinkle bonemeal or bulb food into the area. Start to plant the bulbs.*

2 *When planting, a rule of thumb is to measure the length of the bulb and plant at a depth of 2–3 times that measurement. Once in place (pointed ends up), mix in organic compost with the soil you removed and cover the bulbs well to retain moisture and protect them.*

USING A SHORT-HANDLED AUGER

Bulb planters or augers are useful for planting single, large bulbs. They look like a metal cylinder with a serrated edge at the bottom to penetrate the soil, and have either a long or short handle. They often have a depth measurement.

1 *Hold the auger firmly by the handle and push and twist it simultaneously so that the cylinder cuts into the ground.*

2 *Push the auger right down to the depth required for the bulb that you are planting.*

3 *Pull the auger back up and it will bring with it a section of soil, leaving a planting hole for the bulb.*

USING FERTILIZERS

Plants need three basic life-sustaining elements – light (sun or artificial), moisture (water) and soil (food). We have already established that if you feed the soil, then the soil will feed the plants. If your soil hasn't been fed it can eventually become less fertile and incapable of successfully supporting the edibles, ornamentals and indoor plants you love to grow. Fertilizers come in various forms so no matter what your situation or ability, you can give your soil and plants just what they need.

ABOVE *Plant fertilizers are available in many forms – including liquid, powder and spikes – and are applied in various ways.*

NPK

Whatever you are growing will benefit from regular amendments of organic matter and manures, or enrichment with fertilizers. You need to achieve the right balance, however. While plants do use nutrients, they do so in very minute quantities. There are 13 essential soil nutrients. Here we will be looking at the three primary nutrients – nitrogen (N), phosphorus (P) and potassium (K). Nitrogen helps the plants' foliage to grow strong; it's particularly needed when growing vegetables, lawns and leafy plants. Phosphorus helps roots grow and develop. Potassium, also known as 'potash', is important for flowers and fruit, and woody growth.

When choosing plant fertilizers, you'll see NPK values on the label.

These help to identify the best fertilizer for the plants you're growing. For example, lawn fertilizers are typically higher in nitrogen to promote leafy growth of the grass. A balanced fertilizer is when the three chemical nutrients NPK are included in equal measures, as in the ratio 5:5:5. Tomato and rose fertilizers are higher in potassium.

ORGANIC FERTILIZERS

Fertilizers that are organic are made from naturally occurring mineral deposits and organic material, such as bone or plant meal or composted manure. Organic fertilizers have gone through little processing. However, the nutrient content is low and so larger amounts of this type of fertilizer are

needed. Organic fertilizers tend to be more costly – except home-made compost, or liquid feed made from comfrey or nettles, for example. Many organic fertilizers such as composts add long-term benefits by improving soil structure as well as adding nutrients.

SYNTHETIC FERTILIZERS

Chemically processing raw materials produces a product called a synthetic fertilizer that can deliver high levels of nutrients. These may be more cost-effective and easier to apply, but they need care and attention in storage and application. Another disadvantage is that they can also raise the salt levels in our soil. Finally, synthetic fertilizers tend to feed only the plant, not the soil.

Inorganic amendments

Growmore
(not available in the US)

Sulphate of ammonia

Potash

Superphosphate

Organic amendments

Bloodmeal

Bonemeal

Seaweed

Fish/blood/bone

ABOVE *Raking in slow-release granular fertilizer. This dry, pelleted fertilizer is mixed into the soil or spread over a bed.*

FERTILIZER OPTIONS

Mixing your own fertilizer in water, burying spikes or scratching in pellets and powders are all straightforward ways to keep your plants nourished.

Liquid fertilizer *An economic concentrate of this powder fertilizer uses 1–3 tsp per 1.75 litres (½ gallon) of water*

Fertilizer spikes *These spikes are available for many types of flowers, trees, vegetables and even indoor plants.*

Multi-purpose fertilizer *Gardeners add multi-purpose fertilizer powder to enrich the soil around a young plant.*

Granular spike *This spike fertilizer is shaped in a pyramid and just needs pressing into the soil.*

SLOW-RELEASE FERTILIZERS

Another thing to consider with fertilizers is how quickly they become available to your plants. Slow-release fertilizers are those that release nutrients throughout the season, triggered by warmth and moisture, allowing plants to absorb most of the nutrients without waste by leaching through the soil. While these fertilizers are available in either organic or synthetic form, the organic product is environmentally friendlier.

Processed slow-release fertilizers typically come in pellet, granular or spike forms. Fertilizer spikes are available for many types of flowers, trees, vegetables and indoor plants with nutrients that are specific to the plant you're feeding. Slow-release fertilizers are convenient as they require less frequent applications, but they can be more expensive. Whatever type you select, always read the label carefully.

LIQUID FERTILIZERS

Fertilizers given in liquid form are taken up by plant roots almost immediately. If applied as a foliar spray, they are absorbed even more easily. Look for liquid plant food that has a full blend of major, minor and micro-nutrients. While these fertilizers give plants a quick boost they do little to improve or nourish the soil. Also, without careful application too much synthetic fertilizer can 'burn' foliage and damage your plants.

CUTTING, TRIMMING AND PRUNING

In this section, we'll be thinking about cutting and gathering flowers and how to keep a garden plant – whether a flowering perennial, a shrub, a herb or a tree – within its boundaries and in shape using trimming and pruning. For all the garden activities associated with this process, reduce the potential injury to your plant by using tools that are well-maintained, sharp, clean and appropriate for the job.

ABOVE *Early morning is the best time to cut and harvest the flowers and herbs for your floral arrangements.*

CUTTING

This simple technique is what is required when we collect flowers from our garden for bouquets, gather blossoms for drying or snip pieces of herbs for culinary use. Cutting is a simple task and does not take a lot of energy. This is a great activity for those seniors who may limit their gardening to snipping their rosemary wreath, their lavender plants, or just grooming their houseplants when needed.

The cutting process may also encourage a new growth of blooms but, more importantly, by cutting as low as you can, you minimize the incidence of decaying stems. Coincidentally, the plant will look well cared for and not shaggy if you do this careful full-stem cutting and leave no visible stubby ends.

While cutting sometimes encourages new flowers, it can also mean removing part of the plant that may not grow back – something we want to avoid. Cutting, therefore, needs to be done with some attention to how you're shaping the plant. Try to vary the sides of the plant when you go to gather pieces of it rather than always cutting from the same area. Sometimes cutting from the middle is overlooked but this is often a great way to get a plant opened in its centre, which allows for more light and air circulation.

Always cut as far down the stem as you can because later on you'll need to cut a small length off when you put your flowers into a vase of warm, clean water. Cut all flowers and foliage about 2½cm (1in) from the bottom of the main stem. Make the slice at an angle of about 45 degrees, as this provides a larger exposed area for the uptake of water. It also enables the stem to stand on a point, allowing water to be in contact with the cut surface. Remove

ABOVE *Prune tree branches with well-sharpened tools to make a clean and healthy cut to the limb.*

LEFT *This gardener derives satisfaction from keeping her shrubs and bushes well pruned and shaped.*

ABOVE *Cutting delphiniums for a flower arrangement encourages the production of more flowers.*

the lower foliage that would be submerged. This will retard bacterial growth, which shortens the vase life of flowers and makes the water smell foul.

There's a variation on a saying that goes, "God loved the flowers and invented soil; humans loved the flowers and invented vases." Cutting flowers is a wonderful way to bring the beauty of the garden into your house or apartment, or to share it with friends.

TRIMMING

Many plants will grow too big for their space when left on their own year after year. Some plants become misshapen and need a trim when growth gravitates towards the sun or when other plants restrict them. Houseplants or smaller annual plants in containers benefit most from trimming.

The trimming process is easily done with a pair of sharp scissors, shears or pruners, depending on how thick the stem is. Never cut more than a few inches off a plant when trimming; this helps the plant focus on growing thicker in the area that has not been cut, and will give it a shape that fits the area that it is growing into. You are simply removing excess growth and reshaping

an existing structure. With flowering shrubs, the easiest rule is to always trim shrubs within one month after they finish blooming – this way there is no risk of removing next year's flowers.

PRUNING

Over time, trees and shrubs grow beyond their bounds and need pruning to keep them healthy and cared for. On the following pages we'll focus on

ABOVE *Baskets overflowing with flowers bring the scents and fresh air of our gardens into our homes.*

smaller shrubs, bushes, trees and some vines, showing the basics of when to prune and what tools are best for the job. In some cases, especially when dealing with prized or larger trees, the best method may well be to hire a professional!

CUTTING, TRIMMING AND PRUNING TOOLS

Basic pruning tools include secateurs (pruners), loppers and pruning saws. From heavy-duty blades to those with ergonomically designed handles, there are secateurs for every task. The variety of loppers is impressive too – from those with long-reach handles to mini loppers. Don't be bamboozled by all the options – do your research and ask around and check the effectiveness of multi-purpose options.

If you're still able and willing to prune the existing plants on your property, it's important that you stay on the ground (absolutely no climbing!) and use extension tools to help with the removal of tall limbs and branches, if necessary. When branches are too far away, then consider asking for help or hiring a professional who can safely deal with ladders, and perhaps the necessary power tools. As with all of the tasks that we need to complete in the garden, it's a good habit to pace yourself so you conserve your energy. Pruning can also entail significant debris removal, so reserve some strength for the clean-up.

Basic pruners

For small jobs such as cutting flowers, deadheading, shaping, pruning and houseplant maintenance you can use secateurs with simple sharp blades. These often have a compact design allowing you to use them in dense foliage without damaging the plant. Your cut flowers will keep best if you use clean and sharp tools (never use serrated edges).

Look for lightweight, all-purpose secateurs with soft, flexible, symmetrical handles that reduce blistering and fatigue and work for both right- and left-handed comfort. Sharp, pointed tips give access to otherwise inaccessible areas. Examples include fold-away secateurs for handy storage in your pocket and

ABOVE *Pruning back* Cotoneaster horizontalis *around a windowsill.*

comfort grip options, including soft-loop handles, non-slip and lightweight plastic handles.

Do not use ordinary household scissors for garden jobs since the gauge on scissors is set for paper or fabric, not for flower stems, which are bulkier. Using scissors will crush their vascular systems and prevent proper water uptake. It will also ruin your household scissors.

Garden scissors with soft handle loops

Pocket secateurs

BELOW *For small jobs and light trimming, there are many styles of scissors and secateurs to choose from.*

Garden scissors with ergonomic grips

Floral scissors

ABOVE *Fading hosta flowers are easily removed by cutting their stems off far down at the base of the plants.*

BELOW RIGHT *Pruners come in many styles and strengths depending on the job they are designed to do.*

RIGHT *Bypass secateurs, with their easy scissor-like action, are best for small, less strong hands.*

Bypass hand pruners

Secateurs or scissors with bypass blades allow the cut you make to be clean with no crushing of the plant fibre and are the most widely used of the pruning hand tools. Bypass secateurs have a spring action, so they open automatically when released, and move one sharpened blade past the other in a scissor-like motion and leave clean cuts with minimal damage to branches. They are also available as long-handled, easy reach pruners (*see also* below).

It is not advisable to use bypass secateurs on branches larger than 1cm (½in) in diameter. Their design gives you maximum leverage to reduce cutting effort, and some have a rotating handle that is designed to minimize both strain and fatigue.

Bypass secateurs

Bypass secateurs that can be firmly held in one hand

Long-handled, easy-reach pruners

Long, flexible pruners for hard-to-reach areas

Easy-reach bypass blade pruners allow you to safely prune dense or thorny plants or hedges without stretching or using ladders. For added strength and comfort, these tools can be used with either one or two hands.

Avoid cutting a limb at a larger size than recommended as you may jam the blade or strain your hand, wrist, or arm. As with all garden tasks, assess the job before you start to see if you need a second pair of hands.

RIGHT *Angled pruners such as the one shown here will usually extend from 1.8 to 3 metres (6 to 10 feet). This has the benefit of an adjustable head, thereby increasing manoeuvrability.*

Anvil and ratchet hand pruners

Garden secateurs with an anvil feature usually have a single straight sharpened blade that ends with a flat edge or anvil. Anvil pruners slice just like a knife against a cutting board and effectively remove old or dead wood. They're a little bigger than bypass pruners, making it more difficult to get close enough for crotch cuts.

A stage on from anvil secateurs, ratchet garden secateurs do all that anvil secateurs do with the addition of a mechanism that does the cutting action in stages. They also provide more

General-purpose pruner with a ratchet mechanism

Natural fit anvil pruner with stem holder and soft-grip handles

A lightweight power anvil pruner with a moulded grip

ABOVE *Ratchet and anvil pruners are easy to use for those with arthritis or diminished hand strength.*

leverage for smaller or weaker hands – so that cuts can be made in several easy squeezes. If you are going to do a great deal of pruning, ratchet secateurs can protect your wrists. Most secateurs can handle cutting through a 1–2cm (½–¾in) diameter branch. Ratchet secateurs are ideal for gardeners with weaker hands – find a pair that is lightweight (less than 1kg/2lb) and with the power to cope with heavy work.

Loppers

For anything from 2.5–5cm (1–2in) in diameter, use loppers, which have an anvil ratchet or a bypass action. These come in various sizes; a short-handled one is good for small, tight places, while longer handles offer extended reach and greater leverage. These are useful for pruning thorny shrubs such as quinces, roses and pyracanthas. Lightweight loppers made of aluminium or fibreglass are easier to handle and hold over time. Many have ergonomic designs and gear-driven or ratchet actions, so choose wisely.

LEFT *A good pair of long-handled bypass ratchet loppers gives you leverage and length so you can stand upright (or work from a chair) as you easily slice through the twigs and branches that need pruning.*

Pruning saws

For those gardeners who are still active and maintaining good health, a pruning saw may be just the tool you need when you need to get into a tight space and make a clean cut.

Pruning saws are available in folding and fixed-handled versions and, when sharp, are good for branches up to a 7.5cm (3in) diameter. For thicker branches, you will need a special heavy-duty pruning saw and this is probably a good time to get help. Long-handled saws will enable you to prune without climbing in a tree. When researching a folding saw, look for

ABOVE *Keep this tool nearby – it is portable, easy to use, and deceptively strong. Ensure the blade is covered when not in use.*

one that is lightweight and has a replaceable blade that locks away securely. If in any doubt, ask advice from your local garden centre or an expert.

WHEN TO PRUNE

Timing is perhaps the most important thing to understand about pruning, especially when dealing with flowering trees and shrubs. If you prune them at the wrong time you'll remove the flower buds and there will be no bloom.

In general, prune spring-flowering trees and shrubs immediately after they finish blooming. These are described as shrubs that flower on old wood and they begin to produce next year's flower buds soon after they finish blooming.

ABOVE *Pruning saws are versatile as they are designed to cut through dead wood as well as slice through living, green wood.*

Do your pruning in a plant's dormant period, either in early to mid-spring or in late spring/summer after the blooming period. If severe pruning is required this dormant state is perfect, since it takes some of the stress from the plants.

Prune summer and autumn-flowering trees and shrubs in late winter, before they begin the current season's growth. These are plants that flower on new wood and rely on strong, new growth for a good flowering display.

Early to mid-spring pruning suits plants including the flowering dogwood (*Cornus florida*), glossy abelia (*Abelia* x *grandiflora*), wisteria (*Wistera* spp.) and honeysuckle (*Lonicera fragrantissiam*). If the shrubs are healthy and vigorous, it's fine to prune them back into shape in one session. If you have very old plants or those that are not healthy and vigorous, spread the pruning over a three-year period to reduce the impact of removing so much wood. If in doubt, a general rule is to prune a flowering plant after its final blooms fade.

Prune plants that were damaged by storms or ones with dead limbs quickly to avoid any disease problems.

Lightweight ratchet loppers

Compact loppers for cutting flowers and trimming back plants

Small bypass loppers

Long-handled anvil ratchet loppers with moulded grips

ABOVE *Loppers come in many shapes, sizes and weights and offer various cutting actions to suit individual requirements.*

HEDGE CLIPPING AND RECOMMENDED TOOLS

If you're still caring for the family home you may have hedges that need regular seasonal maintenance. New growth usually needs to be contained, or it will look unruly and, if not checked, will allow the hedge to outgrow its assigned area, and when you do come to trim it, the growth will be thicker and harder to cut through. If your hedges are over 1.2m (4ft) tall, then the maintenance demands are more challenging, so you may be advised to hire someone else to keep them trimmed and shapely. Getting on ladders with sharp tools is unwise for any seniors, but especially so for those who are less agile or have balance problems. The reality is when seniors fall, they tend to get hurt more seriously and take longer to recover.

Hand shears for hedges

If you have a small hedge that can be maintained while you stand on your own two feet, then consider a trimming tool that is lightweight and easy to operate.

Single-handed hedge shears

Telescoping hedge shear

ABOVE *Contemporary hedge shears are innovative and user-friendly with serrated and wavy-edged blades.*

Lightweight hedge shears

Purchase a good pair of hand hedge shears – their superior cutting accuracy means that you will trim only what you need to. Remember, longer blades and handles can prevent backache because you don't have to stoop down as much. But they can also add weight, so it's wise to test some of the newer tools made with fibreglass and aluminium. These still offer superior strength and balance and are lighter than the wooden versions.

To save energy as a senior it might be advisable to avoid shrubs that need regular maintenance to achieve perfect geometric shaping. Look for shrub plantings that are slow, such as leather-leaf mahonia or kurume azalea, and low-growing dwarf varieties, such as hebe or dwarf lavender. You can also

HEDGE-TRIMMING APPROACHES

It is important to use the right tool for the job or choose a tool that is adaptable and serves more than one function. Below are demonstrations of how accessible hedges can shaped by using hand shears – the choice is yours.

Single-handed shears *Opening with a spring action, this design is perfect for shaping topiary, hedges or for edging grass.*

Scissor shears *This traditional one-handed design cuts at any angle and can be operated with either hand.*

Short-handled hedge shears *Use for shearing lavender or the new shoots of an overgrown low hedge.*

Sitting technique *Trim your hedge in a seated position, here shaping the rosemary with lightweight shears.*

use these low-growing varieties as under-storey plantings beneath trees. (*See also* battery-powered hedge trimmers on page 109.)

HAND TOOLS FOR LAWN TRIMMING

A well-maintained lawn looks great, but there comes a time when edge-trimming and hand trimming the hard spots that the mower can't handle becomes more difficult. Those who love their lawns can, however, find appropriate and adaptive tools.

The term 'lawn shears' covers tools designed for trimming difficult nooks and crannies in lawns. Look for those that allow you to stay upright as you trim.

Some blades are based on vertical poles and enable you to stand as you reach around shrubs, borders, and trees. Another edging/trimming device is a long-handled tool with rotating blades that cut at an angle. Some tools have squeeze-grip handles that activate the cutting; others operate by your arms pushing and pulling. Find a lightweight design that fits your height, and is easy on your joints.

BELOW *Edging shears with rotating blades turn full circle to give you the best cutting angle and eliminate bending and stooping.*

USING AN EDGING KNIFE

An edging knife is a tool with a half-moon shaped head, for use when neatening up the edges of your lawn. It cuts cleanly into the turf and creates a sharp edge. A centralized tread gives an even distribution of weight and reduces slippage. It maximizes your digging power and works efficiently because it is designed for this task.

1 *Position the edging knife and put your foot in the foot tread. Press down firmly so that the knife cuts the turf.*

2 *Pull the handle back so that the turf levers up. Remove the turf and repeat the process along your lawn edge.*

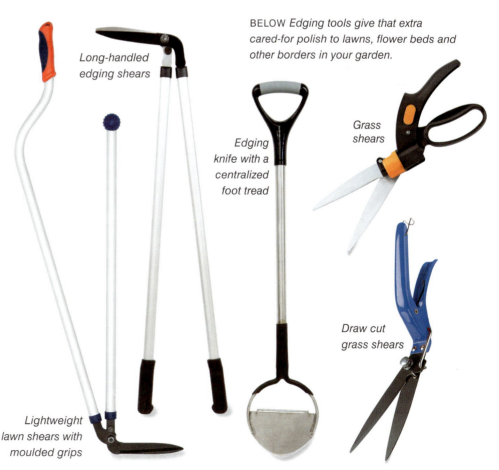

Long-handled edging shears

BELOW *Edging tools give that extra cared-for polish to lawns, flower beds and other borders in your garden.*

Grass shears

Edging knife with a centralized foot tread

Draw cut grass shears

Lightweight lawn shears with moulded grips

BATTERY-OPERATED CUTTING TOOLS

This book does not actively recommend the use of tools that are powered by mains electricity or petrol (gasoline). Even young gardeners can easily trip on an electric lead while working, or accidentally cut through the lead, while petrol-fuelled machines require storage of potentially dangerous fuel.

However, battery-operated, cordless power tools are much more viable.

Battery-operated equipment doesn't have the noise and air pollution of petrol-powered tools. Modern technology also means that such equipment is much easier to keep charged than it was in the past, with longer running times and easier methods of charging. Another advantage of battery-powered hand tools is that they are lightweight and much easier to move and operate than other cutting tools.

Here is a selection of battery-operated hand tools along with larger battery-operated equipment that will make the senior gardener's life much easier.

LEFT *This battery-powered grass trimmer converts quickly from grass cutting to edge trimming. It also has a telescopic shaft that can be adjusted to suit the position and preference of the user.*

Battery-powered secateurs

Using secateurs operated by a battery means that you can do everyday pruning tasks at the push of a button. Depending on the model, features can include a dual blade (a blunt one that guides and a sharp one that cuts), a trigger safety switch and ergonomic handles designed to reduce strain on your muscles.

Battery-powered pole pruners

Pole pruners are long-handled tools with telescoping handles that have a pruning saw with a rope or handle-operated guillotine for reaching high branches. They have either an anvil pruner or bypass pruner attached to a long shaft, which can be made of wood, aluminium or even fibreglass.

The long handle, lightweight design and adjustable height of a battery-operated pole pruner allows you to tackle jobs that manual loppers just

---

USING A BATTERY-POWERED HEDGE TRIMMER

Here are some trimming techniques for battery-powered tools. The size and types of blade (single, double-sided or interchangeable) varies according to the type of hedge you are trimming and its typical height and width.

A long-handled hedge trimmer *with an angled blade makes cutting easier. With no electric cord and no petrol fumes to inhale, this tool is safe and convenient.*

A cordless trimmer *can be small and lightweight, so it is an easy tool to control when trimming small bushes and small-leafed hedges, as well as edging lawns.*

The same cordless trimmer now uses an interchangeable blade, enabling its conversion from trimmer to shaper. It is lightweight and very manoeuvrable.

LEFT *A cordless lawnmower can be as powerful as an electric one and is safer to use, as well as being lighter than a petrol-driven type.*

RIGHT *An automatic lawnmower, a robotic device, takes care of your mowing tasks and saves you time and effort.*

cannot complete. They are much safer than standing on a ladder to cut branches high up in a tree, but are best when used by experienced gardeners, because they can be difficult to control.

Battery-powered hedge trimmers
A cordless hedge trimmer is quiet and pollution-free. Find one that cuts wood up to 1cm (½in) thick so it can tackle most of your hedge-trimming requirements. This option gives you freedom of movement and comfort – and there is no electric cord to cut through.

Battery-powered mowers
There are many examples of electric-powered mowers and you may want to stick to an electrically charged format. However, there are other options that are suited to senior gardeners. A cordless mower will usually be a similar size to the

electric versions, but lighter and therefore easier to manoeuvre. Batteries generally last for about an hour, which is enough time to cut a reasonable area of lawn.

Another option is a robotic mower. These will usually be installed as part of the purchase price, and are driven in conjunction with a perimeter wire buried under the lawn that marks a standard circuit for the mower. Then you press 'go' and just sit back and watch it do all the work. There is usually a remote control option for awkward spaces and for movement to and from its storage space, and they collect the clippings. If robotic mowers are not for you then use a cordless battery-powered model – or get someone to take this job on for you.

Strimmers
A long-handled handheld device, a strimmer uses a rapidly spinning flexible monofilament line, rather than a blade, for cutting grass and plants that won't respond to a mower, or that are sited on surfaces with obstacles that block the movement of a mower. Go for a battery-operated one that is lightweight – these are available with shoulder straps.

Maintaining batteries
Overall, using battery-operated machines is less onerous than other options. You need to recharge the batteries, but this is a straightforward job and doesn't require the awkward delivery and handling of fuel. A typical rechargeable battery life, for those that are used

regularly, might be between four and six years. If you have several battery-operated machines and use the same manufacturer, you can then use the same battery for all your cordless equipment.

Finally, you can also be kind to the environment by recycling old batteries, an option that is usually available through local collection schemes.

RIGHT *This lightweight grass strimmer offers ease of movement since there is no cord to get tangled up.*

DEADHEADING

Keeping flowers from going to seed will encourage new blossoms. So if you have annuals or perennials, keep deadheading and trim off dying flowers so they don't produce seeds. A flowering plant is designed to set seed, so by repeatedly deadheading or trimming off the spent flowers, you activate the plant's system to produce more flowers. An extreme form of deadheading that will give you a second flush of blooms is to shear the plants back to about half their height after their blooms begin to fade.

ABOVE *Deadheading the fading flowers will encourage new blooms and keep the plant growth more active.*

DEADHEADING IN EASY STAGES

The deadheading and trimming process can be overwhelming or therapeutic, depending on the number of plants you have, your schedule and your stamina. If you're still living in your own home and have many flowering plants, frequent walks in the garden will keep you up to date with what is blooming and what flowers are waning.

A consistent message in this book is to do these tasks in manageable and incremental phases. A short walk each morning among the flowering plants can tell you what will need deadheading soon. If you've downsized and have a patio garden, then you're looking at a fairly easy maintenance of your plants.

ABOVE *Walking about in the garden familiarizes you with the maintenance needs of your plants.*

WHAT DEADHEADING ACHIEVES

Deadheading serves two purposes – it keeps plants looking attractive and it stops seed production, which in turn enhances flowering. The general rule is to remove the spent blossoms, making sure you also remove the developing seedpod. Future flowering declines once the plant starts producing seeds, so don't just pull off the petals but go to just behind the flower or in the centre and

LEFT *Gathering flowers for vase displays is also a great time to trim off spent flowers and leaves.*

pinch off the seed-forming pod. Zinnias, marigolds and cosmos will flower all summer if you continually deadhead them. Cut the stem back to the ground or to the next bud or set of leaves.

Some plants, such as busy Lizzies (*Impatiens* spp.) and fibrous begonias, naturally drop their flowers and don't need deadheading. And although perennials generally have a shorter bloom period than annuals, you can extend the bloom time for some, such as black-eyed Susans, by deadheading. Finally, some plants, such as sweet Williams (*Dianthus barbatus*) and columbine (*Aquilegia* spp.), can be cut back to the ground level after blooming and will produce a second flush of blooms.

Most annuals and perennials will look better and give more months of bloom colour and leaf vitality with regular deadheading. Some examples include coreopsis (*Coreopsis grandiflora*), feverfew (*Tanacetum parthenium*), golden marguerites (*Anthemis tinctoria* 'E.C. Buxton'), lobelia, sweet alyssum (*Lobularia maritima*), smaller mums (*Chrysanthemum morifolium*), potentilla, flax (*Linum usitatissimum*), asters, Mexican blanket flower (*Gaillardia*), ageratum, hardy geraniums, other geraniums (especially pelargoniums), petunias, marigolds (*Calendula officinalis*), snapdragons (*Antirrhinum majus*), begonias, campanulas, delphiniums, zinnias,

sweet peas (*Lathyrus odoratus*), salvia and scabious. Even shrubs like rhododendrons and azaleas respond well to deadheading.

Sometimes deadheading is as easy as simply 'pinching back' a dead flower head with your thumb and forefinger under the stem. Often, if you have a

ABOVE *Deadhead your sweet peas by cutting the whole flower stem just as the bloom is beginning to fade.*

quantity of plants that need trimming, small secateurs or scissors are useful. The multi-use hand shear tool discussed earlier is also useful for deadheading.

ABOVE *In the case of common yarrow* (Achillea millefolium) *it is advisable to remove some of the stem below the bloom.*

While it's small enough to fit in your pocket and light to handle, it's amazingly tough. The enclosed grip protects your fingers and adds comfort to your hands.

DEADHEADING

Remove flowers as they begin to fade to allow side shoots to develop and extend the flowering period. However, you can leave some if you want to collect seeds, or if the seedheads are attractive and/or a food source for birds, like teasels.

1 *Leaves or blooms that have faded should be removed promptly. Roses should have any dead or diseased leaves removed along with the withered flowers.*

2 *With fingers or pruners 'pinch' or cut the dead flowers and leaves as close to the next flower stem or bud. Removing just the dead blossom leaves a stem with a blunt edge.*

3 *Visit the flowers often to deadhead since this will keep them from going to seed and will provide you with continuous blooms throughout the season.*

WEEDING AND HOEING

Weeds – can't live with them and can't garden without them. They grow in our garden beds, our pavement crevices and sometimes even our gutters. Weeds are opportunistic; give them a reasonable environment, and they will seize their chance and grow and grow and grow. However, weeding does provide, in the words of garden writer Christopher Lloyd, "a kind of soothing monotony [leaving gardeners'] minds free to develop the plot for their next novel".

ABOVE *A traditional hand fork may be all you need to displace those baby weeds growing in your raised bed.*

ABOVE *Clustering containers full of plants creates a garden that is easy to maintain.*

WEEDS: TO STAY OR TO GO?

The bottom line is that you're going to have to do some weeding. With a little research on the tools on the market you can reduce both your weeds and your physical strain to a minimum.

A weed has been defined as a 'plant that is a hazard or a nuisance or one that causes injury to people, animals or a desired crop'. An example is the holly seedling that sprouts in the vegetable bed. Though probably a desirable plant in a different place, it would be a nuisance to your crop of tomatoes and beans. Thus, the vegetable gardener would 'weed out' that holly tree.

Some weeds may be accepted as attractive plants, if you can keep them within bounds. Queen Anne's lace (*Daucus carota*), for instance, is considered a weed by many gardeners and yet provides a wonderful habitat for butterflies and other beneficial insects, as well as being a delight to look at. Another example is the ground cover, oxalis (*Oxalis oregana*), which fills shady spots with clover-like foliage and pink flowers and creates almost total weed suppression in the beds around it. Some gardeners see oxalis as a criminal in the garden and yet this 'weed' looks healthy and green all year and saves additional weeding chores. As the saying goes, one gardener's weed is another gardener's flower.

ABOVE *Oxalis is pretty, but in some gardens will be invasive and is likely to grow like a weed.*

ABOVE *Cow parsley (Anthriscus sylvestris) is a vigorous grower and is seen as an invasive plant in most gardens.*

ABOVE *Rose bay willow herb or fireweed (Epilobium angustifolium) can be an aggressive plant in a small garden.*

WEED SCAVENGERS

In general, weeds are more offensive than useful. They compete with desired crops such as flowers and vegetables, and they take valuable moisture that we want to conserve for our plants. Because of their vigour, they often shade smaller plants, thus inhibiting or even eliminating the plant's growth. Fertilizers are also scavenged by weeds, robbing our plants of their needed nutrients. Finally, some weeds are poisonous or can expose our skin or lungs to allergies.

Good weed management begins with knowing your weeds by name and something about their life cycle. Is the weed an annual, perennial or biennial? Consider this research as something you do when the gardening season has ended. By knowing how and when to limit seed production you can keep weeds from blooming and producing seeds and you stand a better chance of getting ahead of them.

CREATING A WEED BARRIER

The best way of reducing the time spent weeding is to take precautions before you start work on your bed or border. This can be simply achieved by creating a barrier. There are weed barriers like plastic or landscaping fabric that keep weeds at bay, but they can be expensive. The organic, inexpensive and recyclable method shown here uses newspaper.

1 *Make sure you have an ample supply of organic compost/mulch to cover your garden bed with 7.5–10cm (3–4in).*

2 *Overlap layers of at least 10 pages of newspaper around the perennial plants. Use a layer about 5mm (¼in) thick.*

3 *Water down the newspaper with a sprinkler hose as soon as it is laid on the bed to stop it from blowing away.*

4 *Apply a layer 7.5–10cm (3–4in) deep of the compost or bark mulch collected earlier on top of the newspaper layers.*

5 *You will be rewarded with a bed that has significantly fewer weeds and more space for plants to grow and thrive.*

6 *Here an alternative weed barrier is being created with plastic sheeting. This will then be covered with bedding soil.*

ABOVE *Long-handled weeders allow you to stand as you use a push-pull action to do your weeding.*

WEEDING AND HOEING TOOLS

It has been estimated that gardeners spend 90 per cent of their time weeding and only 10 per cent planting. If these numbers are accurate, it is important that when we weed in our various types of garden spaces, we use the right tool for the job (and weed) at hand. No hoe or weeder is perfect for every gardening task, so it is important to know your physical abilities and to experiment with different designs. Selection is broad, from close-in hand weeders and hoes to those with long handles.

It is a delight to visit nursery centres and garden stores to catch up on the latest stock of newly designed tools. But while it is great to look, read reviews and talk to an experienced tool seller before you settle on a new tool – especially your new weeder – it is most important to 'try on' your new garden buddy. Here we show a range of examples, some standard, some that are specially useful for older gardeners.

Basic requirements

At the simplest level you will probably need a weeding fork, a hand trowel and a long-handled hoe or weeder. But there are many options on the market – in fact a greater variety than any other category, so it's especially important to do your research well.

Weeding or hoeing will normally control small and new weeds as the tool dislodges the green tops from the roots or it may totally expose the whole weed – roots and all. Long-handled weeders or hoes are perfect tools to use as you strive to keep your back straight, also reducing hip and knee strain caused by reaching and bending. Many of these tools come with a metal head but in various shapes that suit different actions. Most of them do the same thing, however – they slice through the weed head with a single stroke. You'll need to find the one that suits you. Here are some of the options.

BASIC WEEDING

Sometimes the only way to get a jump on those small weeds that emerge in the spring is to get up close and personal. For those who can and want to kneel in the garden, using a good kneeler or pad is essential. Use your favourite hand fork to loosen the soil under the plants enabling you to remove the whole weed – leaves and roots!

1 *Remove the flower head, especially if you're just out for a stroll and don't have any tools handy. This keeps the flower from going to seed and prevents it from spreading.*

2 *Using an appropriate weeding tool, here a classic hand fork, plunge your weeder about 2.5cm (1in) from where the weed's stem goes into the ground.*

3 *Pull back on the tool as you lift up the ground surrounding the weed. You may have to make several plunges around the weed base if it is large or stubborn.*

4 *Pull up on the stem as you remove it and hopefully also the root. If you made a divot (a hole in the turf), replace as much soil as you can and gently step on the area.*

Hand weeders

For small beds of flowers or vegetables, hand weeders of various patterns are essential to easy and efficient work. Those shown here are versatile weeders that are designed to provide good balance. A hard, forged-steel blade is welded to a long shaft that has a comfortable wooden handle. The all-purpose blade allows you to get close to plants with the short side of the blade, and you can use the corner to get into cracks, clear large areas with the entire blade or get under most weeds to shave them off like a razor. Its long shaft allows you weed without kneeling and to reach into and under places that your hand won't reach.

Lawn weeders

A collection of different-shaped hand and pole tools, lawn weeders work to remove weeds that tend to grow in the lawn – for example, crab grasses, tap-rooted weeds such as those in the dandelion family and other undesirable grasses.

Push/pull weeders

This design is a fast-action hoe that is used to push and pull the blade back and forward below soil level, in the process cutting the weeds. The wavy dual-edged blade cuts very efficiently. Along with the draw hoe and the Dutch hoe, the technique is simply to stand and push and pull the metal head against the soil surface and cut off unwanted weeds.

Hand weeder *Weeding fork* *Ergonomic hand weeder*

ABOVE *Short-handled hand weeders can be used in combination with a kneeler or when working on a raised bed.*

The draw hoe (*see* second from left) is used with a pulling or chopping action and is more suitable for hard soils than the standard push-pull hoe.

Hoes with adapted handles

The stainless-steel three-tined weeder/hoer is a classic tool and the model shown here (*see* third from right) has a soft-grip, upright-style handle that keeps your wrist and hand in a neutral position and reduces strain. Many models can be used with a telescopic handle to give different lengths, depending on the task you are doing.

Always feel the handles, particularly where you will be gripping the tool. If you have a weak grip because of arthritis, carpal tunnel or other issues, consider tools that have contoured grips that give you more control.

Adding padded grips to handles increases the gripping diameter, which will create more comfort as you work.

LEFT *This selection of long-handled hoes and weeders each have their own purpose. They all enable garden weeding and maintenance with no need to bend over.*

Long-handled push plate hoe

Long-handled draw hoe

Push-pull weeder

Easy-grip forked weeder

Ergonomic weeder with a circular handle

Dandelion weeder

Cobra-head long-handled weeder

This weeder is a universal tool – it weeds, hoes, cultivates, edges and harvests. Its fingernail-like blade is steel and acts as an extension of your hand. The comfortable and efficient handle allows an easy left-hand or right-hand action.

Hula-Ho weeder

Another long-handled scuffle hoe, the Hula-Ho weeder has a band of metal at the end that makes a rectangular hoop.

It's sharp on both edges of the band so with both a forward and backward motion you can achieve a good clean-cutting action. To use this tool, run the metal band through the top layer of soil. This action cuts off the weeds just below the surface. By going deeper, you can reach the roots of many weeds. If you find that blades of grass from the lawn creep into flowerbeds, use the Hula-Ho to cut away the grass. The Hula-Ho keeps the soil in place,

ABOVE *A long- or short-handled winged weeder skims off the top part of most weeds, inhibiting their regrowth.*

instead of piling it all up at one end of the plot or the other. It makes quick work of an otherwise tough job. One gardener who suffered from a bad back said that the Hula-Ho gave her back some dignity as she no longer had to hunch over uncomfortably to weed and the easy back-and-forth motion didn't put pressure on her spine.

Grandpa's weeder

This tool has been around since 1913 and is a favourite among senior gardeners because it allows them to weed without bending, pulling or kneeling. While you might have used it as a hand tool, it now comes with a 90cm (36in) wooden handle. It is an effective and almost effortless weed puller – especially useful when removing dandelions and other lawn weeds.

A press of your foot on the footpad lever will plunge the weeder into the ground around the weed. Removal of your foot and a tilt of the handle towards the footpad lever releases the weed from the soil. An extra bonus of

Hula-Ho weeder

Grandpa's weeder

Pavement weeder

Ball weeder

Winged weeder

Hori-hori knife

Cobra-head long-handled weeder

Circle hoe

LEFT AND ABOVE
This collection of short-and long-handled weeders is a small sampling of the variety of tools available that are comfortable and easy to use. You need to choose the tools that will most successfully attack the weeds in your garden.

this tool is that it can serve as a walking stick as you stroll around your garden looking for weeds. The handle is made of wood and the weeding end is made of cast metal for strength and durability.

Circle hoe

Many gardeners swear by a tool called a circle hoe, which looks a bit like a magnifying glass without the glass. This simple tool allows you to get out and tackle those weeds, but with quite a gentle movement which means there is less stress created on your back, knees, shoulders and arms. Firstly, the circle hoe eliminates much of the need to bend over. Secondly, the blade of the hoe slices through the soil, weeding, aerating and cultivating with a smooth motion. It doesn't drag the soil along, eliminating the extra chore of rearranging the soil.

Ball weeder

This traditional weeder has been around for many years. It has a two-tine fork with a large wooden knob at the base of the handle. The ball creates a fulcrum

support for the rocking motion that is used when weeding. This weeder works particularly well when the ground being weeded is soft because it provides leverage, which weeders with narrow fulcrums do not. It is also useful for removing weeds with spreading roots. Choose one with a reasonably long handle for extra convenience.

Hori-hori knife

This is a digging, scraping, cutting and prying tool from Japan. It is great for serious weeding jobs and has a blade of very hard steel for deep digging and prying, as well as a serrated edge for cutting. It can also be used for dividing perennials, digging holes for transplants – in fact, just about any task in the soil.

Patio and pavement weeders

You can buy specially designed weeders for weeding hard landscaping, such as a tricorner or a winged weeder – useful if you have large areas of patio. Alternatively, use an old screwdriver to remove the weeds between pavers.

Winged weeder

One of the most common and versatile long-handled weeding and hoeing tools in the group of weeders that push, pull, slide or angle (a category called scuffle hoes) is the winged weeder. The sturdy metal head is in the shape of wings and gives you four bladed sides for getting the weed out of the soil on both the push and the pull stroke. It weeds and aerates the soil, skimming just below the soil surface, with an easy push-pull motion. It lets you weed in perennial beds or get dandelions out of your lawn while standing up. If you need to make rows for planting seeds, this tool makes clean straight furrows and will cover the seeds with soil.

The winged weeder comes in three styles: the junior size has a smaller winged metal head to get into tight places, the medium size hand tool allows easy weeding in containers and the larger winged head is for more substantial weeding. Long handles are available in all styles.

ABOVE *Long-handled tools that clean out the cracks of brick pathways make the task easy on the back and knees.*

ABOVE *A knee cushion allows an active gardener to get close to the pavement gaps to remove those small weeds.*

ABOVE *A long handle with interchangeable heads creates a multi-purpose tool to cater for your every weeding need.*

WEEDING: TUNING INTO YOUR ENERGY REQUIREMENTS

Because most of us want to get out in the garden early in the spring, we are often using parts of our bodies that might not have been in action for a while. Before most perennials are poking through the ground and hardly any vegetables are growing, you're likely to have weeds to deal with. But we need to consider the physical stresses of weeding and pace ourselves. This book often talks about the many health benefits of gardening and weeding is no exception: it can help our hearts, burn calories, increase our flexibility and stave off osteoporosis. So we can achieve physical and health benefits while creating a healthy and manageable garden (*see also* warming-up exercises on pages 50–53).

In order to work within your physical capabilities, try to weed or hoe when the conditions are most comfortable. If it is very hot, or there is an icy wind, the work will be more tiring. This can make a big difference in your effectiveness. Each day, do a little more and soon you'll build your stamina so you can stay in the garden longer. This incremental strategy will save you backbreaking hours later on when the weeds have got out of control. Weed a small patch in one go, slowly working outwards, and when you go back next time start in the same spot.

Also, it is better to work with moist soil since weeds will then pull more easily. However, if the ground is really soaked, wait for it to drain a bit because the soil will compact if you walk on it.

WEEDING POSITION

Choosing the right tool for the job is a common theme in this book, for seniors who don't have the stamina they once had. Finding tools that assist us in getting our tasks done more efficiently is becoming easier as we benefit from the wide array of senior-friendly tools.

One consistent caution is that to stay gardening well into our 60s, 70s, 80s and beyond we should avoid stooping over. As much as possible, make it a habit to keep your back straight when you're doing your garden chores.

Keep a lightweight nylon net bag on your shoulder or around your neck so you can collect the weeds you dig conveniently. Remember the 'touch once' theory – clean up as you go!

Long-handed weeding tools and customized hoeing heads give the older gardener an excellent start. If you like to get down on your knees for weeding and if your body is agreeable, it's best to kneel on a cushion or kneeler (*see also* maximizing comfort on pages 54–57).

Kneeling has definite advantages: it creates a stable foundation for your body, enables you to reach into crowded beds with both hands and brings more pressure upon the weeds you are dislodging.

MAKE YOURSELF COMFORTABLE

For spry gardeners who prefer getting on all fours to attack unwanted weeds, try using the combination kneeler/seat (*see also* page 59) – it is portable, safe and allows you to sit or kneel in comfort.

If you don't have a kneeler or a lightweight seat handy a sturdy plastic bucket creates almost the same stability, enabling a close working distance in seated comfort, particularly when using tools with adjustable handles.

Finally, weeding can be discouraging as well as physically challenging. If the weeds seem overwhelming, be patient and tackle a small area at a time, or get help. Top-dress cleared areas with mulch to keep weeds down.

RIGHT *Gentle weeding and bed maintenance in a community garden is a companiable activity.*

USING A GRIPPING WEED PULLER

This tool will remove weeds in cultivated soil. It can be used sitting down and is ideal for one-handed use. Its grabbing action can also be useful for picking up objects.

1 *Push the blade into the ground next to the weed. Release the trigger so that the claw of the weeder closes over the weed.*

2 *Then pull firmly on the weed puller to remove the weed from the soil. The long handle reduces bending to a minimum.*

TRANSPORTING

Whether it's carrying tools, moving plants or taking prunings to the compost, almost every garden job involves moving things. Having the right equipment can make a hard job easy or, in some cases, an otherwise impossible job possible. Remember that transporting things is also a question of keeping safe and not taking on too much. So think about using lightweight containers and lifting anything that needs to be carried in the garden in a safe way (see also lifting objects on page 63).

ABOVE *Lightweight, durable containers are versatile either as attractive pots or to move debris to the compost bin.*

LIGHTWEIGHT CONTAINERS

Many seniors who've chosen to relocate to a residence with a small patio or deck will likely do their gardening in containers. Traditional containers such as terracotta or metal pots are quite heavy even before they are used for planting, so the planted container can be heavy to move. There are moving aid options (*see also* right and opposite) but you can also significantly reduce the weight of your containers by using plastic or fibreglass ones.

Coir and fibre containers are available to use as window boxes or as planters. These lightweight options provide good drainage and air circulation and are environmentally friendly as they will rot down after use, either in your compost heap or planted in a garden bed.

Tough plastic buckets can be used for carrying, mixing, pouring and storing things in the garden. Many of them come with flexible bodies and are frost- and UV-proof.

For those who like a more traditional style there are many fibreglass planters on the market that cleverly imitate terracotta, lead, bronze and copper. This makes them appear solid and permanent within the garden, while maintaining the obvious advantage of being lightweight. They are also frost-proof and survive outside all year round and in all weathers.

Another weight-reducing option for lightweight or traditional-weight containers is to replace up to one half of the soil in the pot with polystyrene beads (Styrofoam popcorn); this adds no weight, takes up space and saves money by not using so much soil. Just cover them with a layer of nylon net before putting the soil in the pot.

However, remember that tall or top-heavy plants need a pot that is heavy enough to prevent them blowing over.

MOVING AIDS

Getting your containers on wheeled coasters will make it much easier for you to have a more 'mobile' garden. Look for a product that is made from extremely strong and durable plastic and has at least four heavy-duty stabilizing rollers. This allows a pot to be simply rolled into a new position.

Pot lifters

While designed for two people, pot lifters are intended specifically to help gardeners and landscapers easily move large, heavy, awkward-to-lift flowerpots, landscaping stones and even root balls. While seniors should

Plastic flower pots

RIGHT *Lightweight fibre boxes and pots are made of biodegradable materials such as coconut husk (coir), bamboo and peat.*

Lightweight fibre window box

RIGHT *When moving a heavy container, use these strap-like supports with a partner for a safe and easy move.*

ABOVE *A wheeled pot mover lets you shift a plant around the patio for more sun and also raises the pot avoiding rot and debris.*

A two-wheel wheelbarrow creates maximum stability.

BELOW Moving soil, debris and plants requires strong and sturdy transports such as wheelbarrows and garden carts.

A one-wheeled barrow needs a stable dual support at the back.

Pot mover

avoid moving heavy things, there will be occasions that you have a tree, shrub or container to move. With a pot lifter and the help of a friend or neighbour any reasonably fit senior can safely move these objects.

Garden bag with tool carriers

Basket for tools and plants

Other transport aids

Most of the time you can be the transporter of your tools. Wearing a pocketed apron, tool belt, or secateurs holster will keep your smaller tools handy and accessible. As you walk about the garden, you can carry what you need with you. Another idea is to have a backpack with your tools, seeds and water bottle. For many of us, having our hands free when we walk about provides us balance and offers us the option to stop, feel, smell and experience the plants.

Carry belt for storing garden tools

Other dual-purpose carry options include stools and baskets – allowing you the convenience of a seat as you garden or a basket for collecting garden items while also keeping your essential tools to hand (*see also* page 58).

LEFT Find ways to keep your tools nearby so your day in the garden is productive and not frustrating.

WHEELBARROWS

While a classic way of transporting heavy loads, wheelbarrows should be treated with caution by seniors with mobility problems or stiffness. A standard one-wheeled wheelbarrow can be useful for sprightly seniors, although it does require upper body strength, offers minimal support while you're moving it forward, can unbalance and puts strain on your back. There are lightweight versions in plastic with wheels with a good-sized tread that can be viable. But for greater stability when transporting garden debris a barrow with two wheels is much more useful. There are also models that are suitable for one-handed use, those with a weak grip and those who have difficulty bending.

A folding wheelbarrow is useful, easily manoeuvrable and easy to store in a small space. These barrows are not recommended for heavy garden duty but work well for grass cuttings, weeds and light organic debris, the kind of transporting seniors are most likely to require.

For all the examples shown here, don't overfill your barrow – it's better to make a few more trips than to stress your back or spill the load.

FOLDING CARTS

There are utility folding carts on the market made of high-grade marine aluminium that is completely rust and corrosion resistant. Loads are dispersed evenly over the axles, offering lots of stability and manoeuvrability even over uneven terrain. A front gate is easily removed and allows for quick, easy, controlled dumping of soil or mulch. When not in use, these folding carts can be easily stored in a closet, garage or storage shed.

GARDEN CARTS

Providing the same service as wheelbarrows, garden carts are safer and more predictable. They're more stable than wheelbarrows and generally can handle larger loads, but can also be more difficult to manoeuvre on rough surfaces. Most garden carts feature two wheels and a large handle similar to that of a lawnmower. They can be pushed or pulled (wheelchair gardeners love this) and give walking support to the pusher. Ultimately, the choice between

A collapsible cart with a removable lining

This leaf cart folds flat and hangs for storage.

This folding cart holds bags for leaves, grass and other soft debris.

a wheelbarrow and garden cart is up to the user; many gardeners find they have need of both.

Garden carts come in all shapes, sizes, weights and materials. There are some very useful smaller carts that are handy for carrying tools, trays of plants or small bags of soil. Some of these come with a cover, so they can do double duty as a place to sit down.

ABOVE LEFT AND ABOVE *Garden carts come in all shapes and sizes, designed to get near the job for an easy clean up.*

Last but not least is the metal garden wagon or garden truck with removable sides. One advantage of these is the highly manoeuvrable handle for going around corners and the rubber tyres for navigating uneven terrain.

USING A FOLDING HAND TRUCK

This lightweight folding hand truck can be a big help when moving awkward and heavier things about the garden.

It can be pushed or pulled depending on the nature of your load, and folds for easy storage.

1 *When folded, this garden cart is light and easy to carry.*

2 *A catch near the handle frees the mechanism. Unfold the step and secure it for use.*

3 *Use the garden cart to transport heavy bags of compost (soil mix) with ease.*

4 *This cart also allows you to transport large pots and plants. Get help when loading the pot.*

ABOVE *The safest way to move heavy loads is on a flat bed cart or wagon that has four wheels to give stability.*

ABOVE *A strong plastic sheet can be all that's needed to move garden debris or a heavy pot from one place to another.*

ABOVE *There are various add-on devices available for motorized carts – such as lap trays, carry bags and baskets.*

WHEELED GARDEN SCOOTS

Garden scoots are invaluable when working in beds that border a level pathway. Essentially a small seat on four wheels, it allows you to sit down about 25–27cm (10–11in) from the ground where you can comfortably garden and then effortlessly roll yourself along to the next part. Look for a sturdy one with wide heavy-duty wheels and a padded seat. Some come with saddlebags or a storage compartment for your tools and supplies.

USE YOUR OWN ADAPTATIONS

Consider using a small luggage trolley to hold your tool basket and maybe a few smaller tools. Having bungee cords available to secure the objects will

BELOW *A wheeled garden scoot lets you work from a seated position and roll in comfort from plant to plant.*

ensure that you don't drop things. An old suitcase on wheels can be perfect, not only to store your tools, seeds and other materials, but also to pull them about. Just make sure that you don't pack it too heavily.

MOVING WITHOUT WHEELS

Now that we've looked at wheeled devices for moving things about in the garden, let's look at other ways. Some of these you may have to hand; others are new to the market.

The 'touch it once' concept applies in the garden as well as the office. To be efficient, always have a disposal unit nearby where you can readily deposit your weeds, pruning debris or raked leaves. Sheets and tarps that you can drag are useful for tidying and for moving lighter piles of trimmings and soft weeds to the compost pile – and old shower curtains can be used in the same way.

A relatively new product is the collapsible pop-up polyvinyl and polyester container, which is ideal for garden debris collection. It usually comes in a 38 litre (10 gallon) and 113 litre (30 gallon) size, with cushioned handles. A toggle-and-loop closure system makes it easy to store on a hook. Ideally they should be made of

tear-proof woven plastic and should be lightweight and easy to store. The 113 litre (30 gallon) size is tremendously useful as it is so capacious – just be careful not to drag it along rough surfaces as the bottom is prone to puncturing.

WHEELCHAIR/WALKER ADD-ONS

If you use a wheelchair or walking aid, look into baskets or lap trays that you can attach to carry tools and sundries. Having your tools and equipment accessible is critical; a mounted tray will enable you to have a small pot or container close so you can do the necessary maintenance. Hanging an organizing panel or attaching a garden belt in an accessible place will provide ready access to your favourite tools. If you use a front-wheel walker there are many attachments that will hold your tools and keep them nearby. Finally, don't forget a place to store your water bottle!

WATERING

No matter where you live, watering is a big part of being a gardener. For older gardeners, it's neither safe nor efficient to be lugging heavy watering cans about the garden or struggling with unwieldy hoses. There are ways to rethink how to get water to beds, containers and hanging baskets as well as trees and shrubs. You can be creative with inexpensive homemade watering systems or look to the professionals for a commercially installed irrigation system.

ABOVE *A simple rain gauge will help you calculate just how much rain your garden gets in an average week.*

WATERING TO SUIT LOCAL CONDITIONS

Because a healthy plant is 75 to 90 per cent water, it requires a consistent and adequate source of moisture to retain its vitality. Of course, a plant's water needs depend on where you live. In any location and climate that has periods of long drought, perhaps with little or no rainfall all year, gardeners have to learn to maintain their gardens through such arid conditions by mulching, growing drought-tolerant plant varieties, mulching again, watering plants deeply but more infrequently and then mulching again. This watering strategy should be a lesson for all of us living in a climate that is changing and where we need to think about conserving water whenever we can.

MEASURING RAINFALL

While not a necessity, a rain gauge helps you determine how much water the garden gets in a week. Find one that has the rain catcher marked with easy-to-read numerical calibrations. If you don't have a rain gauge, you can use empty tuna cans, marking the 2.5cm (1in) level on the inside. If you find that less than 2.5cm (1in) of rain is falling each week you need to supplement the water.

If you are watering with a sprinkler, you can distribute three marked cans about 4.5m (15ft) apart where you are going to water. Check how much water your sprinkler has applied to the area at intervals to work out how long it takes to apply 2.5cm (1in). This will tell you how long the sprinkler must be on to get a designated amount of moisture, and you can then adjust your watering methods.

LEFT *Watering cans for seniors should be lightweight and have a long nozzle and a removable rose (spray head).*

Lightweight watering cans

WATERING TOOLS

If nature doesn't supply your environment with the right amount of rainfall, then you'll need to provide the moisture. Here are the tools to help you water your garden, some new and some traditional. As always, choose these tools to suit the needs of your garden and your own requirements.

Watering cans

Plainly no-one with a garden can manage without a watering can. First used in the 1600s, watering cans were then made of wood and would leak water just as soon as they were filled. Today's watering can has had every modern and practical design know-how applied to it, and allows the gardener to easily tip water directly to the base of the plant, conserving precious water in the process. Using one also enables you to control the amount of water you bring to the plants' roots. For seniors these essential pieces of equipment should have a long nozzle and a removable 'rose' (spray head) and be made of lightweight plastic. Having two handles allows you to use both hands if you need the extra leverage.

ABOVE *Adding a timer to your hose allows you to control the amount of water you use for a set period of time.*

ABOVE *Installing quick-connect hose attachments to taps and hoses makes adding nozzles or sprinklers easy.*

ABOVE *Mounting the hose will keep it off the pathway, allow convenient storage, and make it easy to access and use.*

When choosing your watering can, check to feel whether it is well balanced and has a spout that is long enough for your requirements. If possible, get a brightly coloured one that is readily seen and easy to access. This will also mean that it won't become a tripping hazard. Many of today's watering cans are also ergonomically refined with curved

Standard garden hose

Self-coiling garden hose

ABOVE AND RIGHT *Use lightweight and less bulky garden hoses for easy movement and storage. For additional safety, choose bright hose colours.*

spouts and side handles. Look for a rounded spout (which may be removable). Because the arm and hand strength of an older gardener may be decreasing, purchase a medium-sized can and perhaps only fill it half way. It's also better to carry two partly-filled cans, to reduce strain on your back and shoulders – as long as you aren't leaning on a walking stick or other support.

Garden hoses

Invest in a hose that resists cracks, breaks and kinks. Get one in a bright colour, or at least one that has bright striping, which is especially useful to help those with low vision. If you garden from a wheelchair or scooter, try making the last 7.5–10cm (3–4in) of

your hose rigid by attaching it to a length of a broom handle using twist ties or soft twine. Adding this rigidity avoids the chances of the hose becoming tangled in the wheels of your scooter or wheelchair.

Position the hose in an accessible location where the tap (spigot) is at least 5–7.5cm (2–3in) above the ground. Keep the area around the hose free from slippery mud by laying in gravel, pavers or a sturdy ground cover. Having a lightweight flexible hose no longer than 7.5m (25ft) will also help.

You can add quick-connect hose attachments to the ends of all hoses and taps. These are snap-on-and-off attachments that make adding hose lengths, sprinklers or nozzles much easier on your hands. When researching these, look for the feature of a unique built-in full-flow water control valve – this will shut off water when the attachment is uncoupled and then open to full flow when the fitting is attached. This will save time and energy going back and forth to the garden tap.

ABOVE *Seep or soaker hoses provide slow, deep watering that goes directly to the root zone of the plant.*

ABOVE *Install easy-turn handles to all outdoor taps to make accessing the water easy on your fingers and hands.*

Slow-release soaker hoses

Soaker hoses can be laid along the ground or permanently buried below the surface. Made of water-permeable materials, they allow a low or medium drip of moisture to weep along the length of the hose. Little evaporation occurs and there is no water spraying on foliage, which could cause fungal disease. They may take over an hour to adequately moisten your soil, so use them only when you are around to monitor their effectiveness. To determine if the soil is fully hydrated, dig down to about 30cm (12in); if water has seeped that far, you're done. (*See also* irrigating a wooden raised bed on page 181.)

Easy-turn handles

It can be so frustrating when the outdoor water tap (faucet) is too tight to operate. Often, the tap handle is too difficult to rotate or has become rough and corroded, which makes it unsafe to use. Older hands, especially those with arthritis or Parkinson's, need to have easy access to water without a struggle. A tap with a lever is generally much easier to operate. There are several tap adaptors that make outside taps easy to turn on and off. Tap 'mitts' are simple devices that attach over the existing circular tap and that will keep your hands safe as they give you added leverage to activate the water flow. Other tap adaptations are ergonomically designed to create a comfortable and large gripping area for improved leverage when turning on stiff taps.

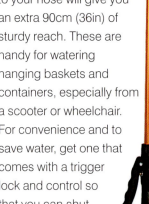

Watering wands

Attaching a watering wand to your hose will give you an extra 90cm (36in) of sturdy reach. These are handy for watering hanging baskets and containers, especially from a scooter or wheelchair. For convenience and to save water, get one that comes with a trigger lock and control so that you can shut off the flow with a finger motion.

Watering wands

MAKING A BOTTLE SEEP TUBE

You don't have to buy elaborate automatic watering systems. The seep system can be used with plastic bottles, which make excellent seep irrigation tubes.

1 *Make some small holes in the cap of the plastic bottle and screw it on tightly. Cut the base off the bottle.*

2 *Push or bury the bottle neck firmly into the ground next to the plant and fill the open end with water, re-firming if needed.*

ABOVE *Hose guides come in many designs to help keep the hose from crushing your plants.*

ABOVE *This 'water computer' comes with adaptors to enable you to connect it to any outside tap.*

ABOVE *An automatic watering system delivers water near the plant or below the soil surface into the plant root zone.*

Hose carts and hose storage

Wheeled hose carts eliminate the need to drag around clumsy hose coils that create tripping hazards. They consist of a reel with a crank that coils the hose on a drum, reducing tangles, knots and kinks. They use a two- or four-wheeled base with a handle for pulling. Buy the most stable you can afford and one with a hand crank that is big and easy to grip. Large, inflatable wheels improve mobility and stability.

Hose attachments and other watering features

Hose guides are a useful feature to help guide your hose around the corners, curves and edges of garden beds as they keep the hose from slipping on to your garden plants. Simple wooden stakes pounded into the ground at an outward angle will prevent the hose form crushing garden plants.

A water distributor can be attached to your tap and allows you to water your garden with the convenience of a battery powered automatic timer. These are supplied with different sizes of adaptor to allow connection to any outside tap. Using the control dials, you simply

need to select the watering start time, frequency and duration and leave the irrigation to manage itself.

Garden sprinklers can be used for watering lawns or garden beds, but are quite wasteful. If you use one, it's best to do it in the early morning or evening, to minimize evaporation. An oscillating sprinkler sprays out a fan-shaped curtain of water, ideal for watering large areas, and the gentle spray is perfect for newly seeded areas and clay soils that absorb water slowly. Look for models that have a timer built in – this is most useful if you are not around to shut off the water. There are models that let you direct the flow of water, reducing waste.

Many seniors may be able to assemble and install a drip system but it is advisable to hire a professional to do the job. While such systems are the most expensive of watering options, they can be custom designed for your garden, soil type and plant needs and can be linked to automatic timers. Use a water breaker with many tiny holes to release water in a soft shower rather than a high-pressure stream.

Hose reel cart with folding handle

Hose reel with recoiling hose

ABOVE AND LEFT *Portable hose storage units are invaluable in patios and small gardens as they are light and mobile.*

WATERING STRATEGIES

If you mulch regularly then you've already reduced your watering chores *see also* page 79). However, as well as mulching, there are other things you can do to conserve water and keep plants healthy.

Try to do your watering in the cool of the morning as this allows the plant roots time to absorb moisture with minimal evaporation loss, giving them strength to weather the midday heat. Watering in the evening when things stay damp can attract pests and encourage fungal diseases. If you do water in the evening, water at the base of the plants, keeping the leaves as dry as possible.

LEFT Hand watering a newly planted perennial can be a calming task – half fill the can as water is heavy.

Water thoroughly but less frequently, rather than often and less generously. The more deeply rooted your plants, the more resilient they'll be in a dry period and frequent shallow waterings will only encourage roots to stay near the soil surface. When you water, do it long enough for moisture to penetrate the top 13–15cm (5–6in) of soil. You can dig a small hole with your hand trowel an hour after you've watered to check.

One strategy to make watering effective is to mound up a 7.5cm (3in) ring of soil around each plant, making a 'dam' at the plant's base. This keeps the water near the plant and allows it to soak down to the roots. Apply mulch around the plant but keep the 7.5cm (3in) ring accessible so the plant can still get water.

WATERING NEWLY PLANTED SPECIMENS

With new perennials, trees or shrubs, dig a hole (or have someone do this for you), fill it with water and allow the moisture to be absorbed. Then put the plant into the

moistened hole and firm soil around the roots and water again. Cover bare soil with 5–10cm (2–4in) of mulch to help retain moisture.

Most shrubs, trees and perennials are best planted in the late autumn when plants are in a period of hibernation. Most of their watering needs are usually met by autumn and winter rains, and the soil is still warm enough for them to put down some roots before spring. Seasonal vegetables and annuals are often small when planted and are vulnerable to dryness. Because they have comparatively shallow roots, they need adequate water, especially during the first few weeks of growth as they build their root systems. To keep new plants moist, water generously once a week if it doesn't rain adequately. After six to eight weeks, gradually cut back on watering.

Fortunately, thirsty plants can extend their roots in in-ground gardens to find moisture when the soil around them runs dry – most established plants can easily weather short periods of dryness. However, if heat and drought are prolonged, then make a point of watering your most valuable plants so they do not get too stressed.

BELOW A new plant among established ones will need regular watering that is targeted to its roots.

BELOW A damn or a circle of soil around a new plant means that the water lingers around the stem base and prevents run-off.

BELOW It is vital to get water directly to the roots of plants; here a pipe is used to channel the water straight into the ground.

ABOVE *Keeping containers well irrigated will ensure their beauty and health throughout the season.*

ABOVE *Plants that like very wet, boggy conditions can be stood in a tray permanently filled with water.*

ABOVE *Turn an empty drink bottle into a mini-reservoir; water seeps through a spike pushed into the compost (soil mix).*

WATERING CONTAINERS

The secret of nurturing a beautiful container garden is to be consistent. Since container plants rely on the gardener to get sufficient water and fertilizer to thrive, closer vigilance is needed than with in-ground gardens. Also, containers need water and food more often than plants in the ground. Potting mediums dry out and will become exhausted of nutrients much faster. The roots can become cramped (or strangle plants), and containers are prone to drainage problems and disease.

Choose containers with a capacity of 14–113 litres (15–120 quarts) and ensure they have good drainage. Small pots dry out more quickly and the area for root growth is restricted. The size and number of plants will determine the container size. Deep-rooted vegetables like carrots, parsnips and potatoes need deep pots. Place your containers

on securely placed bricks or blocks to allow free drainage.

Keep containers near to where you spend regular time. Seeing your plants helps you to get to know their needs. Some, such as fuchsias, require a lot of water and may need to be watered daily.

Succulents require less, and so grouping plants that have similar moisture needs makes watering simpler.

One useful tip for watering containers is to mix water-retaining granules into your soil. Once wet, they release water to the plant roots as the soil dries out.

RIGHT *Spring blooming bulbs can thrive in containers if they are monitored well for their watering and feeding schedules.*

HARVESTING

Many of us garden simply because we love being involved with nature and watching things grow. But we're also thinking ahead to what we might reap from the garden. No matter how old we are, picking colourful bouquets of flowers, gathering nuts and ripe fruits and vegetables, as well as collecting seeds for next year's garden, add to the richness of our experience as gardeners and as human beings. With the correct tools, time and energy, harvesting hearkens back to times when we depended on what we grew.

ABOVE *Using a paper funnel allows you to collect your favourite zinnia or marigold seeds to sow in next spring's garden.*

ASSESS THE POSSIBILITIES

We have already looked at what produce to grow, dependent on what you can manage, but these decisions should also include the ease of harvest. If you have tall fruit trees, picking mature fruit may only be possible with the help of a ladder, which might make it a job that is literally beyond your reach.

Vegetables are generally easier because the growth height is more accessible. If you grow vegetables in a container, your harvesting efforts will be minimal; you can stand or sit as you pluck the cherry tomatoes from the vine, pull off leaves of lettuce or snip parsley. If you added a trellis to your container, then you may need to find a secure place to stand so you can safely reach for the mangetouts (snow peas) or climbing French beans. See the vegetable and fruit garden styles discussed on pages 146–165 to help structure your decisions.

HARVESTING EQUIPMENT

One useful tool to aid the gathering of any hard-to-reach produce is a long-reach or extendable grabber or snapper. Versions can be found for cutting flowers and harvesting fruit. Another useful tool for harvesting fruit is called a telescoping fruit picker. It is lightweight and typically has an aluminium handle that will extend up to 3m (10ft).

If you have nuts in your garden, you can use a long-handled nut collector to save you from bending. The nuts just need to be scooped up and emptied into an available container. Harvesting fallen nuts is fun and easy with a rolling nut picker. It allows you to stand as you gather the nuts and can locate nuts that can't be seen in tall grass.

COLLECTION CONTAINERS

Another practicality to consider for harvesting is the most suitable containers for gathering your harvest. If you have apples, pears or cherries, harvesting them in a picker's basket is best. This is a functional canvas bin that can be cleaned and folded after harvest and stored in a manageable size. A moderate-size picker's basket is intended for a light harvest – so don't overload it. Another option is a wire basket – this will resist rust and corrosion and also has a foam cushion that prevents fruit from bruising. It locks with just a quick turn of your wrist.

BELOW *Having the proper tools to harvest your potatoes, fruits or flowers comes in handy as you carefully dig the potatoes and clip the blossoms.*

Potato harvesting scoop

Lightweight snapper for cutting flowers or fruit picking

Fresh fruit harvester

Nut harvester

ABOVE *A long-handled cut-and-hold tool allows you to secure a flower stem as you cut the flower without losing it.*

When picking flowers use a flower trug, a shallow tray that is perfect for flowers as its shape cradles the delicate blooms and reduces the chance of crushing them. A classic British trug is made of wooden slats, while in the US you can find them made of plaited rush.

If you want to keep both hands free, suspend a milk carton around your neck with twine (use a paper hole punch to make the openings for the twine). This is useful for picking berries and for those with a front-wheeled walker.

Almost any container can become a harvest basket. Just remember how much weight the basket can safely carry and how fragile the crops are. From a woven basket to a tin bucket or a French market wire basket, the options for carrying home your harvest are endless.

COLLECTING SEEDS

Nature is designed to distribute plant seeds, but many gardeners like to collect their own so they can plan where they will grow. Start by collecting annual seeds and sow them in the spring, then you can try perennials, tree and shrub seeds.

There are many easy-to-sow options for annuals, examples being love-in-a-mist (*Nigella damascena*), cornflower (*Centaurea cyanus*) and honesty (*Lunaria annua*). Choose a still, dry day and cut off a seedhead where the pods

ABOVE *A basket of freshly cut flowers and herbs from your garden will make a lovely bouquet to enjoy for days.*

look ready to burst. Put the head into a labelled paper bag in a dry place and wait for the casings to dry out and open. Shake the contents out and separate the seeds from the husks. Put them in a small labelled envelope, and store in a dry place until it is time for sowing.

BELOW *A long-handled nut harvester picks up a collection of nuts in the metal basket without requiring you to kneel or stoop.*

BELOW *Harvesting red runner beans from our lush vines can feel satisfying and uncomplicated as our fingers do the work.*

BELOW *This fruit-picking basket can be used to loosen the fruit, which will then fall undamaged into the bag below.*

TIDYING UP

If you have tidied up carefully, your tasks will be easier and safer the next time you go out to garden. So be sure to save some energy for this final stage of your gardening session. There are many tools and methods that help us keep on top of cleaning up the garden as we go along and as we finish work for the day, but the most important thing is to make time for this process and leave yourself enough energy for what needs doing to keep everything shipshape.

ABOVE *Invest in a sturdy, long-handled dustpan and brush so that you can collect the garden debris quickly and easily.*

TOOLS FOR CLEARING DEBRIS

Many useful clearing-up tools such as light plastic containers, wheelbarrows and trolleys have already been mentioned in the transporting section (*see* pages 120–123), and these will also come in useful at the clearing-up stage. Use a broom for sweeping, and for extra convenience have a long-handled dustpan and brush. Another essential tool is a good leaf rake, especially if you have grass or if you need to collect windfalls. Choose one that is lightweight, has a long shaft to avoid bending over and, for extra practicality, is collapsible.

You can get rakes that have a grab mechanism as well as a rake head, so you can rake and collect at the same time. Hand-grip tools are widely available, enabling the picking up of miscellaneous debris without bending. These can be used in the home and in the garden. Finally, a wheeled cart is a useful investment.

Light and easy to move around the garden, it keeps a refuse bag open for discarding rubbish, and has many handy pockets in which to keep your favourite garden hand tools. At the end of the day, it will fold away for easy storage.

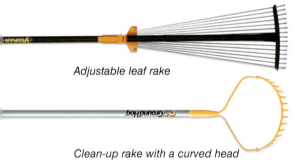

Adjustable leaf rake

Clean-up rake with a curved head

Leaf grabber

RIGHT *A long-handled leaf grabber removes autumn leaves and eliminates the need to bend and stoop.*

USEFUL TIDYING-UP OPTIONS

Here are some of the tools that will keep your garden looking well-cared for. Whatever the season, keeping the garden tidy makes it safer and more enjoyable as we find time to sit down, admire our work and restore our energy.

Raking – *whether you're raking leaves or collecting windfall apples, get a good rake that fits you and your needs.*

Collecting – *this lightweight tool is designed with two large scoops that close together to lift leaves and debris.*

Picking up – *use a hand grip to pick up clippings and other small garden waste, and put them in a debris container.*

Mobile storage – *a rubbish tidy can be moved around so you can dispose of rubbish as you go, and provides tool storage.*

CARING FOR GARDEN TOOLS

The ultimate insult to a garden tool is leaving it outside where it's exposed to moisture from wet ground and dew. Metal rusts and wooden handles splinter quickly on tools that are abandoned like this in the garden bed. Tools that have broken handles or blunt or rusty blades slow us down and give us a less rewarding and productive gardening experience. There are some consistent things we can do to maintain our garden tools regularly so that they endure and are effective for many years to come.

ABOVE *A conservatory is an ideal place for storing tools, as well as for creating a useful work space.*

KEEPING TOOLS DRY AND CLEAN

Because dirt and moisture are the two major offences your tools face, a good basic habit to form is to clean and dry your tools. These simple tasks will keep them in good working order. For shovels, trowels and rakes, wash off the dirt with a strong spray from your hose. Keeping a good, sturdy bristle brush nearby (like the wire brush with which you might clean a cooking grill) can help for a good scrubbing. Most importantly, dry your tools thoroughly with a rag before putting them away.

If you have the space, keep a 19-litre (5-gallon) bucket filled with coarse sand that has been lightly moistened with vegetable oil. Dip the head or tines of each tool several times in the oily sand – this process should help remove stubborn dirt or rust left on the tools.

Smaller tools, like pruners and shears, need the same care and attention as the bigger ones. Towelling off your hand tools will help remove moisture and reduce the occurrence of rust. With very fine grade sandpaper or steel wool, you can get rid of rust. Always be careful when you wipe sharp blades. Lubricating the fulcrums of your pruners with a drop of oil will keep them moving easily.

WOODEN HANDLES

Ash, oak or other wooden handles can last for many years if they are oiled regularly and kept clean. So wipe them after each use and don't leave them exposed to the elements. Once a year or so, sand the handles lightly and, with a cloth, rub in in a coat of boiled linseed oil. Apply another coat if the wood absorbs it very quickly.

KEEPING TOOLS GERM-FREE

Garden tools can carry germs and pathogens from a diseased plant to a healthy one. Carefully washing tools in an anti-bacterial solution may help remove germs from the tools. Full strength denatured alcohol or pine oils can also be used as a sanitizer. You can prepare your own liquid cleaner with one-part bleach to nine-parts water. Use a 13.5-litre (3-gallon) bucket and mix the solution completely before disinfecting your gardening tools.

With a clean cloth, rub the tools lightly to remove any surface dirt, dip the gardening tools into the disinfecting solution and swish or agitate for one minute. Then remove the tools and dry them well. Rubbing oil on the metal will reduce the incidence of rust. Don't save the cleansing liquid – it loses its disinfecting powers after about an hour. Also, don't forget to wash the handles; if they are wooden, a thin rub with linseed oil will keep them smooth and preserved.

BELOW *Good secateurs should be cared for after a hard day's work. Disinfect and dry after cleaning and lubricate with oil.*

BELOW *A tool caked with soil needs to be clean and rubbed after a good session of digging and planting.*

ABOVE MIDDLE A small medium-grain whetstone will keep your hedge shears and secateurs sharp.

ABOVE BOTTOM Keeping secateurs sharp is made easy with this device that quickly and efficiently sharpens both blades at once to the correct angle.

LEFT Sharpening secateurs with a blade sharpener means cleaner cuts and less pressure on your hands and wrists.

COMBATING RUST

The most effective way to prevent rust is to provide a protective coating on the surface of the tool. Look for products that can be sprayed on your shovel, spade or garden fork that will help stop rust. One very effective product is an organic, non-toxic gel. It works well, doesn't contain any harsh chemicals and won't emit strong odours. Some people use a cheap brand of cooking oil, such as rapeseed (canola) or vegetable oil, to coat their gardening tools before they are used. The oil protects the tool and when they are washed later most of the dirt will slide straight off.

KEEPING TOOLS SHARP

Sharp tools are not only more effective, but they will also reduce frustration and unnecessary wear and tear on your body.

Many tools can be effectively sharpened with a small, medium-grain whetstone. When sharpening anvil-type pruners or clippers, sharpen only one blade, but on both sides. For scissor-action bypass lopping shears, sharpen only the outside surface of each blade; this will maintain the cutting surface so the blades will cut cleanly as they slide past each other. In certain instances – especially for your shovels, spades or hoes – this chore should be given to a professional. Garden and hardware stores can recommend reliable services to keep your tools with an edge.

Always wear protective eye gear when sharpening any tool. If possible, secure the tool in a vice or clamp, which will keep your hands free to focus on the job itself.

STORING TOOLS

Have a convenient place to safely store your tools – this should not be so high that you have to strain to reach them, nor so cluttered that you hurt yourself trying to get that rake out. When storing your tools, safety should be your first consideration. This means keeping them in an area where they're easily accessible and free of trip hazards. One simple solution is to purchase a plastic garbage can and stow your long-handled tools in this.

It is a good idea to organize your tools by size and by function. This simple technique will save you considerable frustration when you are looking for the right tool for the job. For example, if you have the space in a shed or garage, hang long-handled

BELOW Diamond sharpeners suit most sharpening requirements. They keep blades in an excellent condition and the tools working to full efficiency.

LEFT Sharpening secateurs with a blade sharpener

ABOVE *If storage is at a minimum, organize your tools, blades downward, in a big plastic bucket, allowing for easy retrieval.*

ABOVE *Keeping water hoses organized in this sturdy tiered device is one way to prevent tripping hazards in the garden.*

ABOVE *Creating storage space for each tool makes finding them easy and keeps them out of harm's way.*

tools together – with their heads down so you avoid being hit in the head and don't need to struggle to balance a heavy tool overhead.

There are many storage systems available using hooks, dowels, clamps and racks that will support the various designs of tool handle. Set up a system that works for you and your space limitations or commission someone else to do this for you. Sometimes labelling the place for, say, your spade helps when others are assisting you with tidying up – having a good system allows others to keep things organized too.

More important, however, is keeping the smaller hand tools that you need for your container or patio garden convenient and accessible. Some people like to store them in a basket with a carrying handle (*see also* pages 120–123). See-through plastic storage bins also are simple and effective ways to stow smaller tools. Another way is to use a pegboard system where you can even draw an outline that denotes the shape of tool

to be hung in that spot. Because each tool has a space, it's more likely that the tool will get put away after use or its absence will be readily seen. Another stroll in the garden will likely find the missing tool. And if you've painted the handles with a brightly coloured band, they are more visible lying in the soil or lawn.

Buckets, the 17–22.5 litre (4.5–6 gallon) size, can double as a sitting stool and a tool-storage caddy. By wrapping a specially designed apron-like tool belt around the bucket you gain about 12 compartments perfect for your hand tools. Get a lid for the bucket and you have a sturdy, comfortable seat from which to garden. This is a great way to recycle old buckets.

Many variations on a theme are available with two- or four-wheeled tool racks. These serve not only to safely and conveniently store all your garden

tools but also to provide the efficiency of bringing the tools with you into the garden (*see also* pages 121–123).

Your tools are your friends. Treat them accordingly. What is more, don't forget to include yourself in the clean-up routine: wash your hands with soap, especially under your nails, for at least 20 seconds – or as long as it takes to get them clean.

RIGHT *A storage shelf made of sheet metal, with gardening tools stored in the individual pockets.*

TYPES OF GARDENS

When you hear the word 'garden', do you think of a bed of fragrant roses, or rows of lush tomatoes ripening in the sun? Maybe you see a rock wall spotted with succulents and dwarf conifers, or a shady spot teeming with ferns and other low-light-loving plants?

Gardens come in all shapes and sizes. As we mature and our life experiences change, we can discover an affinity for gardens that might not have previously appealed to us. Or we may be compelled by circumstances to change the type of garden we're comfortable with. Rather than leave gardening behind, we need to find the right type of garden – one that will keep alive that vital connection we have with things that grow.

This chapter opens up the 'sample book' of garden designs that might suit someone who needs a garden that is low-maintenance and not too demanding or expensive to keep up. We look at flower gardens, vegetable gardens, fruit gardens, herb gardens and patio gardens, then at gardens with features that make life easier for those needing convenient access, such as raised beds and vertical garden structures, and finally at indoor gardens, caring for houseplants in our living environment. So use what follows to find a wealth of inspiring ideas to help you on a new gardening journey.

OPPOSITE *A small patio garden can be made more welcoming with flowering vines, containers and climbing roses.*

ABOVE *Wooden raised beds give easy-to-access gardens for your flowers, herbs and vegetables.*

ABOVE Doronicum orientale *is a tough herbaceous plant that will bring sunshine to your borders in return for very little effort.*

ABOVE *A sunny doorway will accommodate a houseplant, one way to bring the life of a garden into your home.*

FLOWER GARDENS

Flower gardens are like quilts – true labours of love. Although one may have the same colours, shapes and sizes as another, it's the creativity, vision and craftsmanship of the quilter that makes each different and unique. So it is with gardens, but particularly with flower gardens. The colours, shapes, sizes and textures of the flowers we use to create our own unique garden are the elements that make each space different, special and personal.

ABOVE *Radiant blooms of bold colours such as this poppy add interesting textures to your flower garden.*

PLANNING A FLOWER GARDEN

Earlier in the book we discovered how the practical aspects of our garden space influence our decisions about what to grow. We shouldn't, however, underestimate the aesthetic or sentimental aspects of why we choose certain plants. Flowers such as tall pink hollyhocks or fragrant climbing yellow roses may ground our selections, evoking memories of the gardens we grew up in, where we learned to sow and observe the flowers that have played a role in our lives.

MIXED FLOWER GARDENS

For some older gardeners, keeping up a complex flower garden can be a challenge. While we may still yearn to have flowers around us, our enthusiasm

ABOVE *Petunias are familiar perennials that will fill a container with vibrant, season-long colour and shape.*

for their care may wane as we come to terms with limitations of space, energy and mobility. Other senior gardeners may be motivated to maintain a variety of flowerbeds. If your resources allow, it is rewarding to have a colourful mix of perennials, annuals, climbers, biennials, bulbs and ground covers with variations in height and foliage texture.

In larger spaces, flower gardens can be punctuated with small evergreen shrubs or small deciduous trees to give interest when flowering ceases. Annuals, perennials, biennials and flowers grown from bulbs are described in more detail below and overleaf.

Another idea is to grow a three- or four-season garden that has something in flower at every stage of the year – snowdrops and hellebores during the winter; brightly coloured daffodils (*Narcissus*) and tulips throughout the spring; daisies, geraniums and catmint (*Nepeta*) in the summer; and dahlias and chrysanthemums in the autumn.

ANNUALS

Plants that complete their life cycles in one year or less are described as annuals. In this time they germinate, grow shoots and leaves, produce flowers, set seeds and then die. Many tender perennials are treated as annuals in temperate climates, as they are killed by frost, so new plants need to be bought or sown indoors for next year's garden. Examples of annuals are morning glory (*Ipomoea purpurea*), French marigolds

(*Tagetes signata pumila*), and species such as *Impatiens*, *Tropaeolum* (nasturtium), *Zinnia, Nicotiana, Petunia* and *Verbena*. In temperate climates, hardy annuals with more frost tolerance may return the following year, good examples being pot marigolds (*Calendula officinalis*), cornflower (*Centaurea cyanus*), larkspur (*Consolida* spp.), sweet alyssum (*Lobularia maritima*) and Virginia stocks (*Malcolmia maritima*). There are many different kinds of annuals that are reliable bloomers from spring until autumn. They not only provide colour to the garden, but are great for bouquets and flower pressing.

OPPOSITE *Roses climbing on a picket fence adorn a garden, but remember that "Every rose has its thorns".*

ABOVE *Marigolds and Californian poppies (*Eschscholzia californica*) are colourful, versatile plants that liven up a large space.*

PERENNIALS

Flowers that have a perennial habit live for at least two years, and many endure for years. This type of flower reduces our need to buy and replant each season. Most perennials bloom in only one, or at the most two seasons during the year. Because perennials typically bloom in spring, summer or autumn, you should situate them in your garden where you can enjoy them when they are in season.

Even when perennials are not flowering, many of them offer interesting foliage and stem structures that can extend their visual appeal. Coreopsis, coneflowers (*Echinacea*), black-eyed Susan (*Rudbeckia fulgida*), daisies (*Bellis perennis*), columbines (*Aquilegia*) and catmint (*Nepeta*) are a small sampling of rewarding perennials to include in a flower garden. Because it is generally true that perennials are less labour-intensive than other options, these are likely to appeal to gardeners with less time and energy and are explored in more detail on pages 142–143.

BIENNIALS

Flowers that are biennial typically complete their life cycle in two years. In their first year they grow from seed and form leaves and roots but no flowers. They survive winter and then burst into blossom the following year before they set seed and die. Common biennials to have in your garden include sweet William (*Dianthus barbatus*), foxgloves (*Digitalis purpurea*) and hollyhocks (*Alcea rosea*).

BULBS

Generally classed as bulbs are all those plants that die down to the ground every year and survive as an underground storage organ formed from a modified stem, bud or root:

ABOVE *A stone trough contains flowering spring bulbs such as Daffodils (*Narcissus 'Tête-à-tête'*), Chinese Sacred Lily (*Narcissus tazetta*) and low-growing primroses.*

bulbs, corms, rhizomes and tubers. Most of these will flower for many years, often multiplying naturally. Anemones, irises, hyacinths, dahlias, crocus, tulips (*Tulipa*) and daffodils (*Narcissus*) are popular examples of this flower category.

BULBS FOR BORDERS

Planting informal groups of the same bulb can be highly effective and, depending on the size of the border, the groups may be repeated a number of times, with bedding plants or other herbaceous perennials between them. A bed of tulips may be surrounded by forget-me-nots (*Myosotis*) or pansies (*Viola*). Groups of allium may be grown through nearby wallflowers (*Erysimum cheiri*), while gladioli might appear behind penstemons or earlier flowering poppies (*Papaver*).

Lilies are hardy bulbs and can be planted in autumn or late winter. However, they dislike sitting in wet ground, much preferring well-drained soil. If your soil is naturally heavy, add a generous layer of grit in the bottom of the hole as you plant lily bulbs.

LEFT *Well-planned perennial flowerbeds will reliably give continuous seasonal colour, shape and texture.*

Design focus: a flower border for lasting colour

A flower garden is a space with a mixture of flowering plants chosen for their colourful blossoms, interesting foliage and structure. This illustration offers you a guide for planting a simple, yet animated flower border that combines annuals and perennials. Stable stepping stones are placed among the plants so that access to the border is easy. With planning and imagination your flower border can be an exciting combination of colour, height, texture and extended blooming time.

Early in the summer, the yellow 'Stella de Oro' daylilies will produce an abundance of big, showy flowers. The red zinnias, orange-red *Crocosmia* 'Lucifer', and the ever-popular black-eyed Susan were chosen for their mid-season and late blooms. The warm hues of the colour wheel are used – reds, oranges and yellows – and then, for a bit of contrast, some purple flowers and foliage are added.

When you create your design, think about the mature heights of each plant to provide enough room for growth without overpowering other plants. For example, the 'Stella de Oro' daylilies are shorter than most daylilies, so place them in front of taller plants. Forming a floral border with white sweet alyssum defines the garden edge and gives long-lasting fragrant flowers that attract pollinators.

PLANTING LIST

1 Montbretia (*Crocosmia* 'Lucifer')
2 Black-eyed Susan (*Rudbeckia fulgida*)
3 Purple aster (*Aster x frikartii* 'Mönch') (*see* picture above)
4 Purple sage (*Salvia officinalis*)
5 Pink petunia (*Petunia x hybrida*)
6 Daylily (*Hemerocallis* 'Stella de Oro')
7 White alyssum (*Lobularia maritima*)
8 Red dwarf zinnia (*Zinnia* spp.)

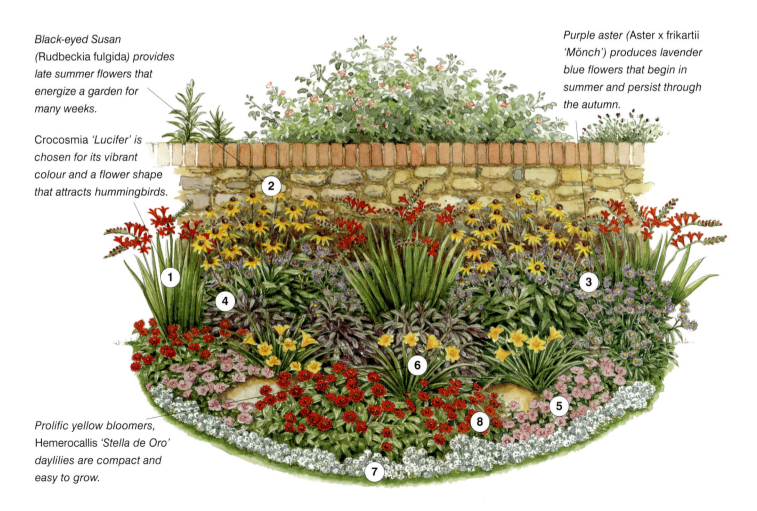

Black-eyed Susan (Rudbeckia fulgida) provides late summer flowers that energize a garden for many weeks.

Crocosmia 'Lucifer' is chosen for its vibrant colour and a flower shape that attracts hummingbirds.

Purple aster (Aster x frikartii 'Mönch') produces lavender blue flowers that begin in summer and persist through the autumn.

Prolific yellow bloomers, Hemerocallis 'Stella de Oro' daylilies are compact and easy to grow.

LEFT Sedum spectabile *is a lush succulent with blue-green leaves and dome-shaped pinkish flowers that appear in the autumn.*

RIGHT *Rose bay willow herb (*Epilobium angustifolium*) is a handsome wild flower that will bloom for about a month. Some dismiss it as an invasive weed, others adore its wild character.*

EASY-CARE PERENNIALS

A perennial flowerbed is an ornamental garden that continues to bloom and grow year after year without the need to replant and spend money on new flowers. This is a popular, low-maintenance choice for senior gardeners. While perennial plants tend to be more expensive than annuals (though some are easy to grow from seed), in the long run your investment pays off in reducing both your labour and the need to replace plants regularly.

Many gardeners like to add new things to a perennial bed each year – colourful annuals, bulbs or even decorative vegetables – to accent the garden during low-bloom periods, but a well-designed perennial garden can stand on its own.

If you would like to concentrate on perennials, research those that do well in your area. You should also assess your garden in terms of its sun and shade conditions and select perennial varieties that will thrive in your microclimate. For example, creating a perennial garden in a shady area will require plants that may not have the most colourful and showiest of blooms, but will allow you to showcase an amazing collection of foliage. If you have a garden in desert-style conditions or in a very sunny and dry area, for example, consider plants from the often-overlooked sedum family, which have a vast array of shapes, sizes and colours.

Perennial colour and texture

Deciding on the colours you want can be one of the most enjoyable aspects of flower gardening. Colour has a great influence on the mood of a perennial garden – cool, pastel shades create tranquillity and calmness while the hot colours inject a feeling of excitement and energy. All the shades of green – usually the colour of the leaves – form the neutral portion of the palette. When making your selections keep in mind that our sensibility to certain colours, especially blue, diminishes as we age, whereas our preferences for other colours such as green and red increase.

LEFT *A thoughtful perennial border starts with spring bloomers, features interesting foliage and uses colours that balance and harmonize.*

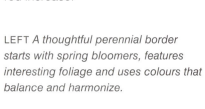

ABOVE *Mixing a variety of blossoms makes an interesting collage of flower shapes that will attract pollinators.*

One strategy to give a bold colour punch to the garden is to choose complementary shades of blue, orange and yellow perennials. Alternatively, you can stay within one section of the colour wheel to create a calming perennial garden with floral shades of pinks and lavenders and subtle sage greens for the foliage.

Texture and form always add interest, so look for plants that have unique structures such as Jerusalem sage (*Phlomis fruticosa*), ornamental grasses, and the Hinoki false cypress (*Chamaecyparis*). These all enhance the personality of the garden by giving it unusual form and airiness.

When perennials are in full bloom the form, structure or foliage is less noticeable, but for 80 per cent of the time all that we see is foliage. So choose plants that have broad, shapely leaves, such as hostas, or the smaller foliage of astilbe, with dazzling green leaves that turn to a mixture of burgundy and purple. Tall spiky ferns can also be attractive.

Controlling perennial choices

Because there are so many varieties of plants available from all over the world, the vast choice can be overwhelming, and it is tempting to pack in as many different flowers as you can. Many gardeners love the chaotic, exuberant effect this creates, while others prefer a simpler design, which can be equally striking if carefully thought out. This is a matter of personal taste, but remember that more varieties will usually mean more maintenance.

Another approach is to create a perennial theme garden. For example, you might choose a fragrant garden with roses, lavender, phlox, stock and dianthus creating layers of scent and pretty blossoms in a sunny area. Alternatively, you could create a butterfly garden that might include plants that are rich in nectar, such as nepeta, salvia, scabiosa, Indian blanket flower (*Gaillardia* spp.) and bergamot (*Monarda*). Butterflies also appreciate flowers that have flat tops like Queen Anne's lace (*Daucus carota*), parsley flowers (*Petroselinum*) and yarrow (*Achillea millefolium*) so they can easily land in the garden, rest on the flat surfaces and absorb the warm sun.

RELIABLE PERENNIAL PLANTS: A STARTER PACK

Galium odoratum *Campanula*

Small trees and shrubs
- Rose of Sharon (*Hibiscus calycinum*)
- Box (*Buxus sempervirens*)
- Hinoki cypress (dwarf variety) (*Chamaecyparis obtusa* 'Nana Aurea')
- Dwarf rhododendron (*Rhododendron* spp.)
- Dwarf hydrangeas (*Hydrangea* spp.)

Tall perennials
- Shasta daisies (*Leucanthemum superbum*)
- Phlox (*Phlox paniculata* 'Franz Schubert')
- Joe Pye weed (*Eupatorium maculatum*)
- Giant fleece flower (*Persicaria polymorpha*)
- Ornamental grasses
- Asters (*Aster* spp.)
- Sneezeweed (*Helenium autumnale* 'Butterpat')

Intermediate-size perennials
- Tickseed (*Coreopsis*)
- Bellflower (*Campanula*)
- Salvia (*Salvia splendens*)
- Gypsyweed (*Veronica officinalis*)
- Heuchera (*Heuchera* spp.)
- Daylily (*Hemerocallis* spp.)
- Gay feather (*Liatris spicata*)

Low-growing perennials
- Alyssum (*Lobularia* spp.)
- Sweet woodruff (*Galium odoratum*)
- Golden-edged thyme (*Thymus vulgaris* 'Aureus')
- Silver brocade artemisia (*Artemisia* 'Silver Brocade')
- Sand strawberry (*Fragaria chiloensis*)

Project: planting and prestaking dahlia tubers

Planting dahlias as soon as the ground is warm to about 15°C (60°F) will give you flower colour all summer long and into the autumn. By choosing healthy tubers, siting them in a very sunny spot (at least 8 hours each day) and preparing the ground, you'll have these quick growers as constant companions in your flower garden. Once you can stake them to support their growth, dahlias are easy to manage and bring colourful rewards.

ABOVE *Dahlia blossoms come in many shapes, sizes and colours and are worth the care required to get them started.*

MATERIALS
- Healthy, firm tubers that are large and free of nicks, cuts or signs of rot
- Equal mix of humus, compost, sharp sand and well-rotted manure
- Shovel
- Stakes
- Soft twine

GARDENER'S NOTE
At step 3, the hole should remain partially filled with just the top of the stem sticking up until you begin to see growth. (Do not add fertilizer or water at this time; wait until you see green shoots appear.)

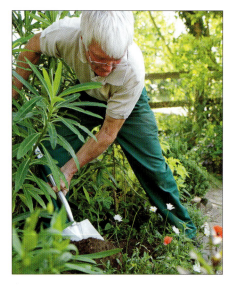

1 *Dig a planting hole at least twice as deep as the length of the dahlia tuber – and equally as wide. Reserve the soil you removed and add a few shovels of the amendment mix.*

2 *For the taller dahlia varieties, drive a sturdy stake near the planting hole before planting. This ensures that the tuber will not be pierced later in the season when staking is necessary.*

3 *Place the tuber horizontally in the bottom of the hole with the eye pointing upwards. Cover with soil to the top of the stem.*

4 *As the plant grows, gradually add soil to fill the hole and feed every 3 weeks with a balanced fertilizer.*

5 *With the taller and the larger-headed dahlias, tie twine around the stem and then to the stake to offer support.*

VEGETABLE GARDENS

"There is nothing … as satisfactory or as thrilling, as gathering the vegetables one has grown". This quote by Alice B. Toklas captures the exhilaration that many gardeners feel when harvesting their homegrown vegetables. For most gardeners, working in their home gardens growing vegetables such as tomatoes, beans and cucumbers has tremendous appeal. They are easy to grow and care for, fun to harvest and there's always plenty to share with others.

ABOVE *Vegetable gardens are both practical and beautiful – here we see squash blossoms and dark green kale.*

HOMEGROWN TRADITIONS

In times of hardship when food was scarce, such as during the Great Depression, growing vegetables was a necessity for many. Potatoes, cabbage, parsnips, carrots and winter squashes were all common crops that would sustain families throughout the winter during these periods. Then there were the Victory Gardens of World War II when citizens were encouraged to grow their own fruit and vegetables to increase self-sufficiency and reduce the need for widespread food transportation. During these times, gardens were planted in back yards, empty lots and urban rooftops and co-operatives were formed where homegrown varieties of fruit and vegetables were shared.

BELOW *A simple and small one-level raised bed is bursting at its seams with salad greens.*

We are facing similar trends now as the 'green' movement encourages us to grow our own food again and keep our lands fertile. Staying connected with our food source and eating locally is the new mantra for gardeners who are taking responsibility for the ways that we grow and distribute our food, both for the good of the environment and our own health.

Growing vegetables is also about sharing knowledge, and about self-sufficiency and independence.

You may already have experienced years of pleasure in growing good things to eat. In this case you have much to share with your children and grandchildren who may have grown up thinking that beetroot (beet) only comes out of a can and spinach from a frozen box. So use your life experience, no matter where you live or what space you may have to garden in, to mentor and enthuse those who might have skipped a generation of gardening. As you do this, you will keep your own roots close to the earth and its bounty as you tend and harvest your favourite vegetables.

IDEAL GROWING CONDITIONS

A productive vegetable patch requires more than six hours of sunlight for a successful yield, although leafier vegetables such as lettuce and spinach grow happily with less sunlight. You'll also need a good-quality soil and good drainage (*see also* pages 73–79).

VEGETABLE CHOICES

Depending on your garden, you may need to choose vegetables that grow most successfully in a limited space, or those that can be easily managed with more limited physical abilities. There is a wide assortment of plants, often hybrids, that ripen more quickly and have a higher yield. We can also plan to counterbalance planting extremes in our gardens, from low-growing dwarf bushes to sun-loving vines.

Vegetables such as green beans are ideal to grow vertically – that is, climbing up stakes or structures – because they make the best use of a limited space. A climbing green-bean yield is two to three times more than a bush bean yield in the same space. Other choices that grow well vertically are butter (lima) beans, cucumbers, melons, peas, squash and tall-growing tomatoes.

If you are new to vegetables or prefer an easy-care option then you can focus on examples such as lettuce, radish, spinach, peas, onions and beetroot. Vegetables that require considerably more maintenance include kohlrabi, cauliflower, leeks, carrots celery or head lettuce.

OPPOSITE *Raised planting beds allow you to grow produce almost all the year round, even where there is no natural soil available. Create them with heavy timber planks and make an allowance for water to drain freely.*

COMPANION PLANTING

Old-style vegetable gardens, sometimes called kitchen gardens, were a mixture of vegetables, herbs and flowers. Today, as we try to reduce our use of chemicals in our gardening practices and strive to attract beneficial insects and wildlife, this type of garden design not only produces a beautiful looking garden but also helps to create an organic system called 'companion planting', which naturally helps to repel pests and diseases.

In general, aromatic plants such as onions, marigolds and tomatoes help to ward off harmful insects. Even particular colours, such as orange and bright yellows, are thought to repel some destructive flying insects. Planting marigolds or nasturtiums near cabbages, radishes, cucumbers and tomatoes helps protect them from their insect invaders. Some

long-time gardeners believe that planting marigolds (the 'workhorse' of pest deterrents) around the entire vegetable garden provides a 'moat' of pungent aromas and bright colours that repels insects.

Another rule of companion planting is to include herbs freely among vegetable crops because they can adversely affect the population of destructive bugs. Chives and garlic deter aphids. Oregano, in the same way as marigolds, is a good all-purpose plant for repelling most insect pests. Rosemary effectively deters beetles that attack beans. So planting a family of basil, oregano, rosemary and chives among the tomato and pepper plants creates a natural way of keeping the insect population under control.

It can also be fun discovering the particular flowers that are beneficial companion plants in your kitchen garden.

Asters and chrysanthemums repel most insects and provide the late-season colour that many gardens lack as they move from summer into autumn. Petunias, which can tolerate heat, will protect beans. Tansy (*Tanacetum vulgare*) has a triple benefit by controlling Japanese beetles, squash bugs and ants. Geraniums, an old-fashioned favourite, are an effective general insect repellant. Finally, the shape of flower petals provides safe landing spots for beneficial insects, so plant companion plants that produce tubular, flat and bowl-shaped flowers.

We've now gained the folklore wisdom and the scientific data that support the importance of coexistence among some vegetables, flowers and herbs. Their abilities to ward off, repel and even confuse insects offer us more options in the varieties of plants we grow and the reduction of chemical use.

ABOVE *Nasturtium works as an effective companion for many plants, keeping away aphids, bugs, and pumpkin beetles, as well as maximizing growth and flavour.*

LEFT *Teeming with produce, this corner bed includes curly kale,* Hemerocallis *'Stella de Oro', strawberry, globe artichoke, French marigolds, Lollo rossa lettuce, fennel, red cabbage, corn and borage.*

Project: growing beans and cucumbers on a trellis

An effective way to maximize your gardening in a minimal space is to grow vegetables together. One idea for this is to plan a tall structure that acts as the central focus on which climbers scramble up. This project demonstrates how you can grow beans and cucumbers together in a small raised bed using either a pre-made teepee structure or one that is constructed with bamboo poles.

ABOVE *This teepee was constructed with nine bamboo poles, but ready-made teepees will reduce time and effort.*

MATERIALS
- Suitable in-ground space or raised bed
- Teepee structure or 7–9 bamboo poles with which to make one
- Twine, string or masking tape
- Seeds of your choice of climbing bean or cucumber variety (soak them the night before for quicker sprouting)
- Plant labels

1 *If you are building your own support structure, start by tying three of the poles together at the top with garden twine, string or masking tape to create a tripod formation. Tie on the other poles at the same point, plant the teepee firmly in the ground or raised bed, and wrap and knot the twine at the top and at stages down the poles to create a sturdy structure.*

2 *If you are using a ready-made teepee, simply open it out to create a circular base and push the legs into the soil. There should ideally be a 5cm (2in) margin around the perimeter.*

3 *Once the structure is solid and firm, plant the seeds (or seedlings) in a circle inside of the base of the teepee stakes. Put the beans on one half of the circular trellis and the cucumbers on the other. Water the seeds or seedlings well.*

4 *As the seedlings grow into longer stems, coax the stems to touch the poles. They will then start to climb up.*

5 *Continue to water them well and remain vigilant about encouraging their vertical growth habits in the early days.*

6 *In the summer you can harvest juicy cucumbers and succulent green beans. Pick them often to get the most tender ones.*

Project: growing potatoes in containers

Potatoes can be grown without a lot of fuss and they can easily be stored for later consumption. There are about 100 varieties of edible potatoes, either mature (maincrop) potatoes or new potatoes, which are harvested before they reach maturity. Growing smaller-variety potatoes in containers is fun, and a good project to do with children. Gathering them without having to bend over the ground makes this crop easy and pain-free to harvest.

ABOVE *The green tops of potatoes and the flowers make an attractive container plant as the tubers fill out.*

MATERIALS

- Plastic container or storage tub
- Drill or knife for puncturing holes
- Multipurpose compost (soil mix) with added garden compost and/or well-rotted manure (or other organic matter)
- Seed potatoes – the following varieties do well in containers:
  'Yukon Gold' – small with golden skin and a rich, buttery taste.
  'All Blue' – a blue to purple skin with blue flesh. The colour holds once cooked.
  'Red Pontiac' – a red-skinned variety with creamy white flesh.
  'Fingerling' – a yellow and small, finger-shaped potato.

1 *Select seed potatoes with at least two eyes and put them, with the eyes facing up, in a well-lit, airy, frost-free place until 2.5cm (1in) sprouts have grown. This should take about 6 weeks.*

2 *Use a 45–75-litre (12–20-gallon) plastic container or storage tub. Drill or puncture several holes in the bottom of the container for drainage.*

3 *Add a third of your potting mixture to the container. Space your potato sprouts on top of the soil about 13cm (5in) apart and at least 7.5cm (3in) away from the sides of the container.*

4 *Cover the potatoes with soil, adding more as they grow (keeping top leaves free). When the soil reaches 2.5–5cm (1–2in) from the top of the container, stop adding soil. Keep well watered.*

5 *When the potato plants turn yellow and lose leaves, it means the tubers are almost mature and can soon be harvested.*

Design focus: a raised-bed vegetable garden

As we age, we may want to avoid having a huge vegetable garden that needs care and attention from the first frost-free day to the first sign of frost in the autumn. This illustration shows how you can create a vegetable garden with a wide selection of produce that is also reasonably low maintenance. This is achieved with raised beds, which eradicate much of the bending and crouching work associated with vegetable maintenance and harvesting.

Having raised beds near the back door will give instant access to your salad garden. Raised beds lessen the strain of maintaining the produce, but when working on your beds you should still use body mechanics that avoid undue pressure being exerted on you, along with appropriate ergonomic tools.

From cold crops such as peas, kale and lettuce to heat-loving tomatoes, peppers and cucumbers, you can plan succession plantings to keep an all-summer-long supply of fresh and nutritious seasonal foods. You can also plant two vegetables in the same bed – radishes and carrots are a good pairing because radishes mature early, leaving room for the late sprouting carrots.

The illustration shows how to plant certain flowers or herbs nearby called companion plants (*see page 148*). These attract beneficial insects to the garden that pollinate and feast on aphids.

Benches are sited nearby so you can take rest breaks and enjoy seeing your produce reach full maturity.

PLANTING LIST

1 Climbing beans (*Phaseolus* spp.) (*see picture above*)
2 Potatoes (*Solanum tuberosum*)
3 Marigolds (*Calendula officinalis*)
4 Onions (*Allium cepa*)
5 Radishes (*Raphanus sativus*)
6 Carrots (*Daucus carota*)
7 Beetroot (beet) (*Beta vulgaris* subsp. *vulgaris*)
8 Chard (*Beta vulgaris* subsp. *cicla* var. *flavescens* 'Northern Lights')
9 Lettuce (*Lactuca sativa*)
10 Peppers (*Capsicum* spp.)
11 Summer squash (*Cucurbita pepo*)
12 Peas (*Pisum sativum*)
13 Tomatoes (*Lycopersicon esculentum*)
14 Borage (*Borago officinalis*)
15 Basil (*Ocimum basilicum*)

Segregating certain crops from one another gives you control over the garden – onions don't need irrigation when they are being 'cured', so they are better separated

Easily accessible water source

Gravel pathway

Shed for storing tools

Summer squash, especially the 'Yellow Crookneck' variety, will give you a steady crop throughout the season – pick them while they are small and tender.

Chard is a versatile and healthy green that can be eaten raw or cooked. One of few greens that rarely goes to seed, it is almost always available for your table.

Project: creating a lettuce garden in a container

Raising your own blend of greens is easy and cost-effective. As well as being convenient, growing leaf lettuces in a container is a way of keeping pests at bay. Position the container where it gets at least four hours of direct sunlight. If need be, put the container on a wheeled dolly so it can be moved to follow the sun. By choosing early and late varieties, you can have fresh salad greens for several months.

ABOVE *Choose varieties of lettuce with burgundy foliage, interesting edges, textures and different flavours.*

MATERIALS

- Young lettuce plants. To achieve maximum colour and texture in your planting choose from the following varieties:
  Early season:
  'Arctic King', 'Black-seeded Simpson', 'Grand Rapids' or 'Winter Marvel'
  Mid-season:
  'Red Fire', 'Freckles', 'Royal Oak Leaf' or 'Salad Bowl'
  Late season:
  'Diamond Gem', 'Esmerelda', 'Galactic' or 'Rosalita'
- Container with good drainage
- Pebbles
- Loose, fertile, sandy loam that is rich in organic matter

1 *Find a container that is not too deep (lettuce has shallow roots). Add a layer of pebbles at the base to aid soil drainage.*

2 *Fill the container with loose, fertile, sandy loam. The soil should be well-drained, moist, but not soggy.*

3 *Loosen the young plants from their pots, then place them on the soil at the spacing recommended for the variety.*

4 *Plant each seedling, at the same depth as it was in the pot, and firm in gently.*

5 *Keep the plants moist but not sodden. When harvesting, select your lettuce leaves from the outside of the plant.*

FRUIT GARDENS

"Live each season as it passes: breathe the air, drink the drink, taste the fruit" are the words of American author and naturalist, Henry David Thoreau. Having access to seasonal, nutritious, sweet and juicy fruit from your own crops throughout the growing season is enormously rewarding. If you choose the fruit wisely, understand the potential and limitations of your growing zone and prepare the soil, then your efforts will reap a harvest of healthy and robust fruits all through the summer.

ABOVE *Hand picking berries is a rewarding way to spend time in the garden or in the berry field.*

GETTING BACK TO FRUIT BASICS

Years ago, you could tell the season simply by viewing the fresh fruit on display in your local grocery store. Today we are bombarded with almost any fruit at any time of the year. While some may regard this as a great way of ensuring a varied diet or, more likely, just accept it as the way things are, longtime gardeners are often disappointed by the perfect-looking berries or melons that are available in all seasons and that are dry and tasteless to eat. Indeed, one of the advantages of being a 'senior' is that we remember how fruit is supposed to taste!

Growing your own fruit guarantees that you'll have fresh and delicious produce, but make sure that you choose fruits that you (or your friends and family) like to eat, since you may get some big crops). If you love it, grow it. Homegrown fruits are also the central ingredients of other edibles that give extra flavour to our meals, especially when they are home-made – desserts, jams, jellies, wines and juices.

SEASONAL FRUIT HARVEST

The seasons of different fruits will influence your choice of what to grow. For instance, you may have several types of strawberry plants or raspberry canes that will welcome the early stages of summer into your garden store. So why not include some blueberry bushes whose fruits will ripen throughout the summer? You can add a small fruiting columnar tree, either apple or plum, or some autumn-fruiting raspberries – and then you have a delicious and accessible fruit garden to enjoy from early summer through to the autumn.

Before establishing a fruit garden, find out the best fruit varieties for your climate (the climate can dramatically affect the fruiting patterns) and the conditions in your garden. Don't forget that many fruits have early, mid- and late season ripening times so you can stretch your harvests out over the summer and into the autumn. There are several types of raspberries that ripen in the early days of summer as well as some varieties that will give you a second and longer fruiting yield later in the season.

OPPOSITE *A fig tree, redcurrants and a columnar pear tree on the trellis makes this garden corner a rich oasis of homegrown produce. For those in tropical climates, choose oranges, lemons and limes.*

LEFT *A garden full of fresh fruit delights: peaches, strawberries, apples, rhubarb, blackcurrants, raspberries and, in the foreground, a mass of blueberries.*

FRUIT PLANTING ESSENTIALS

Locating your garden fruit in or near the vegetable or flower garden will attract many of the pollinators needed for your fruit blossoms. Aim to plant in areas that are free from frost pockets, not exposed to winds and have good drainage. Also, select varieties with the least insect and disease problems. Small fruits thrive best in a fertile, sandy loam soil high in organic matter, but they will give good returns on average garden soil that has adequate fertilization and good cultivation practices.

If space is a limiting factor, small fruits can serve double duty as the ornamental showpieces in your garden. For example, apple trees (*Malus* spp.) provide as lovely spring blooms as any ornamental flowering specimen and will give you a delicious harvest of fruit that a strictly ornamental tree will not.

Likewise, consider using strawberries as a border for a flowerbed or as ground cover. Grapes and raspberries may be planted parallel to flower or vegetable gardens on a trellis or a fence. Plant blueberries to form a dense hedge, or use them as a foundation, planting around the home. You will have at least three seasons of attraction with these – and countless tasty desserts!

Successful home fruit growing should follow the best management practices throughout the year, which means a regular schedule of pruning, fertilizing, watering and pest control. Be assured, however, that the fruits listed in the plant directory (*see* pages 238–241) were selected because they are fairly low maintenance, take little space, and will thrive in containers.

ABOVE *Treat small container lemon trees with the same care as those in the ground – provide good drainage, regular watering, feeding, and high humidity.*

LEFT *A dwarf pear tree is a good choice because the fruit is easily accessible. The fruit will be ready to harvest in the late summer and early autumn.*

GROWING BLUEBERRIES

Blueberries are highly ornamental as well as productive. These attractive, airy shrubs produce lovely white, urn-shaped flowers in the spring. The blossoms turn into delicious, showy berries that decorate each branch with eye-catching shades of purple. Autumn is when these shrubs give us a leaf confetti display of maroons, purples, reds and oranges.

Highbush blueberries are the most popular, and they produce the largest, juiciest fruit, but they need a very acid soil. If you can't provide this, either in the garden or in a container, you could try the smaller-fruited rabbit-eye blueberries (*Vaccinium ashei*), which tolerate less acid and drier conditions.

Ideal planting conditions

If you are growing blueberries in the ground, put them where they have full sunlight for most of the day and where they are far enough from tree roots to avoid competition for moisture and nutrients. They will thrive in porous, moist, sandy, acidic soils high in organic matter. It's good practice to mulch them heavily with pine needles to increase the soil's acidity and keep it moist at all times, but ensure good drainage since they can't tolerate saturated soils.

Mulching is effective when planting blueberries. Many growers combine a layer of leaves at the bottom with 5–7.5cm (2–3in) of sawdust on top. Renewed annually, this heavy mulch retains moisture, keeps the soil cool and adds the required organic matter.

When your bushes are in their third year, you can prune them any time between autumn and either throughout spring or when the new growth appears. Pruning consists mainly of removing low-spreading canes and dead and broken branches. As the bushes mature and get larger, select six to eight of the most vigorous, upright-growing canes for fruiting wood, and remove all others.

Container blueberries

Blueberries thrive best in full sunlight. They also need a large container, so once it is filled and planted it will be heavy and difficult to move. If no part of your garden has enough direct sun, put the container on a wheeled holder so you can move the container easily and safely to ensure that the plant has maximum benefit from the sun.

Plant the blueberry in the container using ericaceous (lime-free) compost (soil mix) leaving a gap of 10cm (4in) below the top of the container for

ABOVE *A mass of ripe blueberries gets sweeter as they bask in the sun, almost ready to be picked.*

watering. Don't bury the plant any deeper than it was in its original container – blueberries have shallow roots and need to be kept at the surface. Water the plant thoroughly with collected rainwater, if possible, and immediately add a bit of light mulch over the top of the roots. The container mulch could be pine needles or coarse bark.

Blueberries need constant moisture, so water them regularly or, better still, provide a drip watering system. In hot weather, you'll need to water them every day. Rainwater is preferable since tap water tends to raise the alkalinity of the soil. They should be fed every month, starting in the spring. You can miss out a month of fertilizing in early to midsummer, but make sure you resume fertilizing them for another month after this. Then wait until the spring to start feeding them again.

FAR LEFT *Birds love ripe blueberries so protect your crop by covering the bush with fleece or netting.*

LEFT *White flowers shaped like upside-down urns let you know that the blueberry season is not far away.*

Project: planting blueberries in a container

You will need to plant young blueberry plants in very large containers, preferably the large, wooden planters that are used for small trees, since these cope well with changeable weather conditions. Make sure that there are plenty of drainage holes as blueberries do not like to have their roots sitting in water. If possible, plant at least two varieties to achieve optimal pollination and a longer harvest period.

ABOVE *Blueberry bushes produce fruit all through the summer if you choose early, mid-season and late fruiting varieties.*

MATERIALS

- Half a whiskey barrel or a container that has approximately 30 x 30 x 30cm (2 x 2 x 2ft) dimensions
- Two parts ericaceous (lime-free or acid) compost (soil mix) mixed with one part leafmould
- Blueberry plants (*Vaccinium* spp.): *V.* 'Sunshine Blue', *V.* 'Northsky', *V.* 'Bluecrop' and *V.* 'Earliblue' all grow well in containers
- Mulch mix – use an equal mixture of pine needles and leafmould
- Protective netting to give the plant protection from hungry birds. A bamboo or metal frame with netting over it can be used for a more permanent structure.

1 *Site your container in a location with a sunny exposure. Create your soil mix using leafmould and potting soil suitable for acid-loving plants.*

2 *Fill the container with the soil mix and pack the mix down firmly.*

3 *If roots are tightly bound, separate them gently. Plant the bush at the same level it was at in its pot.*

4 *Mulch the surface of the soil with a thin layer of leafmould and pine needles. Water well with rainwater.*

5 *When the berries start to form, cover the plant with light netting fabric to discourage marauding birds and squirrels.*

GROWING RASPBERRIES

Raspberries do better in cool temperatures than many soft fruits. They like sun but tolerate partial shade, and need a rich, moist, slightly acid soil. Train them on wires, fixed to stakes at each end of the row. They can become infected with viruses over the years, so when production falls off, usually after about 7–8 years, replace them with virus-free plants, preferably in a different part of the garden. Some varieties are more resistant than others.

There are two types of raspberry, summer-fruiting, which crop heavily over 2–3 weeks around midsummer, and autumn-fruiting (or ever-bearing), which produce fruit continuously from summer until the first frosts. In hot climes, autumn-fruiting ones may produce one crop in early summer on the lower canes, and a second in late summer or early autumn on the top ones. Cropping times depend on the variety: extend the summer-fruiting season by growing the early Glen Clova, for example, and later Malling Admiral. Other good summer varieties are Glen Ample and Tulameen; autumn varieties include Autumn Bliss, Joan J, Bababerry (tolerates hot summers) and Heritage.

LEFT *Raspberry canes tied to wire supports will make your care routine and harvest significantly easier and safer.*

PLANTING AND CARING FOR RASPBERRIES

In most climates, the best time to plant raspberries is as soon as the danger of frost has passed, typically in the early spring. Autumn planting is an option, unless your winters are very cold. Raspberries like soil that has ample compost and organic material worked in. Feed them once in sping and once in summer with a balanced fertilizer or well-rotted manure. Raspberries like 2.5–4cm (1–1½in) of water each week.

1 *Prepare the soil by taking out grass and weeds and spreading organic matter such as peat moss or aged manure to create a loose, porous soil.*

2 *Use garden rows 2.5–3m (8–10ft) long and 38cm (15in) wide. Use a line of string to guide the planting. Dig a hole the same depth and width as the roots.*

3 *Place the plant so that the point where the roots join the stem is 2.5cm (1in) below the soil. Backfill until the hole is three-quarters full. Water well.*

4 *Hammer in metal stakes, at least 1.5m (5ft) high once they have been installed. Attach 3 parallel lines of wire, evenly spaced about 2.5cm (1in) apart.*

GROWING STRAWBERRIES

Strawberry plants (*Fragaria* spp.) are versatile and can be grown in rows, mounds, containers and as a cover crop. They are among the most popular fruits.

There are two main types of strawberries: summer-fruiting, which crop heavily over 2–3 weeks in early or midsummer, and perpetual-fruiting (or ever-bearing), which crop briefly in summer and then over a longer period in autumn, or produce two or three flushes from spring to autumn, depending on the climate. The summer varieties are bigger, juicier and more tasty. There are also alpine strawberries, smaller but with a good flavour; and a recent development, day-neutral strawberries. These are unaffected by day length, so if they are kept warm enough (minimum 10ºC/50ºF) they will fruit at any time of year. Plant them successively from spring to autumn to ensure fruit almost all year round. However, they are smaller and less juicy and flavoursome than the other types.

The cropping period for summer-fruiting strawberries can be extended by growing early (such as Elvira, Earliglow, Honeoye), mid-season (Cambridge Favourite, Alice) and late varieties (Cambridge Late Pine, Domanil). Recommended perpetual-fruiting varieties are Aromel and Flamenco. Plant them in rows or mounds set 45cm (18in) apart. Remove the runners to keep the plant's energy going to the fruit. Water well on planting, and feed with a balanced fertilizer once new growth

appears, then again mid-season. To prevent weeds, retain moisture and keep the fruit off the ground, add a mulch of grass clippings, straw or sawdust around the plant's base. Ever-bearers will need 2.5cm (1in) of water each week during the growing season. When the fruit forms, place a straw layer around the plants, to keep the fruit off the ground and mud free. Replace plants with new stock every 2–3 years, preferably where strawberries have not been grown for at least 3 years. Using a rotation system ensures that there are always new plants at their best. Old plants should be destroyed, not composted, to prevent the spread of viral diseases.

LEFT *For a higher yield, hand-pollinate strawberries by brushing up pollen from the stamens and dusting it over the stigmas.*

ABOVE *Strawberry plants can easily be grown in grow bags on a wooden structure or in hanging baskets on a patio.*

BELOW *Strawberry rows can be planted with landscaping fabric that maintains moisture and reduces weeds.*

Design focus: an easy-access fruit garden

For most gardeners, tasting a sweet berry or juicy apple from their own garden is a delectable experience. This illustration shows an idea for a dedicated fruit garden that is easy to manage, a pleasure to look at and will ensure you a plentiful harvest all summer long. You don't have to interpret it literally – just borrow elements from it that appeal to you to fit within your own garden. So take inspiration from the ideas shown here, but the best advice is to grow fruit that you most love to eat.

Growing fruit in your garden is not difficult – you just need to know what varieties will do well in your climate and what cultivation techniques will help them mature. For example, blueberries are a popular and reliable fruiting shrub, but you need to know that they thrive in very acidic conditions.

Raspberries are low maintenance if they get enough sun, irrigation and wires to keep them in bounds. Growing strawberries in raised beds allows you to give them the slightly acid soil they like, if your garden soil is chalky, and also makes it easier to protect them from slugs. The berries here are chosen so that there is a variety ripening at any point in the season.

Several columnar apples have been developed that take up little space, are easy to maintain, yet produce tasty apples. Asian pear trees produce an abundance of juicy fruit and are typically pest-free and low-maintenance.

PLANTING LIST
1 Blueberry (*Vaccinium* spp.)
2 Asian pear tree (*Pyrus pyrifolia*)
3 Blackcurrant (*Ribes nigrum*)
4 Columnar apple tree (*Malus sylvestris* var. *domestica*)
5 Strawberry (*Fragaria virginiana*)
6 Gooseberry (*Ribes grossularia*) (*see picture above*)
7 Raspberry (*Rubus Idaeus*)

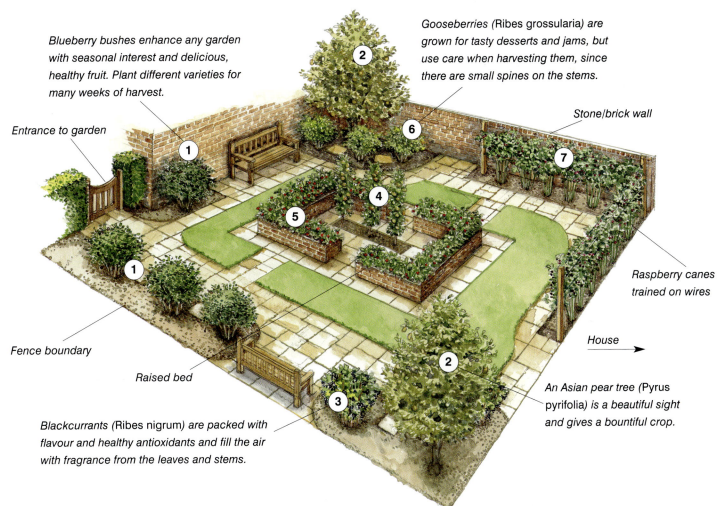

Blueberry bushes enhance any garden with seasonal interest and delicious, healthy fruit. Plant different varieties for many weeks of harvest.

*Gooseberries (*Ribes grossularia*) are grown for tasty desserts and jams, but use care when harvesting them, since there are small spines on the stems.*

Stone/brick wall

Entrance to garden

Raspberry canes trained on wires

House

Fence boundary

Raised bed

*An Asian pear tree (*Pyrus pyrifolia*) is a beautiful sight and gives a bountiful crop.*

*Blackcurrants (*Ribes nigrum*) are packed with flavour and healthy antioxidants and fill the air with fragrance from the leaves and stems.*

Project: planting a strawberry urn

Strawberries are enjoyed for the colour they bring to the garden as well as their sweet taste. The strawberry urn has small side pockets or openings that hold the small plants, so that the roots have access to plenty of soil but the fruits are kept clean, not lying on the ground. The urn must have drainage holes in the bottom. When the planting is finished, be sure to position the urn in full sun.

ABOVE *In the fruiting season keep a careful eye on the maturing strawberries and pick them as soon as they are ripe.*

MATERIALS

- Strawberry urn in terracotta or plastic
- Potting soil mixture
- Pea gravel, small rocks or broken crockery
- Strawberry plants for each hole and additional ones for top surface. Many strawberry varieties are suited to containers (*see* those mentioned on page 161). Look for those that will thrive in your climate and are labelled by the manufacturer as virus free (strawberries are prone to viruses).
- 2.5cm (1in) PVC pipe drilled with holes
- Complete fertilizer

1 *If you have a terracotta urn, place the urn in a tub of water for about an hour, or alternatively wet the urn with a hose or watering can – if you don't do this the clay will wick the water out of the soil.*

2 *Put about 2.5cm (1in) of your soil in the bottom of the container and then cover this lightly with a layer of pea gravel, small rocks or broken crockery. This will help with drainage.*

3 *Fill the urn with soil until you reach the lowest level of pockets. Insert a plant in each of the lower pockets, filling around with soil and firming them in. The crown of the plants must be just above the soil level.*

4 *Water the lower level and each pocket. Then place the PVC pipe down the centre of the pot so that each plant will get adequate moisture. Fill with soil until the next level of pockets. Repeat the planting.*

5 *Stop adding soil when you get to 5cm (2in) below the rim. Add three to four plants in the top, and fill in with soil. In the growing season, water each plant, keeping the soil moist but not soggy.*

GROWING FRUIT TREES

Few things give more pleasure than being able to pluck a healthy apple or plum from your own tree.

As with any new plants, spend time researching the varieties of that will thrive in your climate. Select varieties with the least insect and disease problems. Talk to your local orchard group, horticultural society, agricultural extension or reputable nursery to learn about the trees that do well in your area. Usually the biggest limiting factor when selecting fruit trees is extreme winter conditions. But do your research and you can feel confident about adding a fruiting tree to your garden space.

Dwarf and semi-dwarf trees

Growing fruit need not be a lot of work if you choose the varieties carefully, and even in a small garden you are sure to find something that you can grow successfully. Most of the fruit

RIGHT A fruit salad tree is truly a product of genetic science – it bears five to to eight different fruits of the same family on one plant.

trees grown nowadays are grafted on to rootstocks that limit their growth to varying degrees. This is partly because of lack of space in gardens, and partly because, even for commercial growers, it is more difficult to pick fruit from very tall trees.

Small fruit trees are described as 'miniature' if they reach 1.8–2.4m (6–8ft) in height. Dwarf trees can grow between 2.4–3m (8–10ft), while semi-dwarfs reach 3.6–4.5m (12–15ft). They do have a reputation for being hard to keep healthy, and this is because they have shallow roots and are therefore vulnerable to water shortage. However, keep them fed and watered and the advantages (small size, earlier fruit, easy pruning and harvesting) outweighs any inconvenience.

LEFT A dwarf peach tree (Prunus persicus) can grow in a container on your patio and will give lovely spring blossoms and tasty fruits later in the summer.

BELOW A columnar or 'pillar' apple tree is a great addition to a patio, deck, or other small area. Many accessible fruits form along short, spur-like branches.

Columnar apple trees

As their name suggests, columnar apple trees have the shape of a column (although some people also liken them to bottle brushes), because they grow straight up and have a very small branch length. Growing to an average height of 2.4–3m (8–10ft) and 0.5m (2ft) wide, a fully mature columnar can grow and produce healthy fruit for about 20 years.

Fruit salad trees

Another relatively new option that will add more variety to your fruit crop is a single tree with multiple fruits, often called fruit cocktail or fruit salad trees. Most multiple-fruit trees are grafted on to pest-resistant rootstocks, but you should be careful about the size that these dwarf trees may reach. One version has a citrus theme, with oranges, mandarins, lemons, limes, grapefruit, tangelos and pomelos. Another has stone fruits such as peaches, apricots, plums, nectarines and peachcots. Other versions produce different types of apple, including red, green and yellow skin varieties, or different types of pear, called multi-nashis. Stone fruits, citrus and tropical varieties suit warm and temperate climates while cold climates can grow all types. They can require heavy yearly pruning and shaping to keep them manageable. These are not yet widely available in all parts of the world but are likely to grow in popularity.

Asian pear trees

The Asian pear, also known as the nashi pear, is a vertical grower that has clusters of white, scented flowers that appear in the spring. These trees need little pruning, but you should lightly shape your tree during its first few years. The fruit should be thinned to one or two per cluster, otherwise the tree will probably produce many small fruits and may perform poorly the following year.

The pears are round and are often mistaken for a yellow apple, yet their flesh is very crisp and their taste is a cross between an apple and a pear. Unlike other pears that need to ripen after harvesting for several days, these are at their best straight from the tree – they are already sweet and ripe, with a delicious, crunchy texture. These versatile pears can be used in recipes that require either apples or pears.

Container fruit trees

Most fruit trees can be grown in a large pot – with the exception of cherries, which need larger spaces. While the

ABOVE *Citrus trees are tropical, but with special care and protection from the cold they will survive in temperate climates.*

LEFT *The Asian pear tree (*Pyrus pyrifolia*) produces firm yet juicy, tree-ripened pears in the late summer and early autumn. They taste like a combination of an apple and a pear.*

material of the container won't affect growth, remember that ceramic pots will crack where winters are cold and icy. The key requirement for any pot you choose is that it provides adequate drainage. Generally, you'll want to use a container that measures 45–60cm (18–24in) wide and about the same depth. Larger containers, such as half whiskey barrels, can also be used.

Fruit trees in pots should be grown in fertile soil with a third of the soil mix perlite or vermiculite to keep the soil

from getting waterlogged. Use slow-release fertilizer pellets, or feed the tree every two weeks with small amounts of fish fertilizer. When fruit is on the trees, it is critical to keep them well watered. This keeps the trees healthy and prevents fertilizer build-up in the soil.

To ensure that your potted trees stay healthy and productive, they should be repotted every two years after the leaves have fallen. Once mature, prune the roots about 2.5cm (1in) every other year, then replace the tree in its pot with about 20 per cent new soil.

HERB GARDENS

From ancient times people have been growing and tending herb gardens. The earliest herb gardens, called 'apothecary gardens', were cultivated for medicinal reasons. Some herbs were used to dye fabric. Some of the medicinal herbs, such as mint and camomile, were also used simply to make a refreshing alternative to tea. Nowadays our main use for herbs is to flavour food and drinks, but many herbs, and therefore herb gardens, are also attractive and pleasantly scented.

ABOVE *Muted colours of purple and golden sage create a lovely and accessible back-door container.*

HERBS FOR THE KITCHEN

As we age, we are encouraged to reduce our intake of salt. Using herbs from the garden as taste enhancers can help us cut down on salt without losing the character of the flavours. Sometimes, too, as we get older, our taste buds need more of a boost to detect flavour. Using fresh or dried herbs from our gardens can enhance foods so that we continue to get enjoyment from eating well-seasoned healthy meals.

Whether you're still gardening in your family home, in a new patio garden or in containers, locate your herb garden so you have easy access.

If you place a culinary herb garden in a handy spot, you'll be more likely to use and enjoy your herbs daily. In the garden bed, put the taller plants, like fennel and rosemary, towards the back. Because you'll want easy access to the herbs, place stepping-stones or pavers in the bed so that you can walk safely and easily up to all the plants.

CREATING IMPACT

If you like designing with colours and textures and are not so focused on growing edible herbs, you'll enjoy the creative aspect of making a herb garden. The muted grey and silver foliage of some types of sage (*Salvia officinalis*), lavender (*Lavandula* spp.), silver thyme (*Thymus vulgaris*) and wormwood (*Artemisia absinthium*) inspire herb gardeners to create a quiet and soothing day garden that will also shimmer as a night garden in the moonlight.

A popular approach is to enjoy a combination of edible herbs with other garden plants and shrubs. Used in this way, herbs not only give the garden a rich palette of colour, texture and usefulness, but attract beneficial insects and important pollinators to breathe new life into our gardens. Parsley plants tucked in among annuals will fill a spot with luxuriant, textured green foliage that will outlast many flowers. Sweet woodruff (*Galium odoratum*) and camomile (*Anthemis nobilis*) will embrace the edges of a perennial bed with their sweet scents. A carpet of chives around the base of your favourite roses may help reduce fungal diseases. In short, herbs are low-maintenance plants that are beautiful, edible, and are beneficial companions to other plants. What more could a gardener want?

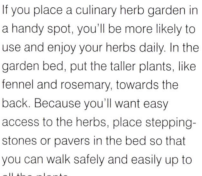

LEFT *Herbs can be tightly tucked in a sunny corner of the garden or as border plants for a path.*

OPPOSITE *A cosy crowd of herbs is happy growing together in their wattle raised beds, creating an old-worldly feel.*

EASY HERB CHOICES

Most herbs are easy to grow given the right growing conditions. From an enormous selection of undemanding options, a first-time herb grower might choose examples such as mint, dill, parsley, fennel, chives, thyme, sweet marjoram, sage, rosemary and rocket (arugula). The choice is great, so there is always something to offer a gardener with only a small garden space.

WHERE TO GROW HERBS

Herbs can be grown in a range of settings, such as custom-designed herb gardens and ornamental borders. They can also be grown as companion plants in the vegetable garden and are eminently suited to growing in containers, hanging baskets and window boxes. They are especially useful if grown near the kitchen, so make sure you have practical and easy access.

Herbs range from tall showy herbaceous plants such as fennel (*Foeniculum vulgare*) and tansy (*Tanacetum vulgare*) to ground-hugging cushion plants such as thyme (*Thymus*

ABOVE *Restrict the spread of invasive plants such as mint by planting them in bottomless pots within the ground.*

vulgaris). The majority of herbs originate from dry sunny environments and so need sunshine to help them develop their essential oils. It is best to site herbs in an open, sunny spot in the garden where they will thrive.

Some herbs may be too easy to grow and prone to spread fast, such as peppermint, spearmint and lemon balm. For this reason, all mints are best grown either in containers, or using the traditional method of sinking a large bottomless pot or bucket in the ground and planting them in that.

ABOVE *Hardscapes such as walls and steps offer distinctive spaces in which to display the many textures and varieties of potted herbs.*

SOIL PREPARATION

Drier sites suit most herbs, and the sunnier and hotter the site the better they will taste. The taste and smell of herbs is usually due to the production of essential oils within the plants. If grown in hot conditions, then the concentrations of essential oils will be greater. Growing herbs in very moist rich soils can accelerate their growth, but will result in a milder flavour. They will also look better and flower less than their 'hot-site' counterparts and be easier to harvest.

Herbs are, however, best grown in a soil that is loamy with some added organic matter. The ideal pH is 6.5 to 7.0.

Herbs may be sown directly in the soil outdoors, just like vegetables, which prefer the same soil pH range. The preparation of the seedbed and the sowing techniques are the same, so herbs can easily be interplanted or block planted among vegetables.

LEFT *A basket-woven rustic hurdle fence keeps a burgeoning garden of mixed herbs in place on this patio.*

Allium sativum

Foeniculum vulgare

Ocimum basilicum

Salvia officinalis 'Purpurascens'

Origanum vulgare

Petroselinum neapolitanum

Rosmarinus officinalis

Salvia officinalis

ITALIAN HERBS FOR YOUR GARDEN

If you plan to use herbs for cooking, select those that deliver your favourite flavours. Lovers of Italian food will most likely want herbs such as basil, oregano, and sage in their herb garden. Mint, saffron and coriander (cilantro) will be important if Middle Eastern cuisine is to your liking. Choosing herbs that complement your cooking will make your choices easy and fun.

A fun way to start is to create a themed garden, such as an Italian selection of herbs. Listed below and illustrated above are some basic herbs you will find in many Italian food recipes. *Mangia tutto!*

Allium sativum (garlic) is unique in that it grows from a bulb and is planted in autumn in temperate climates but in spring in cold areas. These hardy plants will emerge in the spring, so when the leaves turn brown, you can harvest the plump, firm cloves.

Foeniculum vulgare (fennel) is popular because the leaves and the seeds can be used for cooking – the leaves for flavouring salads and sauces, and the seeds for bringing out the flavour that makes Italian sausage so delicious. Harvest the greens when still young, since the plant loses its flavour as it ages. Let a few plants mature and go to seed so that you can harvest these.

Ocimum basilicum (basil) is a tender annual herb that is easy to grow provided you put it in very free-draining soil in a warm, sunny position, sheltered from cold winds. Next to your peppers or tomatoes, basil is said to improve their flavour and keeps away flies and mosquitoes!

Origanum vulgare (oregano) is decorative as well as delicious. At maturity, it sprouts lovely little purple flowers, which are edible. The leaves are used fresh from the plant or dried. Oregano is one of the few herbs that, when dried, has a stronger flavour. It should not be harvested until it has flowered, since the flavour is then at its fullest. Because oregano is a vigorous grower, you may want this in a separate, but nearby container.

Petroselinum neapolitanum (Italian parsley) is sweeter than the curly leaf type and is much more flavourful. The leaves are flat and broad, so the chopping is easier. This is an easy herb to grow in full or partial sunlight. This plant is attractive to bees, butterflies and birds. Use it to garnish vegetables, meats and soups – it will enhance the taste of a wide range of dishes.

Rosmarinus officinalis (rosemary) is a fragrant herb that can grow into a small shrub or can cascade over the side of a container. Pick the form you like to combine with the other Italian herbs, and give it full sun. Rosemary is used extensively in lamb and chicken dishes as well as in breads.

Salvia officinalis (sage), like oregano, is both edible and decorative, with delightful leaf colours and variegations. You can harvest the leaves at any time, but they are at their best just before or just after blooming. The grey leaf variety is the best for cooking but should always be used sparingly as it can be overpowering.

PRUNING LAVENDER

Lavender plants are very easy to manage if you get a pruning routine established. A first-year plant will require little or no pruning, since it produces very few flower stalks. Thereafter you should prune hardy lavenders at the end of the summer just as the flowers fade, so they have time to put on a little growth and overwinter as neat, sturdy bushes.

1 *Time the pruning of your lavender bushes to coincide with the end of the flowering period when all that remains is straggly stems.*

2 *Using secateurs (pruners), cut the foliage back to 23cm (9in) or to a point where you can still see green shoots. Don't cut into the old wood: it will not resprout.*

3 *Regular pruning will keep lavender plants in good shape and should ensure that the bush does not become woody in the centre.*

PLANTING YOUR HERB GARDEN

Herbs can be sited anywhere as long as it is sunny. They often make valuable additions to the ornamental garden. Foxgloves (*Digitalis*), sage (*Salvia officinalis*) and the curry plant (*Helichrysum italicum*) are a few examples that can be used in annual and herbaceous borders as well as in the kitchen garden. Remember to contain invasive herbs such as mint in a pot when growing them among other plants in an ornamental border. Remove the flower-heads from the mint before they have had a chance to seed, as the seed will germinate all over your border.

Because herbs need to be pruned often to encourage fresh, leafy growth, cut off the flowers so that they continue to flourish. When plants flower, it is a sign for them to make seeds and eventually die. Unless they are purely to enhance your garden, be vigilant with flowering herbs such as oregano and basil. Hard as it might be, cut off the flowers as soon as you see them and you will increase your harvest of succulent and tasty herbal leaves throughout the season.

POT-PLANTED HERBS

Herbs make excellent subjects for pots and are wonderful for patio gardens that catch plenty of summer sun, although you need to make sure that the potting mix never dries out. Raised beds, which provide good drainage, are also good areas for growing herbs. Always plant them in a free-draining potting mix that won't become waterlogged.

LEFT *Mix herbs among your vegetables or flowers to create an interesting tapestry of plants and to protect against pests.*

Design focus: a herb circle to delight the senses

This garden plan shows a herb circle, a traditional format for a herb garden originating from the sacred medicine wheels used by the Native Americans, the wheel representing the circle of life and the changing seasons. You may not have the space or inclination to do a whole wheel, but you could design a smaller one, or consider replicating a part of it. Using aromatic herbs, such as lavender, sage and thyme, will create magical aromas with the power to stop gardeners in their tracks.

This herb wheel would have to be sited in a warm, sunny spot as herbs thrive in direct sun. Many herbs have subtle colours and interesting foliage and these can be used, as here, to mix hues and textures in compelling combinations.

Growing the aromatic creeping thyme on the edge of a path or in small cracks between paving stones, where they will be stepped on, will activate the scents of the essential oils. Stepping stones have also been placed near the planting to ensure easy access.

Herbs attract various beneficial insects that prey on garden pests. Having a water receptacle, such as a bird bath, near your herbs will hydrate the butterflies that will visit.

PLANTING LIST

1 Purple coneflower (*Echinacea purpurea*)
2 Purple sage (*Salvia officianalis* 'Purpurea')
3 Rosemary (*Rosmarinus officinalis*)
4 Flowering onion (*Allium atropurpureum*)
5 Creeping thyme (*Thymus praecox* 'Albiflora') (*see* picture above)
6 Golden sage (*Salvia officinalis* 'Aurea')
7 Meadowsweet (*Filipendula ulmaria*)
8 Tarragon (*Artemisia dracunculus* 'Sativa')
9 Yarrow (*Achillea millefolium*)
10 Camomile (*Chamaemelum nobile*)
11 Artemisia (*Artemisia schmidtiana* 'Nana')
12 Santolina (*Santolina chamaecyparissus*)
13 Victoria sage (*Salvia farinacea*)
14 Lavender (*Lavandula angustifolia*)

Paving stones enable people to step right into the herb garden and smell the herbs or harvest them easily.

*Tarragon (*Artemisia dracunculus*) is a popular aromatic herb cultivated for its sweet, anise-like flavour.*

*Flowering onion (*Allium atropurpureum*) is an ornamental herb that provides stunning deep red-purple flower heads.*

Bird bath

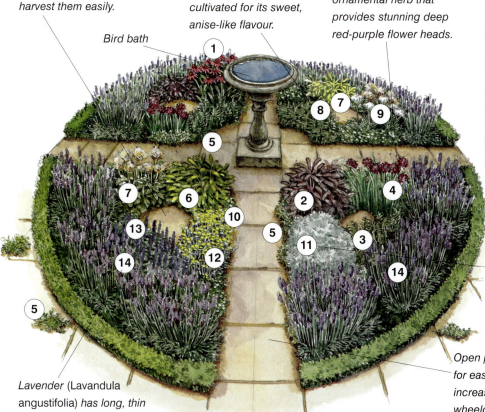

*Artemisia (*Artemisia schmidtiana*) has mounded cushions of ferny, silvery-grey leaves that make lovely edgings to a pathway.*

Open paved pathway to allow for easy access. Width can be increased to accommodate wheelchairs and walkers.

*Lavender (*Lavandula angustifolia*) has long, thin silver-grey leaves and pale lavender-blue blooms from spring until late summer.*

Project: planting a herb container

Herbs thrive on sunshine, so your herb container should get at least six hours of full sun a day in the growing season, and should also be easy to access. The next stage is to choose a selection of herbs – some of the many possibilities are chives, lavender, thyme, savory, tarragon and coriander (cilantro). With a little care, you can have fresh herbs all summer long to flavour your pasta, pizza, salads, meat and vegetables.

ABOVE *Select healthy herb starts and read the labels carefully so you understand the growth habits and required care.*

MATERIALS

- Large container with drainage holes
- Pea gravel, small rocks or broken crockery
- Potting compost (soil mix) with added garden compost and sharp sand or grit.
- Shovel or trowel to fill container
- Herbs such as chives, parsley, lavender, basil and oregano

GARDENER'S NOTE

Most herbs will produce their strongest flavour when grown in low-nutrient soil, but when closely planted in a container they will need a little more feeding than they would in the ground.

1 *Cover the bottom of the container with a layer of drainage material and fill it with compost.*

2 *Place the potted herbs on the container in their pots to lay out the proposed arrangement and spacing.*

3 *Turn the pot upside down, holding the plant with your index and third finger on each side of the stem. Tap the pot or squeeze it to release the plant.*

4 *If the plant is root bound, pull apart some root fibres to encourage new root growth direction. Plant each herb at the same level as it was at in its pot.*

5 *Continue to plant up the container until you have the balance you want. Keep the container well watered until the plants are established.*

RAISED-BED GARDENS

Raised beds are not new. A similar concept was used in the Hanging Gardens of Babylon to create tiers of flowers, and medieval monks used them to cultivate food and herbs. Yet more than any other gardening invention the raised bed has revolutionized the lives of gardeners. Besides providing easy access for those who have problems with bending and flexibility, they have multiple benefits, ranging from the reduction of soil compaction to greater productivity.

ABOVE *This raised bed is built of solid timber lengths that are intersected to create stability and a solid, natural effect.*

ADVANTAGES OF RAISED BEDS

They come in all shapes and sizes. Like clothes, you can buy them 'off the rack' or you can use your creative and mechanical skills to design your own. Raised beds can make a garden accessible to those with limited physical mobility or with low vision, and they add beauty to any garden. Having a raised garden bed also gives you more control in your choice of location and soil quality, and makes it easier to reduce pests. They are undoubtedly a great solution for the smaller urban garden or senior facility.

Probably the most significant advantage to a raised bed is that it minimizes the need to bend over to plant, weed and harvest. In most cases, you can decide the height of your bed so you can make it as comfortable as possible.

Raised beds also enable you to improve the quality of your soil. This will allow you to grow the plants you want, even if the soil in your garden is not suitable. However, if your soil is very chalky, and you are growing acid-loving plants, you might need to lay a barrier at the bottom of the bed to separate the chalky from the more acidic soil.

Because the sides of raised beds are exposed to the sun, the soil warms up more quickly in the spring. This means that you can plant things earlier and, with the soil staying warm throughout the growing season, flowers and vegetables have the advantage of more time to flourish and ripen.

A critical feature of a healthy garden is good drainage. Because the soil in a raised bed is higher than any place water would naturally settle, you can be assured of adequate drainage. In addition, practically speaking, the advantage of raised beds over in-ground rows is that you can work in wet weather without compacting the garden soil and getting your feet muddy.

If you introduce at least one raised bed in your garden space you will see how it improves the quality of your gardening experience. The following pages show you how to build your own from scratch or put one together from a kit. There are many materials that can be used for raising beds, and it's fun and interesting to see how creative you can be!

LEFT *Raised beds not only provide a place to grow all kinds of different plants, they also offer us the best seat in a garden as they bring us close to the trees and flowers.*

RIGHT *Keeping your garden shipshape and undertaking general care and maintenance routines is most easily done if you can sit comfortably as you work, without bending over.*

OPPOSITE *A well-built raised bed can take on different roles, such as both a flower garden and an orchard. So it becomes a mini-garden with complementary elements.*

Design focus: raised beds

The raised-bed garden illustrations here show some of the many materials that can be used for constructing raised beds – wood, pre-made pavers, hay bales, natural stone and brick. While these represent some of the most commonly used materials, the options are endless – more ideas are shown in the panel below right. If your bed is on an in-ground base, you can also plant ground-hugging greenery along the edges to soften and naturalize the structure.

The width of a raised bed should allow you to reach the centre without strain – so no more than 90cm (3ft) if you can access from only one side and 150cm (5ft) if you have two-sided access.

If you are using or making several beds, the path between can be as narrow as 60cm (24in). To avoid mud forming, top the path with fine gravel, or add paving stones.

Because of its long life and ability to resist decay, pressure-treated wood might seem to be ideal for raised beds. If you decide to use treated wood, however, make sure that you get a type that is arsenic-free.

Whatever your needs, raised beds such as these offer an easier, more versatile, more comfortable and safer way to garden than in-ground beds.

RAISED BEDS: CONSTRUCTION OPTIONS

1 Simple wooden raised bed
2 Kit raised bed
3 Paver raised bed
4 Hay-bale raised bed
5 Tall raised bed
6 Raised stone or brick flower bed

ALTERNATIVE MATERIALS

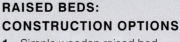

7 Simulated wood planking
8 Railway sleepers (*see above*)
9 Breeze (cinder) blocks
10 Old car tyres stacked together
11 Sturdy, tall, soil-filled plastic bags
12 Galvanized metal water troughs
13 Soil mounds tamped at the edges, with mulch to stabilize the form.

This basic bed can be raised two or three levels by using taller posts and additional boards. Top boards have here been added for seating.

Kits come with real or simulated wood and easy corner connectors that can be stacked to raise the bed. Here, a trellis is added to give the easy-reach advantage of a vertical gardening structure.

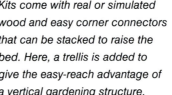

Real or simulated pavers can be stacked to the desired height.

Grouped hay bales allow for a central growing area that is filled with soil as well as planting in the tops of the bales.

This style allows the gardener to stand when tending plants. Leg heights can be altered to allow a wheelchair gardener to get close.

Natural stone makes attractive beds that can be laid out in any shape or size. Brick can be used in the same way.

Project: making a raised bed out of bricks

This raised bed is shaped to fit a corner of the garden. You might not want to do this yourself, but understanding the stages will help you plan where your bed should be sited and the exact dimensions required, before commissioning someone to do it. Obviously the height can be varied according to your requirements. Similarly, as your interests or energy change, the plantings in this raised bed can be easily adjusted for variety.

ABOVE *Concrete or brick raised beds are durable and permanent. They will give you years of consistent access to your plants.*

MATERIALS

- Pointed stake
- Fine sand or line marker paint
- Spade
- Concrete mix
- Bricks and mortar
- Spirit level
- Pointing trowel
- Waterproof paint
- Rubble
- Gravel or pea shingle
- Topsoil
- Good potting medium

1 *Mark out the bed using a stake. Define the lines with fine sand. Dig out along the markings to a depth and width of 15cm (6in). Fill in with concrete to within 5cm (2in) of the top. Firm and leave for 24 hours.*

2 *Build up four or five courses of bricks, and set them into mortar, carefully checking the horizontal surfaces with a spirit level at each stage.*

3 *Clean up the mortar while wet with a pointing trowel. Leave to harden. Before filling with soil, coat with waterproof paint.*

4 *Add a layer of rubble topped with gravel for drainage. Fill in with topsoil and stir in a top layer of potting medium.*

5 *The completed raised bed is here planted with a selection of culinary herbs and wild strawberries.*

BREEZE-BLOCK BEDS

One option for constructing raised beds is to use breeze (cinder) blocks. The technique is to lay levels of blocks with the holes facing up. Work from the corners, ensuring the blocks are touching, and eliminate any gaps. Successive layers should be staggered – use two or three layers depending on the required height.

Fill the block holes around the side of these beds with soil, and plant herbs or drought-resistant plants to conceal the blocks and flow over the edge. Alternatively, cap the blocks to make a seat. The area enclosed by the blocks can be filled and planted as above.

RIGHT *The spaces in the top blocks can be planted with drought-resistant plants.*

Project: building a wooden raised bed

While building from a kit is the easiest way to make a raised bed (see page 180), doing it from scratch isn't complicated. Here is a simple raised bed made with cedar wood and screws. It is constructed upside down and inverted so the vertical posts that are still visible are secured in the ground. Here, three layers of wood raise the height to 45cm (18in), which will suit a wheelchair. Make it yourself if you are active, or ask someone to do it for you.

ABOVE AND OPPOSITE *Wooden raised beds can be narrow (above) or wider to allow for seating (opposite).*

MATERIALS

- 2.5m (8ft) long, 50 x 100mm (2 x 4in) piece of wood (for the corner posts and for the end pieces)
- 6 x 2.5m (8ft) long, 50 x 150mm (2 x 6in) pieces of wood for the sides and ends
- 48 x 90mm (3in) wood screws
- Hand or power saw
- 4 stakes for marking corners
- Post-hole digger
- Drill

GARDENER'S NOTE

You can adjust the height of the bed according to your requirements by changing the number of layers.

1 *Cut the 50 x 100mm (2 x 4in) pieces into four 60cm (2ft) tall corner posts. Cut three of the 50 x 150mm (2 x 6in) pieces in half for the ends. Assemble on a flat surface.*

2 *Mark the corners with the stakes. Dig four holes wide enough for the 50 x 100mm (2 x 4in) corner posts, and deep enough to fit the excess length of the posts.*

3 *Set one of the corner posts on its thin edge, and secure a 1.2m (4ft) 50 x 150mm (2 x 6in) post at one end with the screws. Repeat at the other end. Use a spare bit of wood beneath to protect the work surface.*

4 *Stand one of the end pieces up with the excess on top and attach 2.5m (8ft) 50 x 150mm (2 x 6in) pieces at the end of the construction in three layers.*

5 *Repeat at the other end, and repeat for the two long sides. Then invert the bed construction so that the excess length of the corner posts fits in the dug holes.*

Project: making a raised bed from a kit

You can buy modular systems for creating your own raised bed. With these kits almost everything is pre-cut, pre-measured and relatively simple to assemble. By using the corner pieces that join the sides together, you can put up a modular raised bed in very little time. Some kits allow you to adapt the height. They may be made of wood or recycled plastic, which is lightweight and won't rot or break.

ABOVE *The corner is created by adding the second base board. They are designed to snap in firmly.*

GARDENER'S NOTE

Before you start assembly, measure the area where the raised bed will be located so that it matches the dimensions of the modular kit you are using. If there is existing lawn on the area you will need to remove it by skimming off the turf and exposing the soil beneath.

Level the measured area and then lay a weed barrier – either fabric or a layer of cardboard or newspaper (*see also* page 113). If the kit is light enough you can assemble it elsewhere and carry it across to your site (as shown here).

1 *Kits use dowels, metal pins or corner braces to 'lock' them in place. Here, a corner brace slots into the board. Use the four corner units to join the base boards.*

2 *In this way the raised bed starts to take shape. Ensure that the base remains stable as you work through the manufacturer's instructions.*

3 *This modular system can be built up as high as you require. Here, a second level of boards are being added.*

4 *Once the bed is in position, lay your weed barrier. For a deep bed you can fill the base of the bed with plastic bottles to bulk out the area (reducing the soil required).*

5 *Cover the bottles at the base of the bed with a plastic sheet with drainage holes, or landscaping fabric. You are now ready to fill your raised bed with the soil mixture.*

Project: irrigating a wooden raised bed

Raised beds have a tendency to dry out, so they need more watering than beds in the ground. Having a water source close to the bed makes irrigating them easier. Combining a soaker hose and a regular hose with a hose connector is a good solution, because this saves effort and minimizes waste. Soaker hoses come in a variety of sizes, so choose the length according to that of your raised bed.

ABOVE *Beans and corn are getting their water needs met by a soaker hose snaking its way through the raised bed.*

MATERIALS
- Pencil
- Drill
- Garden hose
- Soaker hose
- Two- or three-way hose connector valve with built-in shut-offs
- 3–4 female hose couplings
- U-shaped wire hose holders

GARDENER'S NOTE
This technique can be adapted for use with a non-wooden raised bed, either by drilling through the material of the bed to make the same hole for the hose to pass through, or by placing the soaker hose at the top of the bed.

1 *Mark on your frame where the entry point of the irrigation hose should be. In one end of the raised bed, drill a hole 5cm (2in) below the top of the raised bed, just large enough to accommodate a hose.*

2 *Calculate the lengths of hose required to cover the distance from the raised beds to the connector and from the connector to the water source. Cut the hose into shorter lengths to suit these calculations.*

3 *Using female hose couplings, attach two pieces of hose to the connector valve. These join one or more hoses to the tap, or to each other. A shut-off valve in each connector arm allows you to redirect the water.*

4 *Insert the other ends of the short hoses through the holes. Inside the raised bed, attach the short pieces of hose to the soaker hose. Attach another length of hose outside using a female hose coupling.*

5 *Arrange the soaker hoses in an S-shape to distribute the water. Place them at the base of the plants in the row so that water is distributed evenly over the roots. You can also bury them beneath the soil.*

PATIO GARDENS

From the open terraces in Italy overlooking the ripening grapevines to the private walled gardens in New York City, we all appreciate that area where the outdoors and the indoors meet, creating a unique garden experience. This area of outdoors offers us tranquillity, rest, fresh air, sun and – best of all – a place never more than a few steps from our door. As we age and look to economize on garden space and effort, patio gardens might be just what we need.

ABOVE *A chair placed in a shady spot on a sturdy, level surface creates a perfect and tranquil garden experience.*

BRINGING THE PATIO TO LIFE

A well-planned patio garden makes the most of a small space. If yours lacks in-ground garden beds, then adding a few containers will make a world of difference to any hard-landscaped area.

Raised beds are another option – small trees, shrubs and even berry bushes can thrive in raised beds and will enhance the atmosphere.

Consider the view you will have from indoors when the weather is inclement. Watching a small maple tree change colour in the autumn or bright daffodil heads nodding in a container gives a sense of well-being when observed through the window.

PRACTICAL CONSIDERATIONS

For anyone who is unsteady on their feet, walks with support or is wheelchair bound, the hard walking surface should be level, smooth and non-skid. If it is made of concrete, colour or tint the cement to avoid reflective glare. Other surfaces, such as bricks or pavers, are good flooring choices, but they should adhere to the requirements above.

It's important that a wheelchair or walker can easily navigate in and out of the doors, so make sure you have an easy knob or door latch to operate. In addition, manual doors should be lightweight so they are easy to open – a heavy door makes it much harder to

access the garden. If required, check that the doorway dimensions accommodate a wheelchair or walker, and don't overlook the threshold, which needs to be as level as possible with little or no elevation to deal with when moving across it.

Provide good lighting in the patio so you can safely enjoy the warm evenings outside. Automatically timed lighting is a safe and practical feature, or select a motion detector light that will illuminate the patio as you enter.

OPPOSITE *Beautiful tiles such as these can make the patio floor a striking feature to set off the plants.*

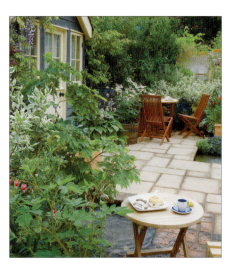

ABOVE *Create a small 'room' in a corner of the patio where you can slip away to read and enjoy a cup of coffee.*

LEFT *Lush plantings and overflowing containers on a patio make a lovely place to sit and relax.*

RIGHT *Sturdy containers full of aromatic herbs and long-lasting flowers can adorn a patio all year round.*

EASY PATIO GARDENING

As we have already discovered, enabling gardeners with physical limitations often involves thinking around a problem, and there is usually more than one option. Using lightweight containers to house your patio plants will, for example, let you move plants around to follow the sun or to rearrange the design. Another successful idea is to raise heavy containers on wheeled caddies, allowing easy movement around the garden (*see also* page 121).

Think about having a hanging basket or two, as they take up no ground space and can adorn any less than attractive blank walls with colourful, cascading flowers. It's a good idea to install an easy pulley system so you can lower and raise the baskets to maintain them.

Make sure you grow some herbs close to the doorway so you can quickly snip a few leaves when you are preparing a meal. A good patio also needs a few comfortable but stable chairs and a small table so you can spend time outdoors and enjoy the natural world around you.

Having a convenient water source is critical to keep your patio plants irrigated. Keep a short, lightweight hose or small watering can nearby to make irrigating your patio garden easy. Place a waterproof box on the patio for your tools, gloves and sunscreen so they are handy but not unsightly.

ABOVE *Hanging baskets create long-lasting confections of flowers and foliage.*

LEFT *A wide doorway in this Victorian-style conservatory leads on to a terrace. Period-style wirework and cast-iron containers complement the planting.*

Design focus: a patio garden for sanctuary and relaxation

A patio can be a private and restorative personal space. Being a manageable size, it requires less physical effort than a large garden to maintain. What is more, it can have ready access to the indoors and sturdy, level surfaces for easy and safe mobility. This illustration shows an enclosed set-up with a table and chairs for summer meals and refreshments. The design could be adapted around other patio formats: a garden corner, a front entrance walkway or a driveway or parking space.

The advantage of patios for senior gardeners is that they have a hard ground surface, creating a sturdy and secure base for those with unsteady feet or balance problems. The surface here has wide, level, square pavers with a contrasting brick pattern that invites you into the space. A similar material is used to define the parameters of the patio.

A selection of year-round plants are suggested here, all relatively easy to maintain. You can also add decorative containers, hanging baskets or wall planters. The symmetrical design is easy on the eye and the wide walkways, the wheeled hose holder and lack of clutter mean that there are no potential tripping hazards.

The simple water feature adds soothing trickling sounds and attracts birds and butterflies. If you have in-ground beds or raised beds, then small deciduous trees such as 'Little Gem' magnolias can be included, along with evergreen shrubs. With all these options, your patio will undoubtedly be an individual statement.

PLANTING LIST

1. Hinoki cypress (*Chamaecyparis obtusa* 'Gracilis')
2. Hinoki cypress (*C. o.* 'Nana Gracilis Glauca')
3. Shrub rose (*Rosa glauca*)
4. Lavender (*Lavandula*)
5. Daylily (*Hemerocallis* 'Stella de Oro')
6. English marigold (*Calendula officinalis*)
7. Sasanqua camellia (*Camellia sasanqua* 'Setsugekka')
8. Vine maple (*Acer circinatum*)
9. Japanese andromeda (*Andromeda* 'Temple Bells')
10. Sweet box (*Sarcococca confusa*)
11. Lady's mantle (*Alchemilla mollis*)
12. Christmas fern (*Polystichum acrostichoides*)
13. Cyclamen (*Cyclamen hederifolium*)
14. Japanese maple (*Acer palmatum*)
15. Busy Lizzy (*Impatiens* 'Dazzler White')
16. Plantain lily (*Hosta fortunei*)
17. Climbing hydrangea (*Hydrangea anomala*) (*see* picture above)
18. Little Gem magnolia (*Magnolia grandiflora* 'Little Gem')
19. Euonymus (*Euonymus fortunei*)

In-ground patch filled with Hosta fortunei

Raised beds

Bench

Stone planter with small sedums

Surrounding brick wall

Wheeled hose cart

Large pavers   Table   Brick patio surface

Project: planting a hanging basket

Using a wire mesh basket as a hanging container for plants allows you to plant not only on the top but also through the sides of the container, camouflaging the base of the basket and giving it a generously overflowing and luxurious look from below. A solid plastic container will not achieve this effect, because you can't plant through the sides. Good news – this basket can be reused each year!

ABOVE *The plants in this basket will soon grow to create a waterfall of colourful flowers and foliage.*

MATERIALS
- Wire basket 35–45cm (14–18in) diameter with a fibre or moss liner
- Scissors or pruners
- Compost (soil mix) (add slow-release fertilizer for a boost)
- Bedding plants in 5cm (2in) pots. Choose from trailing petunias, such as the 'Supertunia', 'Wave' or 'Surfina' series, busy Lizzies (*Impatiens* spp.), ivy geranium (*Pelargonium peltatum*), sweet potato vine (*Ipomoea batatas*), fuchsia (*Fuchsia* x *hybrida*), sweet alyssum (*Lobularia maritima*), trailing lobelia (*Lobelia erinus*), lemon verbena (*Aloysia citriodora*), water hyssop (*Bacopa monniera*) and *Lantana* spp.

1 *Use scissors or pruners to slice through the fibre liner to make the holes. To get full flower coverage stagger the rows. They need to be large enough to pull the plant through but snug enough to hold it firmly.*

2 *Fill the basket with compost to just below where the holes begin. Remove the plant from its cell and, from the outside of the basket, push the roots towards the centre of the container.*

3 *Add more plants so that the growth flows through the side. Add soil to cover the roots and repeat until you reach the top.*

4 *Add more soil to within 2.5cm (1in) of the rim and set 3–4 more plants on the top. Water thoroughly to settle the soil.*

5 *Hang the basket, getting help if necessary – or get someone to do it for you. When irrigating, use a watering wand.*

Project: planting a lightweight container

If you don't have the strength or flexibility to lift heavy containers, the best plan is to decide where you want them and put them in place before planting them up. However, sometimes containers need to be moved – you may be growing tender shrubs that cannot survive outdoors over winter, or perhaps you want to give prominence to seasonal displays. Wheeled trolleys are useful, but it still makes the job easier if the pot is not too heavy.

ABOVE *A small hand trowel and healthy flowers are some of the essentials needed to plant your container garden.*

MATERIALS

- Plastic or fibreglass container at least 45cm (18in) in diameter, with drainage holes
- Lightweight fabric
- Recycled polystyrene beads (mailer pellets)
- Compost (soil mix)
- A mixture of tall, filler and trailing plants. Tall options: canna, colocasia, false cypress (*Chamaecyparis obtusa*) and palm lily (*Cordyline*); filler options: basil (*Ocimum basilicum*), coleus (*Solenostemon*), blood-leaf (*Iresine herbstii*) and Swiss chard (*Beta vulgaris*); trailing options: million bells (*Bidens calibrachoa*), creeping zinnia (*Schizanthus pinnatus*), lobelia and nasturtiums (*Tropaeolum*).

1 *Line the base of the pot with fabric. Fill the pot a third full with polystyrene beads. This will bulk out the volume of the pot without adding to its weight. Then fill with compost to within 2.5cm (1in) of the rim.*

2 *Place the taller plant either in the centre or towards the back of the container, depending on whether the pot is to be viewed from all sides, or put against a wall.*

3 *Plant trailing plants around the edges where they will cascade over the sides of the container to hide the hard edges.*

4 *Set the other plants around the central one, filling in the spaces and mixing varieties of colour and shapes.*

5 *Water the pot until you see water seeping out of the bottom. Keep it watered, fed and groomed throughout the season.*

Project: making a fragrant window box

A window box spilling over with sweetly scented flowers and aromatic foliage will be a delight, from inside and out, and will bring you hours of rewarding scents – and natural aromatherapy. Choose a few strongly-scented varieties that you know you will love, but combine them with some non-scented ones to add colour – otherwise the mixture of fragrances might be overpowering.

ABOVE *A colourful and densely planted window box gives a cheerful welcome to friends and neighbours.*

MATERIALS

- A selection of plants of various heights – used here are scented geraniums (*Pelargonium* spp.), trailing nasturtiums (*Tropaeolum majus*), sweet alyssum (*Lobularia maritima*), ivy (*Hedera helix*) and heliotrope (*Heliotropium arborescens*)
- Window box with drainage holes
- Coffee filter or old piece of wire mesh to cover the drainage holes
- Compost (soil mix)

GARDENER'S NOTE

Other possibilities not included in this project are lavender, dianthus, petunias and trailing sweet peas.

1 *Select your plants by arranging them in a pattern of two or three rows. Put the taller flowers at the back and graduate the heights with the trailing plants at the front.*

2 *Place the coffee filter or screening in the bottom of the window box. This will prevent the compost from falling out through the holes.*

3 *Fill the window box about two-thirds full with compost, and firm it down gently.*

4 *Following your window box planting design, place the plants one at a time in their allocated positions, filling in with compost as you go.*

5 *Add compost to surround the roots, and gently tamp the compost to remove air pockets. Keep doing this as you plant until the level is about 2.5cm (1in) below the top of the window box. Water well.*

VERTICAL GARDENS

Most plants grow vertically as they stretch towards the sun. A garden with vertical elements makes the most of this upward-growing journey of living forms. This approach will maximize space in a small garden and also provide easy maintenance options. Another vertical solution is to use elements in a hanging or raised form, so that plants can tumble downwards, or planted containers can be placed in a shelved structure to create an attractive display and easy watering access.

ABOVE *A tiered, mesh basket structure such as this allows you to be creative in your planting choices.*

PRACTICAL CONSIDERATIONS

Growing plants vertically means that much of your gardening can be done standing up, putting less pressure on your back. Vertical structures also make the most of a limited space and reduce the energy required to care for the garden. Vertical growth also makes it easier to spot problems with pests and diseases – with plants comfortably viewed at eye level.

As well as the obvious ease of access that vertical features bring, growing plants on structures that keep them tall and heading skywards is also a great way to fill less attractive garden areas, such as blank dividing walls and dark corners that may have been bare and neglected.

Growing plants up and over arbours or trellises can create shady areas, and a cool refuge away from the sun. You will need a heavy structure such as a metal arbour to support wisteria or three-leaf akebia (*Akebia trifoliata*).

Formal wooden obelisks can add style and elegance to a garden or, at the other end of the scale, try using a rustic handmade teepee made with bamboo, willow twigs or recently pruned fruit branches.

When planning vertical elements you can use the structure of existing walls and fences to train your plants, or take advantage of the various freestanding support structures available. Three examples of each are illustrated overleaf, along with other alternatives.

OPPOSITE *A wooden arbour offers a pathway to the sun for climbing roses and a perfect spot for a hanging basket.*

ABOVE *Grapevines clothe the whole of the porch structure, giving the area natural shelter and protection from the harsh sun.*

LEFT *Bent willow twigs create an airy and inviting arbour that lends support to lightweight climbing sweet peas.*

CONTAINERS

Breaking up the horizontal perspective of gardens and gaining a height variation is an important design dynamic, with the additional benefit that planting features are more accessible to those who have problems bending. One technique is to add a simple trellis to a pot, giving you a double-impact feature with flowers cascading to the ground and a climbing plant stretching upwards toward the sun.

Another idea is to group containers of various heights. Enhance this by planting a small tree or shrub with an upright growth habit. Make sure that the base is wide and stable. Recommended plants are Japanese holly (*Ilex crenata* 'Sky Pencil') and dwarf alberta spruce (*Picea glauca*).

BELOW *Stacking old tyres creates a practical and whimsical herb, flower or vegetable garden.*

ABOVE *Flower pouches are an easy and economical way to cover a blank wall with a cascade of colour.*

HANGING BASKETS

Another attractive vertical feature is hanging flower baskets that can be used to frame doorways, windows, porches and balconies, thereby combining a dramatic selection of flowering and cascading plants in a restricted area.

You can gain significant height variety in the garden by using baskets and containers at different levels. A successful hanging basket can have tall, spiky plants that are complemented by masses of cascading plants. Wise placement of your baskets will ensure that you get to enjoy the full visual effect of a well-planted container.

The baskets need to be accessible so you can water and deadhead the plants. Pulley systems are available that move the plants to your level. Recommended plants are sweet potato vine (*Ipomoea batatas*), nasturtiums (*Tropaeolum majus*), lobelia (*Lobelia erinus*), wave petunias (*Petunia* x *hybrida*), and trailing begonias (*Begonia solananthera*).

FLOWER POUCHES AND TUBES

An easy and economical way to have bursts of colour hanging on a wall, fence or shed is by using flower tubes

ABOVE *A mixed planting of upright red geraniums and trailing fuchsias creates an attractive hanging display.*

or pouches. These heavy-duty plastic containers come with directions to help you create colourful arrangements that are an eye-catching alternative to the traditional hanging basket. While the casings are not very attractive, they should be hidden once the plants have grown – make sure you choose varieties that will cover them well. The great advantage is that these pouches stretch down and disguise or brighten a much longer vertical length than a basket. You may want to get help hanging them, however, since they are quite heavy once planted up, and make sure you have a stable structure to hang them from. Recommended plants are busy Lizzies (*Impatiens walleriana*), begonias and petunias.

MAINTENANCE

The main care requirement for containers, especially over the summer period, is watering. Any container that is densely planted will need frequent watering, often several times a days in hot sun. Most containers will benefit from regular feeding and deadheading too.

Design focus: vertical planting on walls and fences

Here are three illustrations of vertical planting on existing walls and fences. If your garden is exposed, a well-placed vertical planting, such as a trellis with a climbing clematis, could create privacy or disguise an unattractive feature by increasing the height of an existing wall or fence. Many plants can also be grown over fences or trained on walls. Simple wire grids can also be fastened to the side of a fence to provide guidance for plants that want to seek the heights.

Walls

Solid walls can be used to your advantage in a vertical garden. A lichen-covered stone wall with tiny crevices that are full of mosses or succulents is a thing of beauty and needs no improvement. Other walls of grey cement, breeze (cinder) blocks or new bricks can be dreary and depressing. Shelves can be mounted at various levels on blank walls and these make excellent sites for plant-filled containers.

Another option for walls are espalier structures. These work well on a wall that offers a micro-climate of heat and wind protection. With some initial assistance to build the right foundation, you can create a 'two-dimensional' fruit tree that produces healthy and accessible fruit.

Trellises

These gridded and latticed structures are the workhorses of a vertical garden – they can be free-standing or attached to a wall or fence, and many are strong enough to support heavy plants.

Fences

A practical and uninspiring chain-link fence or a rustic split-rail style can be embellished or disguised with plants that like to climb and twirl on their structure.

1 WALL CLIMBERS
Climbing hydrangea (*Hydrangea petiolaris*) and ivy (*Hedera*)

2 ESPALIER PLANTS
Apples (*Malus* spp.), peaches (*Prunus persica*), plums (*Prunus* spp.) and camellia (*see* picture above)

3 TRELLIS PLANTS
Morning glory (*Ipomoea purpurea*), clematis, star jasmine (*Jasminum* spp.), roses, honeysuckle (*Lonicera* spp.), pole beans (*Phaeolus vulgaris*), scarlet runner beans (*Phaseolus coccineus*), peas (*Pisum sativum*), cucumber (*Cucumis sativus*), pumpkins (*Cucurbita* spp.), squash (*Cucurbita* spp.) and grapes (*Vitis vinifera*)

4 FENCING PLANTS
Wisteria, climbing roses, trumpet creeper (*Campsis radicans*), clematis, three-leaf akebia (*Akebia trifoliate*) and passion flower (*Passiflora caerulea*)

Fan trellis with clematis (Clematis spp.). Wooden fan or decorative trellises that easily attach to walls provide a stable and showy setting for climbers.

Plain trellis with jasmine (Jasminum spp.) and three-leaf akebia (Akebia trifoliata)

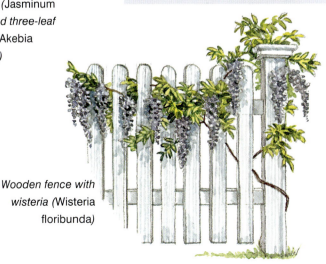

Wooden fence with wisteria (Wisteria floribunda)

Design focus: vertical planting on free-standing structures

Fruit and vegetable gardens have always relied on free-standing vertical structures. These include teepees and obelisks, which look like garden chapel spires with their pointy tips that aim for the heavens and invite sweet-smelling and trailing plants to twist and climb up them. Another free-standing option is a pergola, offering a shady and protective passageway covered with clambering vines and roses that creates a pedestrian connection between a building and the outside world.

Teepees and obelisks

Vegetables benefit from the support offered by teepees and obelisks. Cucumbers will grow straight rather than curved, and beans and peas will hang freely, benefiting from good air circulation and sun exposure. The fruits of squash, melon and pumpkin will need some form of support as they develop to prevent them from breaking off; the small-fruited varieties are best for vertical gardens.

Teepees are fun and easy to make. Bamboo poles, tall willow branches or pliable, recently pruned fruit-tree branches can create attractive and functional tri- or quadri-podded structures for seasonal use. Garden centres also offer a large array of tall, pre-made teepees.

Pergola

The conventional image of a pergola is of a free-standing wooden canopy of crossbeams supported by pillars and covered with climbing vines or roses. It can be any length, depending on the size of your garden.

Arbours and arches

We can be welcomed into a garden by walking under an arched structure covered with leafy, sweet-smelling plants. An arbour goes a step further, inviting us to sit under the shade of the intertwining branches. Fitted with a seat or a bench, this provides a gardener with a place to rest, sip a cool drink and enjoy the view.

1 OBELISK PLANTS

Peas (*Pisum sativum*), climbing beans (*Phaseolus* spp.), butter (lima) beans, cucumbers (*Cucumis melo*), melons, pumpkins, squash, morning glory (*Ipomoea purpurea*) and sweet peas (*Lathyrus odoratus*).

2 PERGOLA PLANTS

Roses (*Rosa* spp.), honeysuckle (*Lonicera* spp.), wisteria (*Wisteria floribunda*), kiwi fruit (*Actinidia deliciosa*) and crimson glory vine (*Vitis coignetiae*).

3 PLANTS FOR ARBOURS AND ARCHES

Clematis, honeysuckle, climbing (not rambling) roses, Chilean glory flower (*Eccremocarpos scaber*), crimson glory vine (*Vitis coignetiae*) and morning glory (*Ipomoea purpurea*).

A-frame structure supporting red runner beans

Teepee structure supporting morning glory

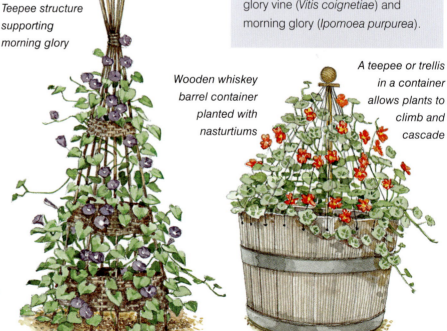

Wooden whiskey barrel container planted with nasturtiums

A teepee or trellis in a container allows plants to climb and cascade

Project: planting clematis

Once established, a clematis will give you years of blooms. The best planting time is in the early spring or autumn, during the cooler weather. Unlike most plants, they are best planted more deeply than they were in the pot, to help them recover if they are attacked by clematis wilt. Clematis like their heads in the sun and their feet in the shade. So plant a small shrub or ground cover at its base like evergreen candytuft (Iberis sempervirens) or an evergreen wild strawberry.

ABOVE *You will find a variety of clematis in flower in every season. The flowers head towards the sun as the roots seek the shade.*

MATERIALS

- Support such as trellis or wires attached to a wall or fence, or free-standing
- Spade
- Fork
- Well-composted organic matter/cow manure
- 2 tablespoons of bonemeal
- Clematis plant. *Clematis* 'Etoile Violette' is a reliable and long-term bloomer as well as a variety that is easy to grow and maintain. Other ideas are *C. alpina* 'Candy', with pink blooms in the spring, and *C.* 'Blue Angel', which has gorgeous sky-blue flowers.
- 2–3 small wooden stakes

1 *Dig a 30 x 30cm (12 x 12in) hole 30cm (12in) from the support. Fork in the organic matter and bonemeal.*

2 *Remove the clematis from its pot and tease the roots out gently if they are pot-bound.*

3 *Plant the clematis so it leans towards the support. Bury the plant crown 5cm (2in) below the surface.*

4 *Insert small stakes to act as an initial guide as the plant finds it way to the trellis.*

5 *Water well after planting and then regularly. Use a fertilizer with a low nitrogen content to encourage blossoms and roots.*

Project: planting up a vertical basket

This tiered vertical planter gives you the opportunity to choose and grow an interesting variety of plants and flowers that offer colour contrast, leaf texture and mixed growing habits. The placement and open design gives easy access to all the plants for watering, fertilizing and deadheading. This structure will also add a distinctive design feature to a space that may benefit from an interesting focal point.

ABOVE *Use plants that have similar water and light needs since they will thrive better and be easier to care for.*

MATERIALS

- Tiered structure with fibre baskets
- Mallet or hammer
- Compost (soil mix)
- Young or plugged plants: shown here are *Skimmia japonica*, *Artemisia stelleriana* 'Boughton Silver', Scotch heather (*Calluna vulgaris*), pepper face (*Peperomia obtusifolia* 'Variegata') and dusty miller (*Senecio cineraria*) (top basket); cyclamen (*Cyclamen persicum*), heather, blue fescue (*Festuca glauca*) and *Helichrysum* (middle basket); cyclamen, heather, snow-in-summer (*Cerastium tomentosum*), trailing ivy (*Hedera helix*) and Michaelmas daisy (*Aster* 'Victoria').

1 *Find a good location and securely anchor the legs of the structure into the ground using a mallet or hammer. Assemble the remaining components, making certain that it is sturdy and straight.*

2 *Select a variety of small plants to grow in each basket (see those mentioned in materials list for those used here). Alternatively, you can choose one larger distinctive plant.*

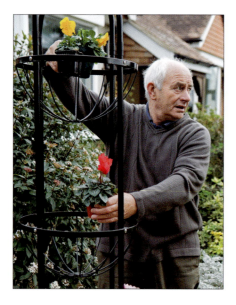

3 *Decide on the combination of plants to fill the pots in each tier. Use a helper so you can stand back to judge the effect.*

4 *Place the selected plants in an empty fibre basket and place this in the wire basket holder.*

5 *Add the compost around the plants and firm them in gently. Water well.*

INDOOR GARDENS

As the weather turns cold, most of us are less keen to spend time in the garden, but we can still keep greenery and living plants around us to animate the interior – and to keep us company. There may also come a time when physical limitations make getting outdoors difficult and inconvenient in any season. Whatever your reasons, creating an indoor garden can improve your quality of life and dramatically boost your emotional and physical well-being.

ABOVE *Forcing hyacinth bulbs indoors during dark winter days brightens up your room and fills the air with sweet fragrance.*

PLANNING AN INDOOR GARDEN

As you would assess your outdoor environment, you also need to survey your indoor space. How much space do you have for plants? How much light do you have and how does it move during the course of the day? Where is your heat source? Are you able to get to the plants easily?

If you are new to keeping plants indoors, start slowly with just one or two. Select the right ones by talking to friends – who may have spare plants as

BELOW *The begonia family offers many interesting varieties that are versatile and easy to care for.*

well as advice – and looking in local nurseries. Remember, too, to find out how big the plants may get.

FLOWERS OR FOLIAGE?

Many indoor plants do not flower but are attractive because of the shape and colour of their foliage – examples include pothos, jade (*Crassula ovata*) and begonia. (Rex-cultorum begonias do have attractive flowers, but are mainly grown for their foliage.) If you'd like a flowering plant, try African violets (*Saintpaulia* spp.), cyclamen (*Cyclamen persicum*), and orchids – with the right care these will stay in bloom for many months.

LIGHT LEVELS

Before buying a plant, think carefully about where you will put it because light level requirements vary from plant to plant. Most flowering houseplants need good light levels, but will tolerate a less sunny position for a couple of weeks as long as they are moved back into the light afterwards. Some indoor plants will benefit from being put outside in summer, but they must be acclimatized gradually.

Artificial lighting can help boost light levels indoors, but it can't replace natural daylight. Most houseplants prefer bright, filtered, natural light. This means that they will need a little shade from the hot midday sun. Garden plants are sheltered by other plants and their roots are buried in deep soil, but houseplants are usually

alone in a small pot, so the roots easily overheat. Cacti and succulents are happy in full sun, as are some of the geraniums, but you need to watch for scorching because sunshine through glass is very different from sunshine outside.

In general, flowering plants need higher light levels than foliage plants, while plants with large, dark green leaves need less light than those with small, silver-grey leaves. *See page 203 for more guidance on light levels.*

OPPOSITE *To grow roses as successful houseplants, make sure they get full sun for part of the day and don't let the soil dry out.*

ABOVE *The giant taro plant (*Alocasia macrorrhiza*) can reach 1.2–1.8m (4–6ft) in height.*

TEMPERATURE AND HUMIDITY

Indoor plants come from a wide range of natural habitats, and their needs vary greatly, so it's important to find out what conditions will suit your plants. However, as a general rule, most – apart from cacti and succulents – like a more humid atmosphere than is usually found in centrally heated homes, and in many cases a cooler temperature, especially in winter.

You can raise the humidity around plants by grouping them together, by regular misting, or by standing them on top of a layer of pebbles in a tray filled with water. The latter method is probably the most effective, but the pot should always be above the level of the water.

Houseplants do well in bathrooms and kitchens because of the higher use of water in these rooms. Conservatories (sun rooms) need good ventilation to prevent them overheating. They should be fitted with windows that open, and some form of shading. Opening windows improves air circulation on a warm day, but can also let in cold draughts. Invest in a device with a digital readout, showing inside and outside temperatures, as well as relative humidity.

Signs of inadequate humidity levels are buds falling off or not opening, leaves turning yellow, drooping and turning brown at the tips. In hot weather, mist plants twice a day when there is no direct sun.

WATERING

Giving your plants the correct amount of water is crucial to successful care. Isolating a plant in a pot means that its roots can't search deep down for water,

ABOVE LEFT *Mist the plant foliage once a day with a mister (with the exception of African violets), twice in hot weather.*

LEFT *One watering technique for indoor plants is to water from below, also a good way of rehydrating dry compost.*

as they would in the ground and that water also drains away less quickly.

Spring and summer are the growing seasons for most plants, when they need regular water to produce new growth. They rest in autumn and winter and need just enough water to keep the compost from drying out. Over-watering is the most common cause of death for plants. Except for bog-lovers, they should never be left with the pots standing in water (other than for a few minutes during the watering process).

Many plants dislike hard tap water, especially the lime-haters, such as gardenias. Ideally, use rainwater for these plants, but, if this is difficult, use cooled boiled water or filtered water. The latter is better because it contains no chemical or other soluble salts. If you use tap water, let it sit overnight so that the chlorine evaporates and the water comes to room temperature. When the surface of the compost feels dry, the plant probably needs water. In the dormant period, it's best to dig down a little way with your fingers – it may still be moist enough.

There are several techniques for watering. The first is to water from above using a small, long-spouted watering can, avoiding the leaves and directing the spout at the soil. To make sure the compost gets wet through, water until the saucer at the base is full, and leave to stand for a few minutes. If the water has just run down the sides of the pot, allow it to soak in thoroughly, and then empty the saucer. Alternatively, water from below, allowing the pot to sit in a tray of water until the surface of the compost feels damp. Discard any surplus. This is a good way to rehydrate compost that has become so dry that the water bounces off the top. If the compost has dried out, add a drop of washing-up liquid to the water to allow it to penetrate more easily.

Another technique is to plunge the pot into a bucket of water until the compost is moist, but not waterlogged; then allow the surplus water to drain away.

ABOVE *Liquid feeds offer a balanced mixture of nutrients designed to enhance the characteristics of each plant.*

FEEDING

Fresh compost has added nutrients, but over time these are used up, so potted plants need an occasional feed with a balanced fertilizer.

Liquid feeds are usually sold in concentrated form and need diluting. The feed should be applied when the plant is in growth or flowering. A foliar feed applied to the leaves works as a quick pick-me-up, but move the plants outside before spraying because the minerals in the feed can leave stains.

Other ways of feeding include sprinkling a few slow-release granules into the compost when planting up or pushing a feeding stick into it.

POTTING AND REPOTTING

Plants bought at nurseries and garden centres come in small plastic pots with the roots already trying to escape through the bottom. At some stage they will need to be potted on into a larger pot with fresh compost.

Check all new plants before bringing them indoors. Ease the plant out of its pot and see if there are signs of vine weevil. The plant may show no sign of disease until it flops in the pot and a colony of white grubs with brown heads are found to have attacked the roots.

Plants can be traumatized by being potted on, but will recover most easily if it is done in spring. Use a container that is one or two sizes larger. Cover drainage holes with a coffee filter or piece of fine mesh screen. Add a layer of fresh potting mix and tap down to remove air pockets. Position the plant about 2cm (^{3}⁄$_4$in) below the rim to allow for watering. Spoon potting mix around the sides of the rootball and pack it firmly around, pushing down with your thumbs to leave a firm surface.

POTTING COMPOSTS

There are two main types of compost: loam-based and soil-less. Sand or grit can be added to both these mixes to improve drainage.

Loam-based compost is made from sterilized loam with added peat-substitute (or peat) and sand, plus fertilizers in varying amounts; John Innes No.1 contains the least, No. 3 the most. Soil-less composts are traditionally based on peat, but to be kind to the environment use peat substitute versions.

Certain plants need specialist growing mediums. Some orchids and bromeliads, for example, are epiphytic and prefer a loose potting mix that allows air to circulate around them. Cacti and succulents also do better in a free-draining cactus potting mix.

PRUNING

Shaping is probably a better word than pruning to describe the needs of most houseplants, but some vigorous plants do need cutting back.

You can encourage some plants to bush out by pinching out the leading shoots, resulting in new growth down the stem. Begonias and ivies respond well to this type of pruning in spring and summer.

Picking off any flowers that have gone past their best, known as deadheading, encourages the plant to produce more. For example, indoor roses will last much longer if they are deadheaded regularly.

If a plant becomes too large, cut it back using a pair of secateurs (hand pruners). The weeping fig (*Ficus benjamina*) responds well to cutting back quite severely. This is best done in late winter or early spring. Stop climbing plants, such as *Jasminum polyanthum*, becoming straggly by cutting back after flowering and tying in wayward shoots to a framework of canes or wires.

ABOVE *Clean plant leaves every couple of weeks. Wash them with water or use a plant polish and buff with a soft cloth.*

ABOVE *Deadheading encourages the plant to produce more flower buds, and keeps the plant looking good.*

PROPAGATING SEMI-SUCCULENTS

Plants are programmed to propagate themselves. As well as producing seeds, many plants have evolved so that a leaf or piece of stem that is accidentally broken off will root and form a new plant if it lands in a favourable spot. Gardeners take advantage of this phenomenon by taking cuttings, using a variety of techniques to give the plants ideal conditions for taking root. The best times are in spring and summer when there is plenty of light and warmth. The larger, fleshier leaves of some succulents, such as echeverias, crassulas and begonias, can be used to form new plants. There are various methods – this technique shows how to propagate from an individual begonia leaf using perlite.

1 *Select a young healthy leaf. Cut it at the plant base and then cut leaving a short stem.*

2 *Using a scalpel, make a 1cm (¹⁄₂in) incision straight across each of the strongest veins.*

3 *Using thin wire bent into a 'U' shape, pin down the leaf on a tray of damp cutting compost.*

4 *Each vein should produce roots. When plantlets develop, separate them and pot them on.*

CARING FOR AFRICAN VIOLETS

African violets (*Saintpaulia* spp.) have a reputation for being tricky to keep healthy. This is not necessarily true, but they do like plenty of light, and they dislike draughts and changes in temperature. If you work around these preferences they should respond well. A reassuring tip is that African violets seem to do best when their roots are tightly confined.

1 *Find a location for your African violet that has bright but not direct sunlight. Make sure the pot is sitting in a tray that can be used for watering.*

2 *Fill the tray with pebbles. Add a moderate amount of water to the tray. The surface soil must dry out between watering. Do not get water on the leaves.*

3 *Each week turn the plant on a half rotation so that all sides get equal light.*

4 *Apply African violet fertilizer every 2–3 weeks to maintain healthy foliage and encourage repeat flowering.*

Design focus: plants and quality of light

All plants need adequate light to thrive. Fortunately, we have choices – some plants like a low light (north-facing windows in the Northern Hemisphere or south-facing windows in the Southern Hemisphere); some need as much light as they can get (south-facing windows in the Northern Hemisphere or north-facing in the Southern Hemisphere). Some plants prefer a more gentle, indirect light, suitable for an east or west-facing window. Here are some of plants that thrive in these light conditions.

PLANTS THAT SUIT A FULL WARM LIGHT

A warm and sunny exposure suits succulents, cacti and bromeliads. The strength of the sun will depend on the latitude, time of year and the orientation of the room.

PLANTS THAT SUIT A COLD, LOW LIGHT

These plants are undemanding in that they do not want to be over-heated, over-watered or overfed. Give them regular mistings of water to create humidity in the air.

PLANTS THAT SUIT A PARTIAL LIGHT

Turn these plants by a third of a rotation every week or two so they grow evenly.

FULL-SUN PLANTS

1 Herbs (basil, oregano, parsley, rosemary)
2 Jade plant (*Crassula arborescens*)
3 Agave (*Agave americana*)
4 Medicine plant (*Aloe vera*)
5 Chives (*Allium schoenoprasum*)
6 Bromeliad (*Bromeliad* spp.)
7 Sage (*Salvia officinalis*)

PARTIAL-LIGHT PLANTS

8 Orchid (various species)
9 Spider plant (*Chlorophytum comosum*)
10 and 11 Begonia (*Begonia* spp.) (see picture above)
12 Prayer plant (*Maranta leucoreura*)
13 Swedish ivy (*Plectranthus australis*)
14 Grape ivy (*Cissus rhombifolia*)
15 African violets (*Saintpaulia* spp.)
16 Japanese aralia (*Fatsia japonica*)

LOW-LIGHT PLANTS

17 Philodendron (*Philodendron*)
18 Cast iron plant (*Aspidistra elatior*)
19 Peace lily (*Spathiphyllum*)
20 Chinese evergreen (*Aglaonema commutatum*)
21 Snake plant/mother in law's tongue (*Sansevieria trifasciata*)

PLANT DIRECTORY

Compiling a plant directory such as this is a bit like being a child in a candy store – there are just so many choices! Because of space limitations not all the wonderful and appropriate plants, trees, shrubs and edibles can be included. But by visiting local nurseries, reading garden magazines and books, joining a garden group, and, if you're so inclined, surfing the internet, you can discover many more interesting plants that will keep your mind and hands busy gardening.

The selections shown here are designed both for ease of maintenance and breadth of appeal. The directory is also meant to be easy to read and to provide necessary information to make good plant choices. This listing is intended to help, encourage and motivate experienced gardeners who may need some additional guidance as they age, maybe moving to a new residence with an unfamiliar garden or learning to live with a physical limitation that affects what is possible for them to do as gardeners. It is also for seniors who are new to gardening – it is never too late to begin learning!

OPPOSITE *Fill your garden space with annuals and perennials, flowers that will keep you company throughout the season.*

ABOVE *Keep the names of your plants documented by using plant labels, useful if you want to check care requirements.*

ABOVE *A selection of herbs, including fennel, sage, hyssop and oregano, grows in a walled garden bed.*

ABOVE *Smaller sized dahlias will bloom earlier and rebloom more quickly, rewarding you with more flowers.*

THE CLASSIFICATION AND NAMING OF PLANTS

The 18th-century botanist Carl Linnaeus devised a system for classifying all living things. He gave plants two Latinized names to show their relationship to all other living things. A plant genus, the first of the two, is a group of plants containing similar species. A species, the second of the two, refers to a group of individuals capable of breeding with each other.

ABOVE *Thunbergia alata, a perky and petite annual vine, loves the sun and provides red, pink, orange and bright yellow blooms.*

SCIENTIFIC NAMES

A plant's botanical, scientific or Latin name, though often derived from Latin, frequently contains Greek and other languages. Some genera contain species that may include annuals, perennials, shrubs and trees, and these may look different from one another even though they are related. Others might contain just one species or a group of species that bear obvious similarities.

A species is defined as consisting of individuals that are alike and tend naturally to breed with each other. Despite this definition, botanists and taxonomists (the experts who classify living things) often disagree about the basis on which a plant has been named. As the science continues to be refined, more old inaccuracies are coming to the fore. Having old names in common usage creates confusion, and plant names often include the old name or synonym (syn. for short) after the correct name. Understandably, gardeners often become frustrated with the seemingly constant name changing, but it is useful to keep abreast of them. Update your library with a good, recently published pocket reference book and take it with you when you shop for plants.

VARIATIONS ON A THEME

In the average garden, you may grow a single species that is represented by small but pleasing differences such as variegated leaves, differently coloured or double flowers. The terms for these variations are subspecies (subsp.), variety (var.), form (f.) – similar to variety and often used interchangeably – and cultivar (cv.). A cultivar is a variation that has been selected or artificially bred and is maintained by cultivation. Cultivars are given names in single quotation marks. So, a cultivar of the Japanese apricot is *Prunus mume* 'Beni Chidori'.

HYBRIDS AND GROUPS

When plant species breed with each other, the result is a hybrid. While rare in the wild, crossing is common among plant breeders and is done to produce plants with desirable qualities such as larger or double blooms, longer flowering time or greater frost resistance. A multiplication sign (x) is used to indicate a hybrid and the name often gives a clear idea of its origins.

A group is a cluster of plants with variations that are so similar they cannot be separated. Their names do not have quotation marks (for example, Andersoniana Group).

BELOW *A collection of smaller containers kept on a garden table can be maintained easily, without bending or physical strain.*

HOW TO USE
THE DIRECTORY

The first category in the directory, on container plants, is designed for those with limited energy and space. The following four categories give examples of plants and then trees that thrive in sun or shade. The next three categories show easy-to-grow edible crops – vegetables, fruit and herbs. Finally, a category on indoor plants suits those with no garden or who prefer to garden inside. A typical entry is shown below, with explanations of the component elements.

ABOVE Salvia farinacea *'Victoria Blue'* (mealy sage) has deep blue flowers and combines well with other perennials.

Genus and species name

The first part of this internationally accepted botanical name, the genus, denotes a group of related plant species (or sometimes a single species); the second part defines a specific species. It may be further defined by a subspecies, hybrid, variant or cultivar name. Sometimes a synonym (syn.) is also given.

Family name

This shows the larger grouping to which the plant belongs. Knowing the plant's family name will sometimes indicate which plants are susceptible to the same diseases.

Cultivation

These notes give a brief recipe as to the best conditions in which to grow the plant, such as the level of sun or shade that the plant either requires or tolerates, with advice on the best type of soil in which it should be grown.

Notes

This section provides relevant and interesting information about the sensory aspects of a plant, its value for crafts or other uses, or a particular cultivar or variety that should be considered. Other information may include details of hybrids (indicated by an 'x' in the name) and recommended varieties and cultivars (featuring names in single quotations) that are available.

Caption

A full or shortened botanical name is given with each photograph.

Photograph

A large number of entries feature a full-colour photograph, which makes identification easier.

- *Foeniculum vulgare*
FENNEL
- **FAMILY Apiaceae**
This handsome perennial will add grace, height and texture. With bright green, finely fern-like leaves and aromatic yellow flowers, it's best planted in the back of the herb or perennial flower garden as it will grow to 90–120cm (3–4ft).
- **CULTIVATION** The plants require full sunlight and well-drained, deep, moderately fertile soil. Best planted in a more spacious garden where architectural structure may be needed.
HARDINESS Fully hardy/Z5
- **NOTES** Fennel attracts bees, butterflies and birds. All parts of the plant are edible – the leaves, stems, seeds and roots. The plants release a chemical that inhibits the growth of some other plants, so do not plant very close to beans, tomatoes or cabbage family plants.
MAINTENANCE Easy. It seeds freely so new seedlings will require weeding to control their spread.

- BELOW Foeniculum vulgare

Common name

This is the popular, non-scientific name. It may apply to the whole or part of the plant genus. There are sometimes a variety of common names.

Genus description

Describes what the plant looks like at different times of year and its popularity. Includes a description of the leaves and, when applicable, the flowers and fruits. The expected height and sometimes spread of a genus or individual plant are often given, although growth rates vary depending on location. Metric always precede imperial measurements. The dimensions of bulbs, annuals and perennials tend to be more consistent than those of shrubs, long-lived climbers and trees.

Hardiness

Each plant's hardiness and zone are given, with the exception of vegetables and indoor plants. The categories are fully hardy, frost hardy, half hardy and frost tender for the UK and Europe, and USDA zones are given for the USA. The hardiness zones give a general indication of the average annual minimum temperature for a particular geographical area. The small number indicates the northernmost zone it can survive in and the higher number the southernmost zone that the plant will tolerate. In most cases, only one zone is given. (*See also* page 255 for details of hardiness definitions, zone entries and a zone map.)

Maintenance

Indicates whether low or moderate care is needed (intensive-care options are not given). Suggestions are often included, and additional information on plant care.

CONTAINER PLANTS

Many elders feel that their gardening days are over when they leave the family home with its in-ground beds, trees and a lawn to tend. However, a smaller garden filled with container plants has options on a different scale, including small, decorative herb-filled pots on a windowsill, large wooden tubs of blueberry bushes and mixed displays of bedding plants outside your back door that bring scintillating colours and perfume to your garden. Even if you no longer have a garden at all, you can grow a surprising range of plants in large window boxes and hanging baskets.

ABOVE *A selection of annuals in a terracotta pot, including* Cordyline australis *in the centre.*

Calibrachoa x *hybrida*
MINI PETUNIA, MILLION BELLS SERIES
FAMILY Solanaceae

This tender perennial produces flowers that look like small petunias. Perfect for containers, they are compact, mounded plants growing 7.5–23cm (3–9in) tall on mostly trailing stems. Prolific bloomers, they produce hundreds of 2.5cm (1in) width flowers from spring through to the first frost. Flower colours include shades of violet, blue, pink, red, magenta, yellow, bronze and white.

BELOW Calibrachoa *'Sunbelfire', Million Bells Series.*

CULTIVATION Grow in light, well-drained compost in full sun. Mini petunias can tolerate very light shade, but flowering will decrease as the shade increases. It dislikes very wet soil, and tolerates drought – in fact it's best to let it dry out between waterings to guard against fungal disease. Set plants out after the last frost.
HARDINESS Frost hardy/Z9–11
NOTES Choose from many hybrids that provide a rainbow of colours as you design your containers and hanging baskets. *Calibrachoa* is a hummingbird attractor.
MAINTENANCE Easy. Self-cleaning, no deadheading necessary. It is susceptible to aphids, but they can be washed off with a jet of water.

Chamaecyparis obtusa 'Pygmaea'
HINOKI FALSE CYPRESS
FAMILY Cupressaceae

This important landscape conifer provides a garden with a graceful slender upright tree with attractive orange-brown stems and nodding branch tips. It reaches a height of only 1.5m (5ft), although it grows much larger in its native Japan. The twisted, deep-green branchlets are held on tiered branches, creating an open habit.
CULTIVATION Dwarf hinoki cypress thrives in well-drained, humus-rich soil in bright shade. If grown in full sun, give careful attention to watering during the summer. It is drought-tolerant in part shade. In hot climates provide protection from the hot afternoon sun.
HARDINESS Fully hardy/Z4–8
NOTES There are many other 'dwarf' cultivars, but most of them are too big for a container.
MAINTENANCE Easy. Protect from the wind. This small tree can be shaped to accommodate tight quarters.

Cordyline australis 'Charlie Boy'
CORDYLINE
FAMILY Agavaceae

Often grown indoors, cordyline is finding a prominent place in stunning annual container gardens, as well as in borders. Providing height, colour and texture with spiky upright leaves, it adds contrast to the bushy and cascading colourful annuals that it shares space with. 'Charlie Boy' has variegated leaves with a burgundy central stripe and bright pink margins and reaches a height of 2m (7ft).
CULTIVATION Plant in a sunny spot in well-drained compost in a container that can be moved. Initial shelter will be needed as it gets established.
HARDINESS Half hardy/Z10
NOTES Suitable for growing indoors.
MAINTENANCE Easy. Dislikes waterlogged soil and temperatures below 8°C (17°F). Move to a sheltered area or wrap in fleece or hessian (burlap) if temperatures drop.

Imperata cylindrica rubra 'Red Baron'
JAPANESE BLOOD GRASS
FAMILY **Poaceae**

This perennial, non-invasive, slow-spreading grass is a striking accent in a container because of its spectacular green, red-tipped foliage. It forms an upright clump about 50cm (20in) tall and wide. As the seasons age into the autumn the blades become redder and finally turn to a dark red maroon. It is a wonderful complement to blue and purple flowers or lovely just as a mass planting in a large container.

BELOW Ipomoea batatas *'Margarita'*.

CULTIVATION This plant loves full sun and prefers being in a well-drained container. In hotter climates it will appreciate light shade. While it is fairly drought-tolerant, don't allow it to dry out during prolonged dry spells, which will cause the tips to brown.

HARDINESS Half hardy/Z5–9

NOTES If possible, position the container of 'Red Baron' blood grass where the morning or late afternoon sun can backlight the leaves, giving off a dramatic red colour glow.

MAINTENANCE Easy. After the blades turn to a straw colour in the winter, cut the plant to the ground.

ABOVE I. cylindrica rubra *'Red Baron'*.

Ipomoea batatas 'Margarita'
SWEET POTATO VINE
FAMILY **Convolvulaceae**

This 'potato' is grown for its fan-shaped leaves that are a bright chartreuse colour. It will trail attractively over the edge of a container. 'Margarita' accents plants with darker foliage. It reaches a height of 10–25cm (4–10in).

CULTIVATION These plants grow best in a sunny location with relatively warm temperatures. Plant in a good, light, well-drained soil. Once established, the sweet potato vine is not particularly thirsty, since the underground tuber retains enough water to get through some dry spells.

HARDINESS Half hardy to frost tender/Z9–11

NOTES 'Blackie' is a variety with dark purple, nearly black foliage and 'Tricolour' has pale green, white and pink margined leaves. Mix these in a container for a lovely show.

MAINTENANCE Easy. Prune often if needed to control for size and to create more branching. It can be kept over winter if the container is protected from frost.

Lobelia erinus
LOBELIA
FAMILY Campanulaceae

Lobelia is a perennial usually grown as an annual for summer bedding and containers. There are trailing varieties, with billowing masses of blossoms, and more compact bedding which seldom exceeds 15cm (6in) in height. The 1–2cm (½–¾in) wide flowers that grow along each stem come in blue, white and carmine.

CULTIVATION Lobelia does best in full sun and in moist, rich soil where summers are cool. It will grow well in hot areas if given partial shade and ample water. Plant out after all danger of frost is past, spacing the plants 10–15cm (4–6in) apart if in the ground.

HARDINESS Half hardy/Z10–11

NOTES A perfect plant for window boxes, hanging baskets, planters, groundcover or border edgings, as it gives a softness of colour and texture. Look for the colour varieties – especially beautiful are the blue palates of 'Cambridge Blue' or the lavender shades of 'Riviera' – and match them with yellows and oranges to create a stunning feast of colour.

MAINTENANCE Easy. Lobelia has virtually no disease or pest problems. Shear the flower spikes after blooming to promote further growth.

Lobularia maritima
SWEET ALYSSUM
FAMILY Brassicaceae

Also known as Carpet of Snow, this fragrant favourite – an annual or short-lived perennial – produces masses of crisp white blooms. Perfect for window boxes and other containers, it grows only 10cm (4in) tall, so works well hugging the outer edges of pots. Ideal for ground cover, too, as its growth is wide spreading and it flowers all summer.

CULTIVATION Grow in full sun to partial shade. Does well in well-drained, light soil.

HARDINESS Fully hardy/5–9

NOTES This sturdy plant adorns coastal gardens as it tolerates wind and salt spray. It attracts butterflies and bees. Alice Series and Easter Bonnet Series cultivars are compact and have flower in white, rose-pink and purple-pink.

BELOW Lobelia erinus.

ABOVE Lobularia maritima.

MAINTENANCE Easy. After first flowering, cut back to enjoy another wave of blooms.

Laurus nobilis
SWEET BAY
FAMILY Lauraceae

This small, evergreen tree is a slow grower. Its height range is 3.6–12m (12–40ft). Its attractive 7.5cm (3in) leathery leaves are long, deep-green, pointed and deliciously fragrant. The small yellow flowers come in umbel clusters that appear over two months in the early summer.

CULTIVATION Likes well-drained, sandy soil with some moisture. Grow in a sunny spot in pots with good drainage. Allow to dry slightly between waterings.

HARDINESS Frost hardy/Z8–10

NOTES The dried leaves are a wonderful addition to soups and stews.

MAINTENANCE Easy. Ensure you can move the container to shelter if temperatures drop below 2°C (28°F).

Lysimachia nummularia 'Aurea'
CREEPING JENNY, MONEYWORT
FAMILY Primulaceae

This vigorous yellow-lime-green leafy creeper is best limited to containers since it has the ability to take over beds

ABOVE *Lysimachia nummularia* 'Aurea'.

and pathways. Managing it in containers will add fabulous colour contrasts and textures to your arrangement. Prolific, cup-shaped, bright yellow flowers (with a diameter of less than 2.5cm/1in) appear in early summer.

CULTIVATION Grow in good potting soil in full sun in a cool climate, or in shade in a warm climate. The yellow hue shows in full sun, while foliage is lime green in shade. Prefers moist soils. Intolerant of dry soils.

HARDINESS Fully hardy/Z4–8

NOTES This plant is mainly grown for its foliage and the way it spills over containers and hanging baskets.

MAINTENANCE Easy.

Pelargonium x *hortorum* 'Mrs. Pollock'
GERANIUM
FAMILY Geraniaceae

This annual, while common in name, offers bold-textured clusters of floral heads from white, pink, red, salmon, orange and violet. Add to this the lush, medium to dark green foliage that has bronze zonal bands and you have an uncommon, reliable and long-blooming container plant.

CULTIVATION Grow these in full sun to partial sun in moist, well-drained soil.

RIGHT *Petunia* x hybrida *Surfinia Series*

A light mulch will cool the roots. They perform well in combination warm, dry days and cool evenings and bloom best when the roots are a little pot bound. Water regularly.

HARDINESS Frost tender/Z9–10

NOTES Another geranium variety includes the 'Martha Washington', with heart-shaped leaves with crinkled edges and showy flowers. This is widely recognized as a first-class potted plant.

MAINTENANCE Easy. Deadhead the spent flowers to encourage continuous bloom. In cold climates they can be brought indoors as a houseplant.

Petunia x *hybrida*
PETUNIA
FAMILY Solanaceae

A popular annual that easily adds a wide range of bloom colour to baskets and containers. Thick and sticky broad green leaves accent the funnel-shaped or heavily ruffled blooms. Colours include deep or pale pink, yellow, red, purple and white. Of the many cultivars, the Surfinia Series are especially suitable for hanging baskets, as they can trail down for as much as 90cm (3ft), with large, showy flowers and bushy growth.

CULTIVATION Plant in full sun using a light, well-drained compost. Like regular

ABOVE *P. x* hortorum '*Mrs Pollock*'.

water and monthly feeding with a complete fertilizer. Heavy rains spoil blooms so if possible, move petunia containers to a sheltered area.

HARDINESS Half hardy/Z10–11

NOTES For small containers or the edging of boxes and planters, choose rosy 'Bright Eyes' with a white throat, rose-starred white 'Twinkle's, light 'Silvery Blue' and white 'Igloo'. The Surfinia Series cultivars have some resistance to rain damage.

MAINTENANCE Easy. Pinch tips to encourage branching, and keep bushy and compact. Remove faded blooms twice a week to improve appearance and encourage repeat flowering.

Salvia farinacea 'Victoria Blue'
SALVIA
FAMILY Lamiaceae

Saliva, or flowering sage, has graced gardens for many years. Over 900 species are available worldwide, so the choice of the attractive 'Victoria Blue' saves you researching all the options. This perennial grows 45–60cm (18–24in) tall, and has intense violet-blue flowers that are densely packed along the stalk. Salvia blooms all summer long. The grey-green foliage is also attractive.

CULTIVATION Salvias like a light, well-drained compost and full sun. In very hot climates, light shade is fine. Give moderate amounts of water to young plants but once established this salvia is able to thrive with low moisture.

HARDINESS Half hardy/Z8–10

NOTES This plant attracts bees, butterflies and other desirable insects and discourages less desirable ones. It can be used in cut-flower arrangements or dried for a longer-lasting display.

MAINTENANCE Easy. Deadheading spent flowers will keep the plant blooming and looking good.

Tagetes erecta
AFRICAN MARIGOLD
FAMILY Compositae

Common African marigold varieties are strong in the orange and yellow colour range, but they also include lovely maroon, red and creamy white shades. Plant heights can vary from 15–90cm (6in–3ft) with flowers from tiny, 1cm (½in) singles to huge, 10–13cm (4–5in) doubles. Marigold leaves are a rich dark green and are finely cut and fernlike.

CULTIVATION Marigold plants are annuals, and are easy to grow from seed. They prefer full to partial sun as well as rich well-drained soil that is not wet. They are very tolerant of average to slightly poor soils and

although they prefer regular watering, they will survive dry periods.

HARDINESS Half hardy/Z8–10

NOTES The related but generally more compact French marigolds (*Tagetes patula*) are often grown as a companion plant, as their strong aroma deters many insect pests. They like similar conditions to their cousins, but the flowers are less susceptible to rain damage than the larger, more frilly African ones. French marigolds offer a much broader colour range, including rich reds, mahogany and bi-colours. Most marigolds are hybrids, so if you save seed from last year's plants, they may not be the same as the originals.

MAINTENANCE Easy. Add a general-purpose fertilizer once a month. Slugs can do major damage, so use an organic slug deterrent or barrier to keep them away.

Tropaeolum majus
NASTURTIUM
FAMILY Tropaeolaceae

A reliable old garden favourite, the trailing nasturtium is an annual that will adorn a container with bright green round leaves surrounded by funnel-shaped flowers in red, orange, maroon and yellow-cream.

ABOVE Tagetes erecta *Jubilee Series.*

CULTIVATION They do best in full sun, in a poor, well-drained compost. Over-fertilizing will promote more leafy growth at the expense of flowers.

HARDINESS Fully hardy to frost tender/Z10–11

NOTES Use as a cut flower or use the young leaves and flowers in salads. 'Peach Melba' is a good choice for containers.

MAINTENANCE Easy. Pick the flowers to encourage further flowering. Aphids like these, but a stream of water from the hose can wash them away easily.

BELOW Tropaeolum majus.

FLOWERS AND PLANTS THAT PREFER FULL SUN

In regions that have hot dry summers or gardens with areas that are sizzling sun traps, you will need a set of plants that will thrive as the temperature climbs and will not create unreasonable demands for watering. Many plants like plenty of light, but a large proportion are content either in full sun or partial shade. Here you will find some that will only thrive well in full sun, and others that are happy with one or the other, or a mixture. Another approach is to concentrate on sun-loving plants native to your region – these will have the best chance of success.

ABOVE Coreopsis verticillata, *the thread-leaf coreopsis, has delicate yellow flowers in loose, open clusters on thin, wiry stems.*

LEFT Allium *x* hollandicum.

Achillea millefolium
YARROW
FAMILY **Asteraceae**

Yarrow produces flattened clusters of red, pink or white flowers on slender stems clad in feathery green foliage.

Plants will typically reach a height of around 60cm (2ft).

CULTIVATION Grow in full sun and well-drained soil. Yarrow is drought-tolerant once it is established. Dividing every other year promotes air circulation, thereby cutting down on problems with powdery mildew.

HARDINESS Fully hardy/Z3–8

NOTES These summer flowers are great for fresh or dried arrangements. Yarrow may suffer from aphids, but also attracts many other insects including ladybirds and parasitic wasps, both of which prey on aphids.

MAINTENANCE Moderate. Yarrow plants should be staked since they do flop down on the ground after high winds. Trimming the plants back after flowering will encourage new blooms.

Allium
ALLIUM
FAMILY **Liliaceae**

Round heads of alliums floating above mounds of foliage are a magical sight. Leave the seedheads as long as you can as they create a good structure for the planting. Provides nectar for bees and other insects. Height varies with variety.

CULTIVATION Alliums like well-drained soil in a sunny location. Plant bulbs 15cm (6in) deep.

HARDINESS Fully hardy/Z6–10

NOTES 'Firmament' and 'Purple Sensation' are robust and long-lasting. For maximum impact, plant bulbs of *A. giganteum* throughout herbaceous or mixed borders.

MAINTENANCE Easy.

Aquilegia
COLUMBINE
FAMILY Ranunculaceae

Columbines are delicately poised garden perennials that grow 38–50cm (15–20in). They produce large, showy blooms of single and bicolour patterns on airy plants with blue-green foliage. The blooms appear from late spring to early summer. Colours include shades of yellow, white, pink, blue, purple and combinations. Add this plant to any garden for years of dependable flowers.

CULTIVATION These grow well in full or partial shade and in average soils that drain well. These plants tolerate dry soil conditions. Once your columbines are established, they will grow well and bloom until the first frost.

HARDINESS Fully to frost hardy/Z4–9

NOTES Columbine is a favourite of both hummingbirds and bees because the flowers contain lots of nectar. A versatile plant, it does well in flowerbeds, containers, as an edging plant and especially in rock gardens.

MAINTENANCE Easy. They self-seed but are not invasive. They don't require mulching or protection in the winter. In mid-season if they look shabby, prune to the ground and you may get a late autumn bloom.

BELOW Aster novi-belgii.

ABOVE Aquilegia canadensis.

Aster novi-belgii
MICHAELMAS DAISY
FAMILY Asteraceae

This aster blooms just as the other summer flowers fade. Its bright and prolific plants produce large clusters of delicate daisy-like flowers in white, purple, lavender, pink or red, from late summer to late autumn. Some grow less than 30cm (1ft) tall, while others are 60cm (2ft) tall or more.

CULTIVATION Asters are happiest when planted in moist well-drained soil but they adapt to most soil types. They love to be in full sun, but will tolerate light shading.

HARDINESS Fully hardy/Z4–8

NOTES Asters are one of the largest families of flowering plants, so enjoy finding the best variety for your garden space. Michaelmas daisies are hybrids of *A. novi-belgii* and *A. novae-angliae*. They are called Michaelmas daisies because they bloom around Michaelmas, or St Michael's Day (29 September).

MAINTENANCE Moderate. Pinch back the tops by 15–20cm (6–8in) around midsummer in order to create a bushier plant and to prolong the autumn bloom. Divide the plant every two to three years by simply digging out half to two-thirds of the plants and leave the remainder in place. Share the divisions with a neighbour!

Briza maxima
QUAKING GRASS
FAMILY Poaceae

This ornamental plant is a graceful and delicate grass that gives elegance to a garden bed or dried flower arrangements. It grows to 30–60cm (1–2ft) high with thin 15cm (6in) leaves. Bunches of straw-coloured nodding seed heads that resemble rattlesnake rattles dangle from the thin stems.

CULTIVATION Quaking grass likes full sun and will be happy in any well-drained soil with minimal water needs.

HARDINESS Fully hardy/Z5–9

NOTES Gather when the heads have changed colour but before they start to break up, and hang them in bunches, heads down, in a cool, dry airy place. Spray with silver and gold to add sparkle to winter arrangements.

MAINTENANCE Easy. May self-seed but new seedlings are easy to control.

Clematis 'Niobe'
CLEMATIS
FAMILY **Ranunculaceae**

This climbing vine is perfect for small spaces and accessible trellises and grows to a height of 2–3m (7–10ft). The lovely velvety, burgundy, single flowers are 10–15cm (4–6in) in diameter with bright yellow anthers at their centres. These stunning blooms will grace your garden all summer, and the fluffy, spiral-shaped seed heads will then stay on for months.

CULTIVATION This plant is easily grown in fertile, medium-moisture, well-drained soil in full sun to part shade. It should be planted 5–7.5cm (2–3in) deeper than it was in the pot, so that if it is attacked by clematis wilt, it will have a good chance of recovery. Clematis in general like their 'feet in the shade and heads in the sun'. Planting a small evergreen bush or dense ground cover around the base will give the roots the shade and coolness they need. Always add thick mulch around the plant in late winter for a good spring growth spurt.

BELOW Clematis *'Niobe'*.

HARDINESS Frost hardy/Z4–9

NOTES There are many different types of clematis, and by growing several you can have flowers from early spring to late autumn. The vigorous *C. montana* will cover a large wall or fence with pale pink or white flowers in spring. Clematis are also lovely when grown through a tree or a large rambler rose – make sure you match the size of the host plant to the potential size of the clematis.

MAINTENANCE Moderate. Feed rose food weekly just before flowering. Because its bloom is mostly from the current year's stems, cut back stems hard in late winter or early spring before new growth appears. (Note that the different types of clematis require different pruning regimes.)

Coreopsis verticillata 'Moonbeam'
MOONBEAM COREOPSIS, TICKSEED
FAMILY **Asteraceae**

A graceful perennial that grows erect stems 45–61cm (1½–2ft) high and about 45cm (1½ft) wide. Its airy foliage forms whorls of finely divided narrow leaves, culminating with pale yellow daisy-like blossoms on the tips of the stems. The plant dances in the breeze.

CULTIVATION Make sure you have a very sunny spot in well-drained soil for the 'Moonbeam', which likes a dry to medium moisture. Hardy and tough, it can thrive in poor, sandy or rocky soils with good drainage. Tolerant of heat, humidity and drought.

HARDINESS Fully hardy/Z6

NOTES 'Moonbeam' is a sterile cultivar, so does not reseed but does spread by rhizomes. A big attraction to bees and butterflies, it also brings birds (especially finches) if you leave the seed heads on.

MAINTENANCE: Easy. For a second bloom, wait until the first flush of flowers wane and then shear the entire plant back. Recovery will be quick, although prompt deadheading of flower stalks can be tedious for a large planting.

ABOVE Crocosmia *'Lucifer'*.

Crocosmia 'Lucifer'
MONTBRETIA
FAMILY **Iridaceae**

This dramatic perennial plant features tubular, nodding, scarlet flowers that bloom on the upper portions of stiffly arching stems. Narrow, sword-shaped leaves rise above a basal clump and salute the other flowers and shimmy in the breeze. A tall grower, it can reach 90cm–1.2m (3–4ft).

CULTIVATION Grown from corms, montbretia likes average to medium moisture, well-drained soil in full sun to part shade. It prefers moist soils if grown in full sun but it is tolerant of summer heat and humidity.

HARDINESS Half hardy/Z5–9

NOTES This old-time favourite is a good cut flower and an eye-catching garden specimen. Hummingbirds are attracted to the colour and the trumpet-shaped flowers. Some other attractive varieties (not 'Lucifer') can be invasive, so plant the corms in a large, bottomless pot or bucket buried in the ground. This way you have that wonderful blast of colour but the plants are controlled.

MAINTENANCE Easy. Watch for spider mites and thrips. In colder regions, the corms can be stored like gladioli, wintered in pots, or mulched heavily outdoors.

Dahlia
DAHLIA
FAMILY Asteraceae

A great plant for adding bold splashes of colour to the garden, dahlias will flower prolifically from midsummer to the first frosts, making them especially welcome when many other plants are past their best. The flowerheads – in many forms from daisy-like to pom-pom-like – can be as small as 5cm (2in) or up to 30cm (1ft) in diameter and in all colours apart from blue. Heights range from 30cm (1ft) to 1.8–2.5m (6–8ft).

CULTIVATION Dahlias need soil warmth to be 14.5–15.5°C (58–60°F). Very wet soil may cause the tubers to rot, so wait for a drying trend when the soil is moist but not soggy. Dig and prepare the planting hole depending on growth size of the tuber. Mix a spadeful of compost, a handful of bonemeal, and a little lime into the soil. For taller varieties, put in a stake when planting (doing it later could damage the tuber).

HARDINESS Half hardy/Z7–10

NOTES 'Alva's Doris' is a warm season, tender perennial with small,

BELOW Echinacea purpurea.

ABOVE Dahlia *'Kay Helen'*.

doubled, semi-cactus flowers in a brilliant red; 'Mary Richards' is a small-flowered dahlia with white flowers and a lavender-pink sheen; 'Fascination' has pinkish-purple flowers and dark bronze foliage; 'Hillcreat Ultra' is a decorative dahlia with small flowers with pink outer petals and lemon-yellow inner petals.

MAINTENANCE Moderate. Deadhead regularly to encourage long flowering. When autumn frosts begin, cut them down to 15cm (6in), dig up the tubers and store, frost-free, in dry sand or peat substitute over winter.

Echinacea purpurea
CONEFLOWER
FAMILY Asteraceae

This perennial flowering plant grows smooth, 60cm–1.5m (2–5ft) stems that support flowers of domed, purplish-brown, hard spiny centres and drooping lavender rays. Bristly oblong leaves grow smaller near the top of the stem. Blooming begins in late spring or early summer. In the autumn, leave the faded flowers in place and watch how the spiky seed heads feed the finches.

CULTIVATION Prefers a deep rich loam and a sunny position. Coneflowers thrive in either dry or moist soil and can tolerate drought once they are established.

HARDINESS Fully hardy/Z4–9

NOTES Some varieties of *Echinacea* are used for medicinal purposes, mainly to boost the immune system, but *E. purpurea* is not one that is used as a herbal remedy. It should only be used as an ornamental perennial.

MAINTENANCE Easy. A robust and sturdy plant that seldom needs staking, and gives a garden several seasons of interest.

Eupatorium purpureum
JOE-PYE WEED
FAMILY **Asteraceae**

Conveniently, Joe-Pye blooms later in the summer when the garden is in need of a boost. Tall sturdy stalks rise like a fountain from a multi-stemmed clump, and then present glorious clusters of rosy pink to light purple flowers. Stems in bloom reach 2.2m (7ft) tall.

CULTIVATION Grow in full sun to partial shade in a moist, rich soil. In the heat, they need regular watering. Plants are slow to emerge in spring, so place markers by the clumps.

HARDINESS Fully hardy/Z4–9

NOTES The flowers attract butterflies as well as a great many other garden visitors. The added bonus of Joe-Pye weed is the subtle vanilla scent of the leaves. Consider using the variety 'Atropurpureum', which has deep purple stems, and the white-flowered 'Album' variety.

MAINTENANCE Moderate. For shorter plants and more blooms, cut stems back by half in early summer.

Hemerocallis 'Stella de Oro'
DAYLILY
FAMILY **Liliaceae**

One of the finest dwarf daylilies with its repeating masses of bright, golden-yellow, trumpet-shaped, fragrant flowers in early summer. They reach 30cm (1ft) tall and wide. You can't go wrong if you have several daylilies in your garden beds.

CULTIVATION It prefers full sun and moist, fertile, well-drained soil.

HARDINESS Fully hardy/Z4–9

NOTES An award-winning hybrid, this dwarf variety works as a ground cover, in rock gardens or as an edging plant. Another good variety is *H.* 'Chorus Line', with abundant pink flowers through to late summer.

MAINTENANCE Easy. Divide every 3–6 years when clumps become crowded.

ABOVE *Passiflora caerulea.*

Passiflora caerulea
'Constance Elliot'
BLUE PASSION FLOWER
FAMILY **Passifloraceae**

The flowers of this tendril climber are highly distinctive: ten outer petals surround a crown of central filaments, inside which are the prominent, theatrical stamens. The flowers are white with filaments banded blue, white and purple and are in bloom from mid- to late summer. Most passion flowers are hothouse plants, but *P. c.* is reliably hardy in a sheltered spot in cold areas. It can be evergreen, but if cut down by frosts will usually regenerate from ground level. Can reach a height and spread of 10m (30ft) or more, although this will be less in cooler climates.

CULTIVATION Can be grown in any well-drained soil in sun in a sheltered position. Protect in winter in cold areas. Provide support for tendrils.

HARDINESS Frost hardy/Z8–10

NOTES The creamy white flowers with red stigmas are followed by edible orange fruits.

MAINTENANCE Easy.

Penstemon x gloxinioides
GARDEN PENSTEMON
FAMILY **Scrophulariaceae**

Penstemons are versatile flowers and will grace a rock garden or enhance a perennial border. They have delicate narrow bell-shaped, lipped flowers in a colour range including periwinkle blue, plum, red, pink, white and rarely yellow – these bloom from mid-spring until midsummer. Compact and bushy, they have narrow lance-shaped green leaves, and come in varying heights, up to 1m (3ft).

CULTIVATION Plants like an open, sunny spot with good drainage so if your soil is heavy, add plenty of sand and grit. Roots are sensitive to disturbance and too much moisture, so do not mulch the base of the plant.

HARDINESS Fully to half hardy/Z6–10

NOTES The blossoms are magnets to hummingbirds and butterflies. They will do well in containers with a mixture of multi-purpose potting compost (soil mix) with added grit to aid drainage.

MAINTENANCE Easy. After flowers fade, cut back for repeat blooms.

BELOW *Penstemon x gloxinioides.*

Phlox paniculata
SUMMER PHLOX
FAMILY **Polemoniaceae**

A majestic herbaceous perennial, the elegant flowers start to bloom in mid-summer and are a good choice for providing late summer colour in the garden. The tall flower heads reach up to 1.2m (4ft) high, and produce tubular, scented, white, purple or pink flowers that are ideal for attracting butterflies and moths. Long, mid-green leaves are carried right up the stem; they are lance-shaped with toothed margins.

CULTIVATION Summer phlox will grow in almost any soil but prefers rich, moist but free-draining ground in full sun or semi-shade. Propagate by division in early spring, or basal cuttings can be taken in the spring.

HARDINESS Fully hardy/Z4

NOTES Often used in herbaceous beds, mixed borders or in a specialist butterfly border. The many cultivars include 'Blue Ice' (pale blue), 'Bright Eyes' (pale pink with red eyes), 'Eventide' (pale blue), 'Fujiyama' (pure white), 'Hampton Court' (lilac-blue) and 'Le Mahdi' (violet).

MAINTENANCE Easy.

BELOW Phlox paniculata.

ABOVE Rudbeckia fulgida *var.* sullivantii *'Goldsturm'.*

Rudbeckia fulgida var. *sullivantii* 'Goldsturm'
BLACK-EYED SUSAN
FAMILY **Asteraceae**

An old favourite in cottage gardens, this perennial flowers throughout summer and into the autumn. It grows up to 60cm (2ft) tall with wide, hairy, dark green, lance-shaped leaves. The 7.5cm (3in) yellow flowers with black central cones will brighten the character of any garden.

CULTIVATION This plant can tolerate clay soils and mild droughts, but will thrive in well-drained, moist soil. Does well with high heat and humidity as well as in freezing climates. Plant during the growing season, 45cm (18in) apart, and add mulch to retain moisture.

HARDINESS Fully hardy/Z4–9

NOTES A great cutting flower that reblooms later in the season with bouquets to harvest. Leave seed heads on in the autumn for the birds.

MAINTENANCE Easy. Divide every few years when the plants become crowded. 'Goldsturm' has few pest or disease problems.

Sedum 'Herbstfreude'
SEDUM
FAMILY **Crassulaceae**

This lovely perennial is a succulent with fleshy green leaves about 7.5cm (3in) long. On long, sturdy stems, clusters of pink blossoms show in late summer that age to coppery rust. Bees and butterflies love them. This variety dies completely back in winter. Grows to a height and width of 30–60cm (1–2ft).

CULTIVATION 'Herbstfreude' prefers average to dry, well-drained soil in full sun. Division seems to be the easiest method of propagation. Will tolerate drought.

HARDINESS Fully hardy/Z3–9

NOTES Sedums are native to many parts of the world and come in all sizes, shapes and colours. Some are cold hardy, others are more tender. *S. acre*, the stonecrop, is also hardy and will form a low, dense mat, smothered in yellow flowers for a long period.

MAINTENANCE Easy. Divide clumps every 2–3 years and share the beauty around the garden.

Stachys byzantina
LAMBS' EAR
FAMILY **Lamiaceae**

The texture and colour of this plant's foliage make it ideal for a perennial ground cover. The light purple flowers on tall spikes 30–45cm (12–18in) are not the showiest. It is the leaves' velvety texture and the silvery green colour that get the attention.

CULTIVATION Grow in full sun. This perennial flower thrives in poor soil that is well drained. Its drought-tolerance makes it perfect for rock gardens and a low-maintenance beds.

HARDINESS Fully hardy/Z4–9

NOTES If young children visit your garden this plant will be fun! Just seeing the foliage will spur them to reach out and touch the softness. The leaves press well. Lambs' ear plants are also deer-resistant. Honey bees and other beneficial insects love this plant.

MAINTENANCE Easy. Cut the flower spikes soon after they tend to flop. These plants will spread but removing clumps will keep them under control.

Thunbergia alata
BLACK-EYED SUSAN VINE
FAMILY **Acanthaceae**

This is a cheerful and fresh twining evergreen climber, bearing bright yellow or orange, open flowers, 3–4cm (1¼–1½in) across, with a dark, tubular centre. If grown as a perennial (kept warm over winter), it reaches 2.5m (8ft) high, as an annual 1.5–2m (5–7ft).

CULTIVATION Set plants out in a sunny location after the last frost and when the weather is warm. This vine needs regular water and rich, well-drained soil.

HARDINESS Half hardy/Z10–11

NOTES Does well in containers and in the ground. The latter will encourage it to really take off. Train on to strings or install low trellis if in a container.

MAINTENANCE Easy.

Viola x *wittrockiana* cultivars
PANSY
FAMILY **Violaceae**

A 'flower for all seasons', pansies are perennials usually grown as annuals, and some varieties will flower right through mild winters. Pansy blooms are single with five petals that are rounded in shape. The coarsely notched leaves are medium green, oval or heart-shaped. Grows to a height of 15–25cm (6–10in).

CULTIVATION Need rich, fertile soil, so add manure, leafmould or compost and turn it several times. They like sun in the morning and dappled shade in hot afternoons. Regular water is adequate.

HARDINESS Fully hardy/Z4–8

NOTES Another variety to try is *V. odorata*, the old-fashioned, very fragrant violet. It only reaches 20cm (8in) high, so you need to get close to get the full scent. Another is *V. alba*, the Parma Violet variety, less hardy than the others, but is intensely scented and does well in containers. Pansy blossoms are easy to press and beautiful to use on cards and bookmarks for craft projects.

MAINTENANCE Very easy. Just remember to take time to deadhead.

BELOW *Viola* x *wittrockiana*.

ABOVE Zinnia elegans.

Zinnia elegans
ZINNIA
FAMILY **Asteraceae**

If sown successively, zinnias will give you flowers over a long period in summer. The leaves are lance-shaped and sandpaper-like in texture. Hybrids come in dwarf, intermediate and tall varieties. Flowers range from tiny button-like heads to large heads with double petals, in almost every colour except blue. Depending on the variety, height varies from 60–65cm (2–2½ft).

CULTIVATION Choose a site in full sun, although zinnias like a little afternoon shade in especially hot regions. Provide rich, well-drained soil. Keep soil somewhat moist by mulching. They can survive in soil that's on the dry side but will wilt in very dry conditions.

HARDINESS Half hardy/Z3–10

MAINTENANCE Easy. To produce bushier plants, pinch the tops out of young plants when they are 10–15cm (4–6in) high. Remove faded blossoms during the season to keep them producing. 'Cut and Come' will give many weeks of blooms if you keep harvesting it.

FLOWERS AND PLANTS THAT THRIVE IN THE SHADE

Defining the word 'shade' can be a lively and complex vocabulary game. The dimly lit area beneath evergreens will be different from the space under or near deciduous shrubs and trees. The terms used here are 'light shade' where there is a predominance of lightly dappled shade cast by trees and shrubs, 'partial shade' where there is four to six hours of more heavily filtered sunlight from surrounding trees or shrubs and 'full shade' where there is less than four hours of daily sunlight and dense shade from trees and shrubs.

ABOVE Asarum caudatum, *a dark green ground cover of heart-shaped leaves, creates a spicy, gingery perfume.*

Alchemilla mollis
LADY'S MANTLE
FAMILY **Rosaceae**

This charming perennial does well in sun or partial shade. The sweetly scented yellowish-green flowers seem to float above the soft-looking scallop-edged foliage, which has a bluish cast. Reaches 50cm (20in).

CULTIVATION Lady's mantle prefers moist, humus-rich soil, but will tolerate drought. It likes an application of mulch, which keeps it cool and moist. Root dividing or digging up the volunteer plants will let you share them generously. If they become messy or too numerous, simply divide them or thin them out.

HARDINESS Fully hardy/Z4–8

NOTES The velvety leaves hold beads of water on their surfaces that look like tiny round diamonds. The flower clusters nicely accent bouquets.

MAINTENANCE Easy. It can naturalize easily when it drops its many seeds, so keep it deadheaded if you do not want multiple plants in odd places.

Asarum
WILD GINGER
FAMILY **Aristolochiaceae**

This attractive, fast-growing ground cover forms lush carpets of green heart-shaped, leathery leaves. Spring bloom brings unique but shy bell-shaped brownish-red flowers that are tucked under the leaves. In a naturalistic setting such as a woodland shade garden, this plant complements the evergreens and wildflowers.

CULTIVATION Because this plant is native to woodland settings, it really wants full shade. Wild ginger can grow in heavy soils with lots of water but prefers a looser humus-rich soil that is slightly acidic.

HARDINESS Fully hardy/Z6–8

NOTES Roots and leaves have scent similar to culinary ginger but should not be used as seasoning. Look for varieties that provide silvery markings, such as *A. shuttleworthii,* which lends interest to the front edges of a garden, and *A. caudatum*, which is evergreen and more drought-tolerant.

MAINTENANCE Easy. However, you may have to protect the plant from slugs and drying winds. Feel free to divide this plant in the spring or autumn – you will have plenty of divisions to share!

LEFT Alchemilla mollis.

ABOVE Aspidistra elatior.

Aspidistra elatior
CAST-IRON PLANT
FAMILY **Liliaceae**

Though a popular Victorian houseplant, this sturdy long-lived plant can be a staple for the shade garden. With its wide, lance-shaped, leathery, evergreen leaves it makes a striking accent to the outdoor garden. It will reach 30–60cm (1–2ft) high and wide.

CULTIVATION The cast-iron plant likes a moist but well-drained, fertile, sandy soil. It can survive in hard, poor soils, but it won't tolerate soggy conditions and if in the direct sun the foliage will burn and turn brown. It needs a sheltered position, and should be protected in cold winters with fleece or similar.

HARDINESS Frost tender/Z7–10

NOTES The leaves of the cast-iron plant are especially long-lasting in flower arrangements.

MAINTENANCE Easy. Aspidistra thrives on neglect and will do fine unless the soil is practically devoid of nutrients, so fertilize during period of active growth for the best appearance. Red spider mites might need to be controlled.

Astilbe
ASTILBE, FALSE SPIREA
FAMILY **Saxifragaceae**

This light, airy plant that carries feather-like flowers on slender and wiry stems is a treasure in the shade. The dark green, delicately cut leaflets give a foundation to the rise of small white, pink or red plume-like flowers. If not deadheaded, the flowerheads turn an attractive shade of brown and look good throughout the winter. They can grow from 15–90cm (6in–3ft) or taller.

CULTIVATION Astilbe likes moist, humus-rich soil. If the site is consistently moist, or even boggy, it will thrive in full sun; in drier soil it does best in partial shade. It will tolerate full shade but bloom may not be as robust.

HARDINESS Fully hardy/Z5–8

NOTES Look for the drought-tolerant variety, *A. chinensis*, which grows to 60cm (2ft) high and wide, and has dense, pinkish-white flowers in late summer. *A.* 'Deutchland', at 50cm (20in) high, produces its white flowers in late spring.

MAINTENANCE Easy. Will benefit from being fed during the summer. Deadhead faded flowering stems and every 4 or 5 years divide the clumps.

BELOW Astilbe.

ABOVE Begonia x tuberhybrida '*Non-Stop*'.

Begonia x *tuberhybrida*
BEGONIA
FAMILY **Begoniaceae**

This tender, winter-dormant perennial tolerates little light and is a bonus to a shade garden. Tuberous begonias offer a rainbow of colours on single- or double-frilled or plain petals and bloom all summer. Some grow upright with large, arrow-shaped leaves on brittle stems to 75cm (30in). Pendula begonias are ideal for hanging baskets on a shady tree limb.

CULTIVATION Tuberous begonias grow best in light shade or the foliage will scorch. They need rich, well-drained soil high in organic matter. Allow soil to dry between waterings.

HARDINESS Frost tender/Z10

NOTES Begonias are divided into a different types and groups, with flowers in almost every colour except blue, and including some that bloom through the winter. *B.* 'Can-Can' is an upright Tuberhybrida type, whose yellow flowers have a striking, frilly, pinkish-red edge.

MAINTENANCE Moderate. To encourage continued bloom and shape, keep deadheading and pinching back leggy stems. To save tubers for next year, dig them up and store in a cool, dry area.

ABOVE Campanula persicifolia.

Campanula persicifolia
PEACH-LEAF RED BELLFLOWER
FAMILY **Campanulaceae**

Bellflowers are a group of plants that light up a garden with their bright blue flowers that grow on long, slender, flexible stems. Heights (including other species) vary from 60–1.8m (2–6ft). The flowers appear in early summer and, as the name implies, the leaves of *C. persicifolia* look very like the leaves of a peach tree.

CULTIVATION Grow in light shade or full sun. These plants love cool summers and regular water. Native to open woods, they like well-drained soil that is high in organic matter.

HARDINESS Fully hardy/Z4–8

NOTES The variety *C. carpatica*, known as Carpathian harebell, is a delight since it stays low 15–30cm (6–12in) and is long blooming. Add to a rock garden or as a bed border.

MAINTENANCE Easy. Watch for slugs.

Cyclamen
SOWBREAD
FAMILY **Primulaceae**

This delightful genus is native to the Mediterranean. The flowers are unique and distinctive, with their swept-back petals. The hardy species of cyclamen are invaluable in the garden, as they belong to a select group of plants that thrive in dry shade and are therefore excellent for planting beneath trees, where in time they will build up large colonies. The leaves are usually beautifully marked.

CULTIVATION Prefers moderately fertile, moist but well-drained soil in partial shade, but will tolerate drier soils.

HARDINESS Hardy/Z5–10

NOTES *C. coum* flowers from late winter to mid-spring, in a variety of colours from purple-violet to pink and white. *C. persicum* has scented flowers that appear in winter and spring.

MAINTENANCE Easy. An annual mulch of leaf mould is beneficial.

BELOW Cyclamen coum.

Dicentra spectabilis
BLEEDING HEART
FAMILY **Pavaveraceae**

This is perennial favourite of partially shaded gardens. The common bleeding heart has lobed green foliage that gives a delicate feel to this plant, which grows up to 75cm (30in). The key features are the abundant red heart-shaped flowers that hang from arching stems.

CULTIVATION They thrive in partial shade with rich, moist and slightly acidic soil. It should not be too wet. They bloom later in the spring and into early summer. Foliage dies down even in mild climates, but in hotter climates the plant usually lasts for just one season.

HARDINESS Fully hardy/Z4–8

NOTES These flowers are a visual treat and are wonderful to press.

ABOVE Dicentra spectabilis.

MAINTENANCE Easy. When blooming is finally over, the foliage will turn yellow and the plant can then be cut to the ground. Plant flowering annuals to fill the areas.

Epimedium grandiflorum
BISHOP'S HAT, FAIRY WINGS
FAMILY **Berberidaceae**
An excellent perennial ground cover in shady areas. The heart-shaped foliage is

BELOW Epimedium grandiflorum.

attractive all year round and grows on stems 7.5–10cm (3–4in) high. The leaves are light green, but in the spring will have a pink to bronze tint. The foliage will remain all winter if the plant is in a protected location. In late spring, star-shaped, four-petalled flowers dangle in clusters and, depending on the cultivar, they may be white, cream, rose, lavender or yellow in colour.
CULTIVATION Does its best when grown in light to partial shade. Prefers a rich, moist, well-drained soil, with the

BELOW Galium odoratum.

addition of compost and leafmould. Epimediums are propagated by division in the spring or autumn.
HARDINESS Fully hardy/Z5–9
NOTES A great ground cover under trees because it will happily cohabit.
MAINTENANCE Easy.

Galium odoratum
SWEET WOODRUFF
FAMILY **Rubiaceae**
This perennial ground cover is best suited for informal plantings with its white, star-shaped fragrant flowers that bloom in mid-spring atop stems that are covered with shiny, whorled leaves. Reaches a height of 15cm (6in) and spreads to 30cm (12in) or more.
CULTIVATION Grows well in full shade and moist, well-drained soil. Too much sun will stunt the plant and it may die back.
HARDINESS Fully hardy/Z5–8
NOTES The whole plant is fragrant and brushing against it will release its fresh odour. The plant was often used to flavour May wine and in medieval times the most fragrant variety, *G. verum*, was used to stuff mattresses, which is why another common name is 'bedstraw'.
MAINTENANCE Easy. Prune plant back in spring to prevent it from getting too leggy. In cold areas, winter protection is recommended.

Gaultheria procumbens
WINTERGREEN
FAMILY Ericaceae

This versatile evergreen ground cover has upright stems about 5–15cm (2–6in) high with oval glossy dark green leaves. When bruised, the leaves emit a strong wintergreen fragrance. Scarlet berries follow urn-shaped summer flowers of pinkish white.

CULTIVATION With light to full shade, this plant will thrive in rich, moist, acidic soil. While wintergreen can tolerate some drought, it will keep looking its best with regular watering.

HARDINESS Fully hardy/Z3–8

NOTES Wintergreen was once widely used as a medicinal herb, both externally and as a tea, and the oil was used to flavour root beer and toothpaste. It is still used in making perfumes. The plant is an effective ground cover, spreading by rhizomes to form mats 1m (3ft) across.

MAINTENANCE Easy. A regular mulch of conifer needles will help to increase the soil's acidity.

BELOW Geranium macrorrhizum.

ABOVE Gaultheria procumbens.

Geranium macrorrhizum
CRANESBILL
FAMILY Geraniaceae

This cottage garden favourite forms an attractive ground cover through summer and autumn. It is an excellent perennial, clump forming and spreading by rhizomes. It typically grows 30–38cm (12–15in) tall and can spread to 60cm (24in). Five-petalled, deep magenta flowers with dark red sepals, 2.5cm (1in) across, appear in clusters above the foliage from mid- to late spring and may rebloom later. The palmate, deeply lobed (5–7 lobes), medium green leaves (basal leaves 10–20cm/4–8in wide) are hairy, sticky and aromatic.

CULTIVATION Easy to grow in average, dry to medium, well-drained soil in part shade. Tolerates drought due to thick rhizomes as well as hot and humid summers. The removal of flowering stems is all that is usually necessary for maintaining an attractive plant appearance. If foliage decline occurs as the summer progresses, individual leaves may be removed as they yellow. If flowering stems are not removed, some self-seeding may occur in ideal growing conditions.

HARDINESS Fully hardy/Z4–8

NOTES This plant is sometimes called bigroot or bigfoot geranium due to its thick, fleshy rhizomes. The leaves acquire attractive red and bronze tints in the autumn. Flowers give way to cranesbill-like seed heads. A multi-season plant.

MAINTENANCE Easy. It makes such a dense ground cover that it chokes out most weeds. Good news – plants of this species do not need to be cut back, sheared or otherwise trimmed after flowering.

Helleborus orientalis
LENTEN ROSE
FAMILY Ranunculaceae

This evergreen perennial enlivens a shade garden with handsome and glossy dark green leaves that are finely serrated. This plant can stand alone as a showpiece or be joined by others in scattered groupings in a woodland scene. The Lenten rose gets its name from it approximate bloom time – early spring – with 5–10cm (2–4in) single white or pink rose-type flowers that seem to rise out of the soil without any connection to the foliage. They last for many weeks and as they age some flowers turn pinkish green or purple. Since the flowers hang downwards and are often hidden under the leaves, some people like to grow them in raised beds or containers, or to remove some of the leaves – though this does weaken the plants.

ABOVE Hosta fortunei aureomarginata.

CULTIVATION Hellebores will do well in light shade and prefer rich, moist and well-drained soil. Lots of organic material will keep this nourished since feeding it nitrogen may damage the roots. It grows slowly from spreading rhizomes and is not invasive.

HARDINESS Fully to half hardy/Z5–9

NOTES A warning: the variety *H. niger*, the Christmas rose, while just as lovely as the Lenten rose, is highly toxic to humans and animals.

MAINTENANCE Moderate. Feed once or twice a year. Try not to move since it takes them several years to re-establish after transplanting. In early spring clip the over-wintered foliage as close to the ground as possible.

Heuchera sanguinea
CORAL BELLS
FAMILY Saxifragaceae

A versatile plant for a rockery, shady border or container. It forms a tidy clump of scalloped, round leaves, 7.5–15cm (3–6in) high. The delicate clusters of large, red, tubular flowers are borne on tall, wiry stems and brighten a low-light area. *H. s.* is ideal for a border front in dappled shade.

CULTIVATION Plant in sun or partial shade in rich, fertile soil and set the crowns above soil level. The leaves are likely to scorch in full sun. They can tolerate some drought once established but excellent drainage is critical in the winter.

HARDINESS Fully to frost hardy/Z3–9

NOTES *H.* 'Santa Anna Cardinal' has vibrant rose-red flowers over a long period in summer. This variety is a delight to see and to add to bouquets. It is attractive to bees, hummingbirds and butterflies.

MAINTENANCE Moderate. Annual mulching is recommended, since the rootstock tends to push upwards. It is best to lift and replant every few years, or replace with new plants. In a mild climate, watch for mealy bugs at the base of the plants.

Hosta
PLANTAIN LILY
FAMILY Liliaceae

Hostas are grown for their lush foliage in heart, lance, oval and even round shapes in colours from dark green to chartreuse, grey or blue, with many variegated versions. The delicate spikes of flowers rise form the centre of the clump in summer, in pastel shades of pink, purple, cream and white.

CULTIVATION Grow in rich, consistently moist but well-drained soil in a shady, sheltered site.

HARDINESS Fully hardy/Z4–9

NOTES Hostas are good container plants, too. Those with textured or waxy leaves tend to attract fewer pests. Leaves make long-lasting and wonderful additions to cut flower arrangements. The patriot hosta (*H. fortunei*) is an especially good beginner plant.

MAINTENANCE Easy. However, protect them from slugs and snails. Those with textured or waxy leaves attract fewer pests. Plants go completely dormant in the winter, collapsing to a pile of yellow leaves. Remove these and wait for their re-emergence in late spring.

BELOW Heuchera sanguinea *'Monet'*.

ABOVE *A formal edging border with* Impatiens walleriana.

Impatiens walleriana
BUSY LIZZIE
FAMILY **Balsaminaceae**

Mostly tender annuals or perennials, busy Lizzies are a universally popular bedding plant, grown for their brightly coloured flowers, produced over a long period. They come in all colours apart from yellow and blue (bright red, orange, pink, purple, violet or white) and have narrow glossy green leaves on succulent pale-green stems.

CULTIVATION Grow them in partial shade in fertile but well-drained, humus-rich soils in cool sites. They can be pinched back to encourage bushiness or planted slightly closer. They require constant moisture levels but not standing water.

HARDINESS Half hardy/Z10–11

NOTES Look for the many cultivars, including the Super Elfin and Tempo Series, including doubles, variegated leaves, and uprights.

MAINTENANCE Easy.

Lamium maculatum
SPOTTED DEAD NETTLE
FAMILY **Lamiaceae**

Spotted dead nettle is a popular ground cover because of its silvery foliage that brightens up dark, shady areas. With a height of up to 15cm (6in), it is a low spreader, 20cm (8in) wide, with variegated 2.5cm (1in) crinkle leaves with rounded teeth. Lavender flowers with upper and lower lips bloom from spring to late summer. These plants can tolerate shady areas that have dry soil.

CULTIVATION Plant spotted dead nettles in an evenly moist, well-drained, moderately rich soil in partial shade. They prefer cool temperatures.

HARDINESS Fully hardy/Z4–8

NOTES The metallic hue on the leaves makes this useful for designs with creative colour schemes. The 'White Nancy' variety stays relatively short – only 15cm (6in) – but spreads to 1m (3ft) or more. 'Anne Greenway' offers an exquisite blend of chartreuse, silver, medium-green and mint green foliage, making this ground cover breathtaking even when not in bloom.

MAINTENANCE Moderate. It is best to cut this plant back after the first bloom to promote compact growth.

Pachysandra procumbens
PACHYSANDRA, ALLEGHENY SPURGE
FAMILY **Buxaceae**

This ground cover gives clean and compact growth with grey-green oval leaves. It reaches 1.8–3.6m (6–12ft) high. The two-toned foliage is richly patterned and persists through most winters. A second-storey layering of fresh green leaves follows the fragrant white flowers that appear briefly in the spring. They do not compete with tree roots so are perfect for hugging around a shady tree trunk. Can be evergreen or deciduous.

CULTIVATION Ideal for shady areas in moist, acidic soil. Plant 2.5cm (1in) apart as they spread by underground runners.

HARDINESS Fully hardy/Z4–8

NOTES Handles full shade or part sun but too much sun will hamper growth and turn leaves yellow. Each year give bed well amended organic mulching.

MAINTENANCE Easy.

BELOW Lamium maculatum.

Polygonatum biflorum
SOLOMON'S SEAL
FAMILY Liliaceae
This woodland perennial fills the back areas of gardens with grace and elegance. The stems tend to arch and lean over to one side. Leaves are 15cm (6in) long and 10cm (4in) wide and are spaced close together along the stem. From late spring to midsummer, small, white, bell-shaped flowers hang in pairs from the leaf axils. Bluish-black berries appear once the flowers are finished. Grows to a height of 1.5m (5ft) or more.
CULTIVATION Grow in full or partial shade, in fertile, loamy soil. Fairly rugged, the plant will tolerate less than ideal conditions but does best with regular water. Foliage persists all summer.
HARDINESS Fully hardy/Z3–8
NOTES Occurs in both high-quality and degraded woodlands, which makes it a versatile garden plant. The nectar and pollen of the flowers attract various bees, including bumblebees, and the Ruby-throated hummingbird, which also sucks the nectar from the flowers.
MAINTENANCE Easy. The plant dies down after the first frost and rises again in spring warmth. It grows from thick, fleshy rhizomes that can be divided and transplanted. The leaves are often damaged by slugs and sawfly larvae, but the plants usually recover, once established.

Polystichum acrostichoides
CHRISTMAS FERN
FAMILY Dryopteriaceae
Dark evergreen leaves that grow 30–45cm (1–1½ft) tall in symmetrical clumps about 90cm (3ft) wide. Looks best when mixed with other woodland type plants. Fronds stay upright and offer lovely contrast to snow in colder climates. In spring, lovely light green fiddleheads emerge.
CULTIVATION Grow in rich well-drained soils in mixed woodland plantings or against a wall in shady areas.

ABOVE Polygonatum biflorum.

HARDINESS Fully hardy/Z3
NOTES There are many other species with interesting frond shapes, colours and textures. Florists use the fronds for fresh and dried arrangements.
MAINTENANCE Easy. Cut old fronds before fiddleheads emerge to keep tidy.

Primula
PRIMROSE
FAMILY Primulaceae
Every shade garden needs to host a collection of primroses. They are valued for their colourful spring blooms as well as the textured green round or oblong leaves that form a tight, rosette base.
CULTIVATION Does well in partial shade and grown in organically enriched soil that is slightly acidic and well drained. They do best in cool and humid climates.
HARDINESS Fully hardy to frost tender/Z5–6
NOTES Varieties include *P. helodoxa,* with its small umbels of rose or lilac flowers, *P. japonica* with its tubular, deep red flowers, and *P. vulgaris* with its flat, soft yellow flowers. Don't forget *P. veris*, better known as cowslip, with nodding clusters of fragrant yellow flowers.

MAINTENANCE Easy, especially in areas with chilly winters and cool summers. Deadhead to ensure longer blooming. In the autumn, dig and divide overcrowded clumps.

Solenostemon
COLEUS
FAMILY Lamiaceae
Grown for its vividly coloured leaves in many patterns, this tropical plant is a tender perennial that will be killed by the first frost. Sizes range from 60cm (2ft) tall to dwarf versions. The large leaves do particularly well in the shade. While the blue flower spikes are attractive, they are often pruned since they detract from the plant's shape.
CULTIVATION Plant outdoors when temperatures are warm in neutral pH, moist and well-drained soil. Propagate from stem cuttings or seeds.
HARDINESS Frost tender/Z10
NOTES Great for borders, indoor and outdoor containers. The hybrid Kong Series comes in vibrant reds, roses, mosaics and scarlet.
MAINTENANCE Easy. Late summer blooms should be pinched off to encourage leaf growth. Highly resistant to disease or insect problems. Feed regularly with nitrogen-rich fertilizer.

BELOW Primula japonica.

TREES AND SHRUBS THAT PREFER FULL SUN

If your garden is a sunshine oasis, a mixture of sun and shade, or has a sun-drenched wall or corner, then you will need trees and shrubs that will thrive there. Here is a selection of those that do well in the sun, others that can cope with alternating sun and shade and all with preferences for soil and moisture conditions that can be chosen to suit your climate. From the drought-tolerant abelia and the fragrant Chinese witch hazel, to the cool-climate-loving blue spruce and the Californian lilac with its intense violet flowers, here is a sampling to inspire you.

ABOVE Amelanchier arborea *(common serviceberry) is well suited to small gardens and has a mass of white spring blossoms.*

Abelia x *grandiflora* 'Little Richard' ABELIA
FAMILY Caprifoliaceae

This mounding, compact shrub may be semi-evergreen depending on climate and has clusters of small white bell-shaped flowers from summer right through the autumn. Grows 3m (10ft) high and wide.

CULTIVATION A non-complaining shrub, abelia thrives in soils from clay to loam. It is drought- and salt-tolerant. Does well in full sun but also performs well in light shade.

HARDINESS Half hardy/Z6–9

NOTES Wildlife such as hummingbirds

BELOW Abelia x grandiflora *'Little Richard'*.

and butterflies love this shrub. Foliage turns a deep copper colour, adding to its already impressive winter display.

MAINTENANCE Easy. Do not shear but select a few branches and prune at ground level. This selective pruning will open the centre and give better shape.

Amelanchier arborea SERVICEBERRY, JUNEBERRY, SHAD BUSH
FAMILY Rosaceae

This small tree offers four seasons of interest with white and fragrant spring flowers with showy white petals that occur in elongated, drooping bunches. Red to purple round berries hang in small clusters as they ripen in early to midsummer. The fruits are edible, so are a great attraction for birds. It has wonderful autumn colours ranging from bright yellow, peach and apricot to orange and deep red. Plant with an evergreen backdrop and create a lovely landscape scene. Can reach a height of 10m (30ft) with a narrow spread.

CULTIVATION Grow in an average, medium, well-drained soil in full sun to part shade. It is tolerant of a wide range of soils and needs regular watering.

HARDINESS Fully hardy/Z5–9

NOTES Edible berries can make great pies if you can harvest them before the birds steal them.

MAINTENANCE Easy.

Ceanothus thyrsiflorus CALIFORNIAN LILAC
FAMILY Rhamnaceae

Small, glossy, dark green holly-like leaves are abundant on this low-growing evergreen shrub. Dark violet blue 2.5cm (1in) clusters of flowers cover it in early spring. Reaches a height of 60–90cm (2–3ft) and a width of 2.5–3m (8–10ft). Other good varieties are *C. gloriosus exultatus* 'Emily Brown' (ground cover), *C.* 'Gloire de Versailles' and *C.* 'Concha'.

CULTIVATION Give them light, well-drained soil and occasional summer watering. They do tolerate heavy soil.

HARDINESS Frost hardy/Z7–9

NOTES Provides habitat and cover for songbirds as well as seeds eaten by

bushtits, mockingbirds, quail and finches. Attracts bees and bumblebees.
MAINTENANCE Easy. Control growth by tip pruning during growing season.

Cornus kousa
KOUSA DOGWOOD
FAMILY Cornaceae

This small deciduous ornamental tree has dense growth with delicate limbs that spread horizontally. It bears white, star-shaped flower-like bracts in late spring to early summer. Showy red fruits that look like a big, round raspberry persist throughout the summer. The autumn foliage colour is red to maroon. Even the bark offers special interest in that initially it is smooth and light brown but as it ages it exfoliates into small patches forming a tan and brown camouflage pattern. Can reach 7m (22ft) in height.
CULTIVATION This dogwood likes to grow in in full or partial sun. It is a slow grower, with very low water requirements, and has tolerance for salty soils.
HARDINESS Fully hardy/Z5–8
NOTES *C. k.* var. *chinensis* has larger flower heads and more narrowly pointed bracts. The berries are edible and wild birds love them.

BELOW Cornus kousa.

ABOVE Euonymus alatus *'Fireball'*.

MAINTENANCE Easy. This is a good choice because it is resistant to typical dogwood anthracnose disease and dogwood borer moth.

Euonymus alatus
BURNING BUSH
FAMILY Celastraceae

This deciduous twiggy shrub that grows to a height of only 3m (10ft) and a width of 90cm–1.5m (3–5ft) accents a landscape for several seasons. The summer foliage is dark green and the shrub will do best in full sun. It's drought-tolerant after the first year of getting established but not if in a container. Waiting for its brilliant autumn show of fiery red foliage, however, is one of the reasons to have this in your garden.
CULTIVATION Plant in full sun to achieve vibrant autumn colour. It is tolerant of a variety of soils.
HARDINESS Fully hardy/Z4–9
MAINTENANCE Easy. If you choose to prune to keep its shape, do so in the autumn or early winter after the leaves fall. When shaping, prune out the entire branch, removing it from the base of the plant.

Hamamelis mollis
CHINESE WITCH HAZEL
FAMILY Hamamelidaceae

This slow-growing small deciduous tree or shrub can reach up to 4m (12ft) high. It presents a vase-shaped silhouette with bare outstretched limbs waiting for the early and lovely yellow spring flowers to adorn them. They are fragrant and have been described as looking like shredded coconut or spiders.
CULTIVATION Thrives in well-drained, fertile, humus-rich soil, in full sun. It also grows well under the bright shade of tall trees or with a half day of sun and a half day of shade. Provide regular water during summer dry spells, watering deeply to encourage a deep and extensive root system.
HARDINESS Fully hardy/Z5–9
NOTES This wonderful tree/shrub has many interesting features but its spring and autumn displays are perhaps their periods of crowning glory. You can bring in a branch in winter and force the fragrant flowers to bloom indoors.
MAINTENANCE Easy. Prune only to guide its shape and growth or to remove suckers.

BELOW Hamamelis mollis *'Pallida'*.

ABOVE Lagerstroemia indica.

Lagerstroemia indica
CRAPE MYRTLE
FAMILY **Lythraceae**

This four-season deciduous tree is a treasure. It comes in sizes to fit large or small spaces and has showy flowers and bark as well as great autumn colour and winter fruit. Flowers are borne in summer in big clusters and come in white and many shades of pink, purple, lavender and red. The fruits that follow are brown or black. When mature they dry and split, releasing disc-shaped seeds.

CULTIVATION Provide moist soil and it will grow rapidly, but once established it will tolerate dry conditions. Careful pruning is recommended to remove crossing or overly dense branches.

HARDINESS Frost hardy/Z7–10

NOTES Look for the newer varieties which can survive in colder temperatures.

MAINTENANCE Easy. Prune lightly in the dormant season.

Oxydendrum arboreum
SOURWOOD, SORREL TREE
FAMILY **Ericaceae**

An exquisite four-season slow-growing deciduous tree. It has drooping, long-lasting sprays of fragrant flowers in early to midsummer and lights up the garden with its soft red, luminescent maroon and yellow foliage in autumn. If this is not enough, add the pyramidal pendulous branches, chunky bark, reddish new wood and shimmery spring leaves, and you have an outstanding specimen tree. Grows to about 15m (50ft) high and 7.5m (25ft) wide.

CULTIVATION Propagate by softwood cuttings in summer or by seed in autumn. Thrives in acidic, richly organic soil. Roots are shallow, so avoid planting under the tree or use ground covers that are shallow rooted. Cooler summers are best for this tree.

HARDINESS Fully hardy/Z5–9

MAINTENANCE Easy.

Picea pungens 'Baby Blue Eyes'
BLUE SPRUCE, COLORADO SPRUCE
FAMILY **Pinaceae**

A slow-growing pyramidal semi-dwarf tree with sky-blue stiff needles in neat rows. The rough grey bark adds texture to the landscape. Can reach 15m (50ft) high and 5m (15ft) wide.

CULTIVATION Does best in full sun to part shade. Give it moderate water and rich, well-drained soil. The shallow root system likes cool climates.

HARDINESS Fully hardy/Z3–8

NOTES Ideal as an accent tree for small areas. Birds are attracted to spruces for shelter and food.

MAINTENANCE Easy. Resistant to spider mite. Needs no pruning since it grows only 5–7.5cm (2–3in) per year.

Stewartia pseudocamellia
JAPANESE STEWARTIA
FAMILY **Theaceae**

This excellent four-season deciduous garden tree grows slowly to 20m (70ft) tall and 6–9m (25–30ft) wide. Pyramid shaped, it is often multi-trunked. Older bark exfoliates creating a camouflage pattern of orange, green and grey. The deep green foliage is elliptical with finely serrated margins.

CULTIVATION Grows best in humus-rich, acidic soils with good drainage and even moisture. Mulch in light soils and during dry seasons.

HARDINESS Fully hardy/Z7–9

NOTES A good showpiece tree in woodland gardens. Throughout the summer it bears white camellia-like flowers with orange anthers. Autumn foliage turns orange, red and then purple. A brown pointed triangular fruit appears and persists, giving winter interest.

MAINTENANCE Easy. Needs little to no care beyond the removal at intervals of weak and exhausted wood.

BELOW Stewartia pseudocamellia.

TREES AND SHRUBS THAT THRIVE IN THE SHADE

As gardens come in all shapes and sizes, their rates of exposure to the sun also differ widely. The location, the landscape design, its proximity to other buildings, and the growth of trees over time can create a garden that is defined by shade. While tending a garden with little direct sun may be challenging, with research, nursery shopping and observation of local gardens, you can find interesting trees and shrubs that will thrive in such conditions. Moreover, tending a shade garden is often less work and always offers a cool and relaxing spot to rest in.

ABOVE Calycanthus *is a versatile four-season shrub – enjoy the spicy, cinnamon aroma of the burgundy flowers and bark.*

Acer circinatum
VINE MAPLE
FAMILY Aceraceae

This deciduous tree can grow in the understorey of moist forests where its shape is often sprawling and crooked. In open areas it is more of a symmetrical small tree that has an upright habit. Lovely greenish-red circular leaves turn orange and scarlet in the autumn. Perfect for a woodland landscape surrounded by ferns. Grows up to 5m (15ft) or more.
CULTIVATION Needs an evenly moist, well-drained soil, and moderate water.
HARDINESS Fully hardy/Z6–9
NOTES A four-season jewel for a shady garden – the twisty, leafless branches offer delicate patterns against a winter sky.
MAINTENANCE Easy. Prune in late autumn to midwinter.

Acer palmatum
JAPANESE MAPLE
FAMILY Aceraceae

This small, slow-growing deciduous tree has year-long interest. Early spring growth glows red and the delicately cut green leaves turn brilliant colours in the autumn. Height and spread of 6m (20ft).
CULTIVATION Growth is best in moist, well-drained soils that are high in organic matter. Give protection from hot, drying winds. They are happy with conditions that have filtered sunlight. Because they are shallow rooted, do not cultivate the surrounding soil and avoid planting them near established shallow rooted trees (such as beech or large maples). Mulch to prevent weeds.
HARDINESS Fully hardy/Z5–8
NOTES With so many varieties, this is an enjoyable tree to research.
MAINTENANCE Moderate. Prune lightly if it becomes too big.

Calycanthus occidentalis
SPICE BUSH, CALIFORNIA ALLSPICE
FAMILY Calycanthaceae

This clump-forming deciduous shrub is perfect as a background plant or for giving privacy to a space. It can reach 3m (10ft) high and wide. Leaves start out a lime-green colour and darken through summer and then turn yellow in the autumn. Late spring or early summer brings brownish red flowers that resemble small water lilies. Both foliage and blossoms have fragrance.
CULTIVATION This shrub can be trained to be a multi-stemmed tree. Likes shade or sun and regular water. Can tolerate sand, clay, poor drainage and seasonal flooding.
HARDINESS Fully hardy/Z6–9
NOTES Easily grown from seeds, but the seeds are toxic, so be cautious.
MAINTENANCE Easy. Remove twiggy stems annually to tidy. Avoid hard pruning.

BELOW Acer palmatum 'Nicholsonii'.

Camellia sasanqua
WINTER-BLOOMING CAMELLIA
FAMILY Theaceae

These broad-leaved evergreen shrubs
will make you smile on a dark winter's
day. Flowers are produced in late autumn
and winter along stems with shiny, dark
green leaves. Blossoms come in single,
double and semi-double forms. These
are fragrant and come in pastel pinks,
roses and whites, with a few of them
deep rose, deep pink and bright red.
Growth ranges from 45cm–3.6m (1½–12ft)
high and 1.8–3.6m (6–12ft) wide.
CULTIVATION Likes well-drained, acidic
soil rich in organic material – older plants
are fairly drought-tolerant but younger
ones like regular watering with rainwater.
HARDINESS Frost hardy/Z7–9
NOTES Tolerates more sun than other
varieties. They can be trained onto a
trellis and do well in pots.
MAINTENANCE Easy. Prune after
flowering. In the spring, keep roots cool
by placing 5cm (2in) of mulch that does
not touch the trunk base.

Cornus stolonifera 'Flaviramea'
RED TWIG DOGWOOD
FAMILY Cornaceae

This woody, deciduous, multi-limbed
shrub is grown for its stunning red

BELOW Camellia sasanqua.

ABOVE Cornus stolonifera.

autumn foliage and winter twig display.
Grows 2.1–2.75m (7–9ft) high and
spreads 3.6m (12ft), but pruning can
manage shape. Summertime creamy
white flowers appear in 5cm (2in) clusters
that later bear white or bluish berries.
Truly a plant for all seasons.
CULTIVATION Thrives in cold and warm
temperatures. Tolerates poor soil but
will do better with moderate water. Cut
down severely in winter while dormant.
HARDINESS Fully hardy/Z2–8
NOTES Good for preventing soil erosion
and space filling. Lovely against a pale-
coloured wall in the winter as the red
bark lights up the area.
MAINTENANCE Easy. Spreads by
underground runner, so use a spade
to cut off roots.

Hydrangea quercifolia
OAK-LEAF HYDRANGEA
FAMILY Hydrangeaceae

A four-season shrub that reaches 2m (6ft)
tall and wide. Has attractive, deeply lobed
leaves that resemble those of oaks, and
gives fabulous autumn colour. It bears
large elongated clusters of white flowers
in late spring and early summer. They turn
a lovely pinkish-maroon by the autumn.
CULTIVATION The perfect exposure will
get morning sun and afternoon shade.

Needs excellent drainage in slightly
acidic soil, but withstands hotter
temperatures than other varieties.
HARDINESS Frost hardy/Z5–9
NOTES 'Sikes Dwarf' and 'Pee Wee'
work well in smaller gardens.
MAINTENANCE Easy. During dry
spells it will appreciate regular deep
waterings about twice a week.

Kalmia latifolia
MOUNTAIN LAUREL,
CALICO BUSH
FAMILY Ericaceae

This slow-growing handsome evergreen
shrub grows to 1.8–2.4m (6–8ft) high and
wide. It has glossy, leathery, oval leaves –
turn them over and see the yellowish
green undersides. Delight in the late
spring light pink or white cup-shaped
flowers that have showy stamens
resembling stars.
CULTIVATION This shrub needs moist
soil that is rich in humus and is acidic.
It should be sheltered from drying winds.
HARDINESS Fully hardy/Z5–9
NOTE Look for varieties such as
'Carousel' or 'Kaleidoscope' that have
flowers with contrasting colours.
MAINTENANCE Easy. Because *K. l.*
is a slow grower, very little pruning will
be necessary.

Pieris japonica 'Temple Bells'
ANDROMEDA
FAMILY Ericaceae

This attractive shrub is a slow-growing,
dwarf broadleaf evergreen with tiered
branches. New foliage emerges as a
bronze-apricot colour and over time turns
to dark green. Large white flowers in
dense drooping clusters appear in late
winter or early spring. Grows to 6m (10ft)
tall and wide.
CULTIVATION Prefers an acidic, well-
drained soil that stays moist – a yearly
mulch with pine needles keeps it damp
and acidic. Likes cool summers and will
become stressed with too much heat.
HARDINESS Fully hardy/Z6–8

ABOVE Sarcococca confusa.

NOTES It is a good choice for containers near entrance ways since it has year-round interest.
MAINTENANCE Easy. Prune by removing spent flowers.

Sarcococca confusa
SWEET BOX
FAMILY **Buxaceae**

This evergreen shrub is a delight all year, even though its seasonal features are subtle. It's a reliable shade shrub that has a few varieties – some are low growers while the tallest may reach 1.8m (6ft). Ideal for small spaces or grouped as a hedge, this bush has dark, waxy green leaves and tiny white blossoms in late winter. The flowers have a powerful fragrance, which is the main reason for growing this plant. Sweet box grows slowly and keeps an orderly and polished appearance all year.
CULTIVATION A shade lover, this shrub thrives in organically enriched soil.

Growth is slow and orderly, so pruning is rarely needed. Likes moderate water.
HARDINESS Fully hardy/Z6–9
NOTES *S. humilis* is the low-growing variety and can be used as a ground cover. Birds love the berries!
MAINTENANCE Easy. But make sure you weed the seedlings that want to overpopulate the garden.

Styrax japonicus
JAPANESE SNOWBELL
FAMILY **Styracaceae**

A springtime showpiece, this small deciduous tree may grow to 10m (30ft) and has a slender and graceful trunk. A profusion of white, bell-shaped fragrant flowers hang in clusters, and these later form into fruits that dangle into the autumn.
CULTIVATION Provide good soil that is well drained. This tree has deep-growing roots but they won't take over.
HARDINESS Fully hardy/Z5–9
NOTES Best to plant in a raised bed or on a berm (a mound of earth with sloping sides) where you can look up

into the tree to appreciate the lovely display of white flowers and scallop-edged green leaves. 'Pink Chimes' offers an upright form with pink blossoms.
MAINTENANCE Easy. Prune to keep shape and keep lower branches cut to reduce bushiness.

Taxus cuspidata 'Nana Pyramidalis'
YEW
FAMILY **Taxaceae**

This slow-growing dark evergreen conifer grows more slowly than most other yews and forms a textured and dense broad pyramidal shape. Dark, thick green foliage is tufted along each stem. Red fruit appears in early autumn. Once established, it is tolerant of shade, coastal conditions, and drought conditions. Reaches a height of 5m (15ft).
CULTIVATION Adaptable to many soil types, but pH levels should not be too alkaline or acidic. It prefers shady areas away from surfaces that radiate heat.
HARDINESS Fully hardy/Z5–7
NOTES This variety is great choice for a privacy screen or a windbreaker. It can be easily sheared to make hedges.
MAINTENANCE Easy. Minimum shearing is needed to maintain its appearance. An excellent choice for a low-maintenance hedge.

BELOW Taxus cuspidata.

VEGETABLES

As we rethink how to garden as we get older, we also need to redefine the concept of a garden and how it might suit our abilities. This is especially true when we plan our vegetable gardens. As the following list illustrates, no matter what your gardening environment, vegetable-growing options are wide. If you are still tending an in-ground vegetable garden, it may be time to cultivate fewer rows, limit the number of varieties you plant and select varieties that are easy to cultivate and harvest. It is always better to have a well-maintained smaller vegetable plot than a large one that can get out of hand.

ABOVE Capsicum *'Santa Fe Grande'* peppers add great colour and are seen as one of the best varieties for pickling.

ABOVE Allium cepa *(onion).*

Allium cepa
ONION
FAMILY Amaryllidaceae

There are many varieties of onion – most are round, but some are torpedo-shaped. Golden varieties are good for storing, but reds and whites provide sweeter and milder flavours. Plant the miniature bulbs, called 'sets', in mid- to late spring when the soil is warmer.

CULTIVATION Plant in an open position in rich, well drained, loose soil that has been manured the previous autumn. Since onions are shallow-rooted, they need moisture near the surface.

NOTES Choose an inappropriate variety for your area. Plan them as part of a crop rotation scheme.

MAINTENANCE Moderate.

Beta vulgaris 'Boltardy'
BEETROOT (BEET)
FAMILY Chenopodiaceae

Raised for their edible root, beetroot greens are also a nutritious part of this versatile vegetable.

CULTIVATION Beetroot does well in sun and shade. It likes loose, well-drained soil that is high in organic matter and is not acidic. Remove soil clods or rocks and keep the soil moist. Thrives in almost any climate but where it is hot sow in early spring so that plants mature before the extreme temperatures. Grow as an autumn, late-winter and early-spring crop.

NOTES All beetroot is easy to grow, but 'Boltardy' is the easiest. Use old favourites with round dark maroon roots such as 'Mr Crosby's Egyptian' or 'Detroit Dark Red'. Newer varieties include 'Chioggia' which has rings of red and white. Also tasty vegetables, golden yellow beets are becoming more popular.

MAINTENANCE Moderate. Beetroot does not transplant well, so thin seedlings to 7.5cm (3in) apart and eat the thinned seedlings as you would spinach.

BELOW Beta vulgaris *'Boltardy' (beetroot).*

ABOVE Beta vulgaris *subsp.* cicla *var.* flavescens *(chard).*

Beta vulgaris subsp. *cicla* var. *flavescens*
RAINBOW CHARD
FAMILY **Chenopodiaceae**

Part of the beet family, chard is grown for its vitamin-rich leaves.

CULTIVATION Chard tolerates poor soil, inattention, frost and mild freezes. Plant as soon as the soil can be worked – it's an early sprouter. In mild climates, one planting will last the entire year, so plan a permanent place for it.

NOTES Rainbow chard or 'Bright Lights' chard is as beautiful as it is delicious. When the weather starts to cool down, and most other crops are finished for the season, chards of all types will continue to grow. Just cut the leaves as you need them!

MAINTENANCE Easy. Slug-resistant.

Capsicum
PEPPERS
FAMILY **Solanaceae**

These are attractive bushy plants that grow from 30cm (1ft) to 1.2m (4ft) high. They produce hot and sweet varieties.

CULTIVATION Because peppers are of tropical origin plant them when temperatures are 21–26°C (70–80°F) during the day and 15–21°C (60–70°F) at night. Several weeks before

planting, work the soil 20–25cm (8–10in) deep. The soil should not be sticky. Add ample amounts of organic matter, especially if your soil is heavy. Mulching is crucial for all peppers, especially sweet peppers, because their roots tend to be shallow. Use a material that is slow to break down and will last for the entire season.

NOTES In temperate climates, peppers do best under glass, as they need a long season of warmth to ripen.

MAINTENANCE Moderate. To harvest peppers, snip the stem with secateurs.

Cucumis sativus
CUCUMBER
FAMILY **Cucurbitaceae**

There are two main types of cucumber: greenhouse varieties and outdoor or ridge varieties. A cucumber vine typically bears small yellow flowers that form into cucumbers. Plants for growing under glass are tall climbing ones that bear long, tasty, slender fruits. Outdoor varieties are bushier in habit, produce shorter fruits and use little space. Shapes vary from the slicing type to the pickling or novelty Asian round variety.

CULTIVATION Wait until warm weather (15–21°C/60–70°F) to plant the seeds. Cucumbers perform best in fertile, well-drained soils in full sun.

BELOW Cucumis sativus *(cucumber).*

ABOVE Cucurbita *'Black Forest' (squash).*

NOTES 'Sweet Success,' 'Fanfare' and 'Lemon' are good bush varieties, suitable for a small garden.

MAINTENANCE Easy. Frequent, shallow cultivation and hand pulling will keep weeds down until the vines cover the ground. Water plants once a week during dry weather.

Cucurbita
SUMMER SQUASH
FAMILY **Cucurbitaceae**

Squashes can be divided into two main groups: summer and winter types. The former are best used fresh, the latter will store well. Summer squashes come in bush and vine forms; all need plenty of room. Crookneck squashes are a summer type with a long, curved neck. One or two vines of these, if kept under control, will give you an early harvest.

CULTIVATION Cultivate the garden spot until the soil is crumbly and fine, and till in plenty of organic matter.

NOTES Do not water in the evening. Harvest when small and tender. There are numerous varieties of climbing squash, including the summer 'Custard Squash', the summer bush variety 'Tender and True' and the winter 'Turks Turban'.

MAINTENANCE Easy. Give regular moisture, but leaves and stems should be kept as dry as possible.

ABOVE Daucus carota *'Early Nantes'*.

Daucus carota sativus
CARROT
FAMILY **Apiaceae**

Delicate fern-like green foliage is produced above sweet, tasty roots.

CULTIVATION Prefers light, sandy soil and full sun. Sow the seeds as soon as the ground can be worked and more seeds should be planted every few weeks throughout the summer. The seeds are tiny, which makes sowing them difficult, but you can always use a seed tape or precision seed sower (*see* pages 88–89). If over-seeded, thinning is easily accomplished by snipping off the tops – there is no need to pull.

NOTES Cultivar options are 'Nantes', 'Chantenay', 'Touchon' and 'Short n' Sweet'. Today, various shapes (such as round carrots) and colours such as purple and white are available.

MAINTENANCE Moderate. Avoid irregular watering since dry-to-wet conditions cause the root to split.

Phaseolus vulgaris
FRENCH BEANS, RUNNER BEANS, SNAP BEANS, STRING BEANS
FAMILY **Fabaceae**

Edible, tender, and fleshy pods grow on self-supporting bushes or climbing vines. Plants have bright green leaves and the flowers are white or purple.

CULTIVATION Plant seeds after the soil reaches 18°C (65°F) and there is no more danger of frost. They like well-drained and fertile soil, which has not recently been planted with beans, potatoes, tomatoes, lettuce or cabbage.

NOTES Bush types are easier to manage, but pole types take up little space and are easier for harvesting. There are many varieties that have both bush and pole growth habits, such as 'Blue Lake', 'Contender' and 'Kentucky Wonder'.

MAINTENANCE Easy. Keep well watered. Harvest when foliage is dry to avoid spreading disease. Rotate crop each year.

Lactuca sativa
LETTUCE
FAMILY **Asteraceae**

Lettuce comes in four main types: loose-leaf, crisphead, butterhead (Boston) and cos (romaine). The leafy varieties are recommended since they stand the heat better, grow faster and give a longer harvest.

BELOW Lactuca sativa *(lettuce)*.

CULTIVATION Use loose, well-drained soil and barely cover the seeds after sowing. Feed plants lightly and frequently during the growing season. Plant every 2 weeks for prolonged harvests.

NOTES Loose-leaf types come in green and red.

MAINTENANCE Easy. Protect from slugs. To harvest, clip off outer leaves.

Lycopersicon esculentum
TOMATO
FAMILY **Solanaceae**

Lush and leafy, these plants can be bushy and require little or no staking. Other types are trained as cordons and will need the support of canes or wires.

CULTIVATION Tomatoes require plenty of sun. Set out seedlings after the air and soil have warmed up. They do better if seedlings are planted deeper than they grew in the pot. Plants will be more anchored and sturdier, and roots will develop along the buried portion of the stem. Add compost or manure to the soil.

NOTES Among the best varieties are 'Gardener's Delight', 'Sungold', 'Celebrity', 'Big Rainbow', 'Brandywine' and 'Enchantment'.

ABOVE Lycopersicon esculentum *(tomato)*.

MAINTENANCE Moderate. When plants are about 90cm (3ft) tall, remove the leaves from the bottom 2.5cm (1in) of stem to prevent fungus spread. Bush varieties need no training, but for cordons, remove sideshoots as they appear, leaving a single stem, and keep tying it in to the support. Nip out the top when the plant reaches the right height.

Pisum sativum
GREEN SNAP PEAS
FAMILY **Leguminosae**

Both the bush and climbing varieties that produce shell (shelling) peas, mangetouts (snow peas) and sugarsnap (snap) peas will give a generous harvest despite their delicate appearance.

CULTIVATION Sow seeds early in spring as soon as you can work the soil. Peas love cooler temperate climates and when temperatures exceed 21°C (70°F) most varieties stop producing pods. They grow in most soils but prefer a medium well-dug soil with plenty of organic material. Do not add nitrogen!

NOTES Bush types are easy yet can take up valuable space. Consider climbing or pole types that take up little ground space and are easier for harvesting. Varieties include 'Alderman', 'Sugar Snap', 'Oregon Trail' and 'Super Sugar Mel'.

MAINTENANCE Easy.

Raphanus sativus
RADISH
FAMILY **Brassicaceae**

A satisfying crop since it germinates quickly and within 2–3 weeks you can be harvesting. Though grown for its root, radish greens are also tasty and nutritious. Most familiar types are the round red or red-and-white varieties. Choose from many varieties that are all white ('White Icicle' or pink ('French Dressing'), or long and narrow. Daikons are radishes that have the hotter flavours.

CULTIVATION Sow seeds during the short, cool days of spring and autumn. During these times, radishes are perhaps the easiest and fastest vegetable to grow. Simply sow seed directly into the soil. As you harvest a row, plant another and enjoy radishes all spring and summer long.

NOTES Varieties include 'Cherry Belle', 'White Icicle' and 'Scarlet Globe'.

MAINTENANCE Easy.

Solanum tuberosum
POTATOES
FAMILY **Solanaceae**

Potatoes are undoubtedly one of the most popular vegetables. The foliage part of a potato is an attractive small bush of divided dark green

BELOW Raphanus sativus *(radish)*.

ABOVE Solanum tuberosum *(potatoes)*.

leaves that in time are companions for the star-shaped, clustered, pale-blue flowers.

CULTIVATION You need to 'chit' the seed potatoes by arranging them, with the 'eyes' facing up, in the light in a cool but frost-free room. They are ready for planting when the sprouts have reached 2cm (¾in) in length, which will take approximately 4–6 weeks. Before planting, loosen up the soil 20–30cm (8–12in) deep and mix in some compost – leaf mould is also a good option. It is best to plant in moist but not sodden soil. Plant no earlier than 2 weeks before your last frost with a soil temperature above 7°C (45°F). Cut the seed potato into egg-sized pieces, leaving one or more 'eyes' on each.

NOTES If an in-ground garden bed is not available or too low for you to tend comfortably, potatoes can be grown easily and abundantly in large 75-litre (20-gallon) containers or bags. Keep near your kitchen and you can have fresh potatoes when they are in season.

MAINTENANCE Easy. Always make sure that developing tubers are covered with soil to keep skin from turning green (this can be toxic to eat).

FRUIT

One of the advantages of being a senior is that we remember how fruit is supposed to taste! Growing your own guarantees that you'll have fresh and flavourful fruit that will delight your taste buds. The varieties listed here require fairly low care and maintenance, often take little space to grow, and some will thrive in containers. To lengthen your berry harvests, take note of the early, mid, and late ripening options. Finally, even gardens with limited space can be home to at least one fruit tree since new breeding has created varieties that are compact and columnar shaped. Always choose fruits that you enjoy eating.

ABOVE *Blueberries, strawberries and raspberries brighten up your garden and can then be harvested for use.*

ABOVE Cucumis melo *'Iroquois' (cantaloupe melon).*

Cucumis melo
CANTALOUPE MELON
FAMILY **Cucurbitaceae**

This delicious fruiting annual has trailing, soft, hairy vines that can cover a good deal of ground. The small rounded fruit has a 'netted' skin pattern with the edible flesh varying from light green to reddish orange.

CULTIVATION Melons prefer fertile, humus-rich, well-drained, sandy soils. Warm-season crops, cantaloupes should be planted when all danger of frost has passed. The ideal climate consists of a long, frost-free season with plenty of sunshine and heat, and relatively low humidity. Plant in the spring when the soil temperature is 18–29°C (65–85°F).

NOTES In areas with a short growing season, use transplants to get a head start. Cantaloupe can be trained to a fence, trellis or grown in a large pot. As the fruit grows, support it with cloth slings since the weight may damage the vines.

MAINTENANCE Moderate. Look for varieties resistant to mildew and other diseases. 'Ambrosia', 'Classic Hybrid', 'Hales Best', 'Mission', 'Rocky Sweet' and 'Summit Hybrid' are all excellent.

Ficus carica
FIG
FAMILY **Moraceae**

CULTIVATION Figs thrive in a spot with full sun, preferably near a sunny wall. They are not fussy about soil, but give them space. They appreciate regular water and excellent drainage. Figs do not need other varieties for pollination.

NOTES Fig trees will grow quite large before producing good crops, unless the roots are restricted. They are traditionally planted in 60cm (2ft) deep and wide pits, with paving stones forming the sides and broken bricks or stones at the bottom. 'Brown Turkey' is a reliable variety and 'Negronne' is a dwarf variety which grows to only 1.8m (6ft) high.

MAINTENANCE Easy. Figs are best planted when dormant – in autumn and winter. They need only minimal pruning. Protect fruit from birds by using netting.

BELOW Ficus carica *(fig).*

Fragaria x *ananassa*
STRAWBERRY
FAMILY **Rosaceae**

These low growers, which are 1.8–2.4m (6–8ft) tall, have toothy, roundish leaves and white flowers. They spread by runners to about 30cm (1ft) long.

CULTIVATION These plants like well-drained and acidic soil. Grow in full sun or bright partial shade. When planting, hill the centre of the hole and position the crown of the plant at soil level. Spread the roots down the slope and cover with soil so that it reaches just halfway up the crown. Plants need regular moisture during the fruiting season. In the winter, mulch with a layer of straw or other weed-free light organic material. Strawberries grow well with bush beans, spinach, borage and lettuce.

NOTES Buy your plants from local suppliers using types that do well in your climate. Strawberries will thrive in containers where the soil and drainage conditions can be controlled.

MAINTENANCE Easy. If you cut off the runner plants early you will encourage larger fruit. Use straw or pine-needle mulch between rows in spring to keep the ground moist and the fruit clean.

Fortunella margarita
KUMQUAT
FAMILY **Rutaceae**

Kumquats have been called 'the little gems of the citrus family'. Shrub types grow 1.8–4.5m (6–15ft) while dwarf versions reach only 90cm–1.8m (3–6ft), ideal for a small garden. They are slow growing with thornless branches that are light green and angled when young. The lance-shaped leaves are a glossy dark green. Sweetly fragrant white flowers appear and then form small oval fruits with golden-yellow to reddish-orange peel.

CULTIVATION Kumquats are among the most cold-hardy citrus trees on earth. They love climates where the summer days are hot but the nights are chilly.

ABOVE Fortunella japonica *(kumquats).*

They grow reliably in most types of soil, but prefer a sandy loam.

NOTES The kumquat has a thin, sweet peel and a zesty, somewhat tart centre. Eat kumquats unpeeled, as you would eat grapes. They taste best if you roll them between your fingers first as this releases the essential oils in the rind. Another tasty variety is *F. japonica*.

MAINTENANCE Easy. Needs very little pruning, just a little for shaping. Each year apply a few doses of nitrogen fertilizer such as fish emulsion. Whenever the temperature drops to 4°C (24°F) or below try to protect the fruit by wrapping it in hessian (burlap), or if it is in a container, move it to a sheltered spot.

BELOW Fragaria *x* ananassa *'Calypso' (strawberries).*

Malus sylvestris var. *domestica*
COLUMNAR APPLE TREE
FAMILY Rosaceae

Many gardens do not have the space to grow full-size apple trees so a new type of apple tree has been created, the columnar. Mature trees average 2.4–3m (8–10ft) tall and only about 60cm (2ft) wide. They can grow and produce healthy fruit for about 20 years.

CULTIVATION Plant in full sun and provide good, well-drained soil. In cold climates container-grown trees will need winter protection.

NOTES They work well as potted plants, making them portable. Early producers, they may grow fruit on their first year. 'Northpole' and 'Golden Sentinel' resemble Golden Delicious in taste.

MAINTENANCE Easy.

Prunus cerasus
SOUR CHERRY TREE
FAMILY Rosaceae

These small cherry trees grow from 4.5–7.5m (15–25ft) tall. Their compact size allows for easy maintenance and harvest. Many produce a mouth-watering crop of plump, juicy fruit that ripens in midsummer. They are dependably hardy, with huge harvests for pies and preserves. These trees are self-pollinating so you do not need multiples for successful pollination.

CULTIVATION Like full sun. Avoid heavy clay and wet soils – they prefer rich, well-drained, moist soils. Do not soak for over 24 hours prior to planting.

NOTES The 'North Star' variety produces full size fruit even though it grows only 1.8–2.4m (6–8ft). The sour fruit has light red skin, perfect for pies and pastries.

MAINTENANCE Easy. To avoid disease do any pruning in the summer and not during the usual cool dormancy months. They need more nitrogen and water than sweet cherries so use a slow-release fertilizer high in nitrogen.

Pyrus serotina
ASIAN PEAR TREE
FAMILY Rosaceae

This is an excellent ornamental espalier or deciduous shade tree. In spring it's covered with white blossoms and the glossy attractive leaves are tinged with purple all summer and into autumn. It can reach 7.5–9m (25–30ft) high and 4.5m (15ft) wide.

BELOW Prunus incisa *'Oshidori'* *(dwarf cherry tree).*

ABOVE Rubus idaeus*.*

CULTIVATION Grow in full sun in deep well-drained soil. Trees can tolerate heavy wet soils. Ripening happens from late summer to autumn.

NOTES Asian pears are sometimes called apple pears because they are round like apples but juicier and with a different texture. Unlike most European pears, the fruit ripens on the tree. Another variety of Asian pear is *Pyrus pyrifolia*.

MAINTENANCE Moderate. With prudent pruning, tree size can be reduced to half. Thin fruit to one pear per cluster to have larger fruit.

Rubus idaeus
RASPBERRY
FAMILY Rosaceae

Raspberries may be red, black, purple or yellow-fruited. There are summer-fruiting types, which crop once in midsummer, and autumn-fruiting (ever-bearing), which fruit continuously from late summer to the first frosts (or, in hot climates, may produce an early and a late crop).

CULTIVATION Raspberries do best in full sun but will tolerate slight shade.

NOTES Apply a general all-purpose fertilizer in late winter, one that is low in nitrogen since too much of it can result in bushy plants and less berries.

MAINTENANCE Moderate. Fruited canes should be cut down after fruiting, and autumn varieties trimmed again in spring. The most common disease is fungus so keep the plants thinned to allow air circulation. Insects are not a common problem. Plants will need replacing every 7–8 years, as they are often weakened by viruses and lose productivity.

Ribes nigrum
BLACKCURRANT
FAMILY Grossulariaceae

Currant bushes are deciduous and fast growing under optimum conditions. They grow a multiple-stemmed clump, up to 1.5m (5ft) high and wide, but can be pruned for shape. Blackcurrant leaves are pale green, while those of the red currant are deep blue-green.

CULTIVATION Currants like morning sun and afternoon part-shade with ample air circulation. Intense sunlight will scorch leaves. Frequent cultivation will damage the shallow and superficial roots, so keep them well mulched. Water until harvest.

BELOW Ribes nigrum *'Ben Sarek'* *(blackcurrant bush).*

ABOVE Ribes uvacrispa *(gooseberries).*

NOTES Plants are thornless and fruits are small (pea-sized), produced and harvested in a grape-like cluster called a 'strig'.

MAINTENANCE Moderate. They need protection against various pests, including birds.

Ribes uvacrispa
GOOSEBERRY
FAMILY Grossulariaceae

This multi-stemmed bush grows between 90cm–1.5m (3–5ft) tall and wide, and produces translucent, round, green berries with stripes. The leaves resemble those of a maple and give a lovely autumn colour.

CULTIVATION These cold hardy plants prefer cool, moist, well-drained sites. Plant in a medium-weight soil that is well drained but not dry. If the fruit is to develop fully, moisture is required. However, in very fertile soil, the plant produces too much green growth at the expense of good fruit.

NOTES Gooseberries make jams, jellies, preserves and pies, and some are sweet enough to eat raw when ripe. 'Pixwell' is hardy and almost thornless.

MAINTENANCE Easy. To prevent fungal disease, select planting sites with good air movement.

Rubus spp.
BLACKBERRY
FAMILY Rosaceae

The berry varieties suggested here are thornless, self-supporting canes. The firm berries are conical and are bright glossy black. The leaves usually have three or five oval coarsely toothed, stalked leaflets.

CULTIVATION Blackberries grow best in fertile and well-drained soils that get regular moisture throughout the growing season. Fruit will ripen best in hot summer.

NOTES Disease-resistant blackberry varieties include 'Ouachita', 'Navaho' and 'Arapaho'. Other popular varieties are the easy growing, thornless 'Loch Ness', the flavoursome 'Fantasia' and the large, delicious fruits of 'Sylvan'. Plants are vigorous so need sturdy supports. Watch out for thorns.

MAINTENANCE Moderate. Fertilize at bloom time with a food high in nitrogen.

Vaccinium corymbosum
BLUEBERRIES
FAMILY Ericaceae

While grown for the fruit, blueberry bushes make handsome hedges and borders. They give visual interest nearly all year round as white or pink urn-shaped flowers appear in spring, and then spectacular autumnal leaf displays.

CULTIVATION Blueberries prefer full sun and a very acid soil. Buy several plants so you can benefit from blueberries from early summer right through to late autumn.

NOTE If your soil is neutral or alkaline, grow blueberries in containers but keep them well watered at all times.

MAINTENANCE Moderate. Water regularly in the spring and summer and use rainwater whenever possible. Use an ericaceous (azalea/camellia-formulated) fertilizer when spring growth begins, and again after harvest. Prune old growth to encourage younger branches.

HERBS

Herbs have an established history as garden plants and are still used for their medicinal properties, their flavours and their scents. Most herbs are small flowering plants. In many cases it is the leaves of the herbs that are used, but sometimes it is the flowers or the stem or root. The following list introduces a selection that will give a garden varied colours, textures and growth habits. Many have an important role in providing food for birds and butterflies. All those included here have the potential to tantalize the senses of smell, touch, sight and taste. They are all easy to grow and need minimum care.

ABOVE Lavandula angustifolia *is all that a plant should be: fragrant, beautiful, fast-growing and irresistible to bees.*

Allium schoenoprasum
CHIVES
FAMILY Alliaceae
Closely related to the onion and garlic, and also to the many ornamental alliums, this clumping plant has hollow tubular grass-like leaves that are flavourful in salads. In late spring, light purple flowers appear on 30cm (12in) stalks.

CULTIVATION Provide an open, sunny situation and free-draining soil. Grows well if left undisturbed for several years to form large clumps. Easily propagated by seed in autumn, or by dividing the clumps in spring.

HARDINESS Fully hardy/Z3–9

NOTES Chives can be grown inside or out. Also a great companion plant: a large area of chives planted under roses will help to ward off blackspot.

MAINTENANCE Easy.

Foeniculum vulgare
FENNEL
FAMILY Apiaceae
This handsome perennial will add grace, height and airy texture. With bright green, finely fern-like leaves and aromatic yellow flowers, plant fennel in the back of the herb or perennial flower garden as it will grow to 2m (6ft) tall.

BELOW Foeniculum vulgare.

CULTIVATION The plants require full sunlight and well-drained, deep, moderately fertile soil. Best planted in a more spacious garden where architectural structure may be needed.

HARDINESS Fully hardy/Z4–9

NOTES Fennel attracts bees, butterflies and birds. All parts of the plant are edible – the leaves, stems, seeds and roots. The plants release a chemical that inhibits the growth of some other plants, so do not plant very close to beans, tomatoes or cabbage family plants.

MAINTENANCE Easy. It seeds freely so new seedlings will require weeding to control their spread.

Lavandula angustifolia
LAVENDER
FAMILY Lamiaceae
One of the most popular herbs, lavender plants can be a small shrub reaching up to 90cm (3ft) in height. It provides fragrance, beauty, and there are many uses for its grey-green leaves and spikes of purple/lavender flowers.

CULTIVATION Likes well-drained soil with abundant sun. It is best propagated by cuttings. If winters are severe, some varieties will need protection.

HARDINESS Fully hardy/Z6–9

NOTES The 'Hidcote' variety works well along paths, as it is erect and has a neat habit. 'Munstead' is ideal in containers. The French cultivar

'Grosso' is a heavy bloomer, with flowers that have a strong fragrance. When dried, the flowering stems make excellent everlasting bouquets and have uses in many crafts.

MAINTENANCE Easy. Cut back after flowering is over.

Mentha spicata
SPEARMINT
FAMILY Lamiaceae

This is the most popular culinary mint because of its wonderful flavour and scent. It is a crisp-looking plant with pointed crinkly leaves and purple flowers in the summer.

CULTIVATION Like most mint plants, this one likes full sun and rich, moist soil. Because of its tendency to become invasive, grow mint in a bottomless container that is buried in the garden bed to contain its spread.

HARDINESS Fully to frost hardy/Z5–9

NOTES Grow spearmint near an outside doorway (in a container works well) – then, on a hot day you will benefit from its refreshing scent wafting through the air. Blossoms attract bees, butterflies and other beneficial insects.

BELOW Mentha spicata.

ABOVE Monarda didyma 'Garden View'.

The birds like to feast on the seed heads so leave some for their autumn-time forage. Dry the leaves just before flowering for future use.

MAINTENANCE Easy.

Monarda didyma
BEE-BALM, BERGAMOT
FAMILY Lamiaceae

This handsome perennial is a dramatic filler where height is needed in a bed. The 1.2m (4ft) stems rise from strong clumps and form spiky scarlet blossoms and a welcome splash of colour and texture. The lemon-scented leaves resemble those of mint.

CULTIVATION Plant bee-balm in full sun in a well-drained soil that retains some moisture. A good mulching helps since the plant is not drought tolerant. Divide to propagate.

HARDINESS Fully hardy/Z4–8

NOTES This vintage plant will attract bees, hummingbirds and butterflies, as well as other beneficial insects to your garden.

MAINTENANCE Look for varieties that are resistant to mildew. With vigilant deadheading, you can have flowers for eight weeks or more.

Nepeta x *faassenii*
CATMINT
FAMILY Lamiaceae

This member of the mint family is not invasive. Its soft silvery grey-green heart-shaped foliage grows on graceful thin twigs. It grows 45cm (18in) high and wide and spikes of lavender flowers appear from late spring to summer.

CULTIVATION Catmint is happiest in a well-drained soil in full sun. While drought tolerant, in hot climates it appreciates some afternoon shade. It has a moderate need for water. Rock gardens are perfect settings for catmint, as are border fronts, herb gardens or naturalized plantings.

HARDINESS Fully hardy/Z4–8

NOTES The leaves of this hybrid are fragrant and less attractive to cats than some species. The blooms are useful as fillers in bouquets. Butterflies and hummingbirds are attracted to their nectar, but deer and rabbits are repelled by mint-scented foliage. 'Walker's Low' is a lovely variety.

MAINTENANCE Easy. No serious insect or disease problems. Shear flower spikes after initial flowering to promote a continuous blooming.

BELOW Nepeta x faassenii.

Ocimum basilicum
SWEET BASIL
FAMILY **Lamiaceae**

One of the most popular herbs, sweet basil is an annual that thrives in warm temperatures. The tender green leaves grow on stalks.

CULTIVATION An easy plant to grow from seed. When the plant is 10–15cm (4–6in) pinch back the tips to encourage new growth and remove the flowers to ensure the leaves continue to grow.

HARDINESS Frost tender/Z8

NOTES 'Dark Opal' has large, bronzy purple leaves and is a great addition to borders, planted among other ornamentals.

MAINTENANCE Easy. All you need to do is prevent the basil from flowering so you have a longer harvest of tasty leaves.

Origanum vulgare
OREGANO, WILD MARJORAM
FAMILY **Lamiaceae**

An upright-growing herb with square stems and broad, oval-shaped green leaves. In summer white flower clusters are borne, which bees love. Can reach 45cm (18in).

CULTIVATION Oregano likes full sun and poor to moderately fertile, well-drained soil. The best ways to propagate are by planting seeds or taking tip cuttings.

HARDINESS Fully hardy/Z4–8

NOTES To keep the flavour, prune off most of the flowers – but let a few stay to attract the pollinators such as bees and butterflies.

MAINTENANCE Easy.

BELOW Origanum vulgare.

ABOVE Petroselinum crispum.

Petroselinum crispum
PARSLEY
FAMILY **Apiaceae**

The world's most popular herb, parsley, is widely known as the limp green garnish on our dinner plates. But this tightly curled balm-scented dark-green leaf plant can enhance a garden border, flowerbed or container with appealing texture and substance.

CULTIVATION Parsley needs a good amount of light and will do best when it gets around 6 hours of sun. It will also tolerate partial shade. It likes a well-drained, moisture-retaining, fertile, humus-rich soil. (If you grow it in containers do ensure there are adequate drainage holes.) Set out transplants from the nursery after the last risk of frost.

HARDINESS Half hardy/Z4–9

NOTES Parsley leaves can be cut all season long. You can continue cutting all winter if you have it in pots under glass; the leaves can be dried, but have little flavour. Parsley attracts many beneficial creatures such as lady beetles, green lacewings, spiders and hoverflies; all use the parsley flower as a safe landing site and an egg repository.

MAINTENANCE Easy. Parsley can overwinter if it is lightly mulched during extremely cold weather. Remove the flower stems when they appear – this will keep the plants producing leaves.

Rosmarinus officinalis
ROSEMARY
FAMILY Lamiaceae

This frost-hardy evergreen perennial blooms from mid-spring to early summer, and often again in autumn. Upright varieties reach a height of 90cm–1.8m (3–6ft) and low trailing types do very well in containers. It has narrow, highly fragrant leaves and abundant pale blue flowers.

CULTIVATION Grows best in sun and in well-drained soil. Place in a sheltered location. Propagates easily from cuttings. Grows well in containers.

HARDINESS Frost hardy/Z7–9

NOTES Though not fully hardy, it can survive down to -10°C (14°F) in well-drained soil. Fresh leaves can be cut at any time for culinary use. To dry leaves it is best to take cuttings just before the plant blooms.

MAINTENANCE Easy.

Salvia elegans
PINEAPPLE SAGE
FAMILY Lamiaceae

This impressive perennial grows upright to a height and width of 90–120cm (3–4ft) and has bright green leaves with a strong aroma of ripe

BELOW Rosmarinus officinalis.

ABOVE Salvia elegans.

pineapple. In mild areas, it blooms from autumn to spring, showcasing bright red delicate tubular flowers. Hummingbirds love this herb.

CULTIVATION Salvia loves full sun, good air circulation to deter mildew and moist but well-drained, humus-rich, modestly fertile soil. Good soil drainage helps keep the plant from waterlogging and having roots that freeze in winter. Easy to propagate from cuttings or seeds or dividing the roots.

HARDINESS Frost hardy/Z8–10

NOTES 'Scarlet Pineapple' grows to 90–120cm (3–4ft). The hybrid 'Frieda Dixon' can be used as a ground cover.

MAINTENANCE Easy. Tall varieties, if grown in part shade, will need staking.

Salvia officinalis
COMMON SAGE
FAMILY Lamiaceae

This shrubby perennial has oval, grey-green, velvety leaves – these are aromatic and the plant is frequently used as a culinary herb. In late spring and summer lavender blue flower spikes emerge. Many colourful varieties are available from variegated leaves to those

blushing with red violet. Grows 30–90cm (1–3ft) tall and 30–60cm (1–2ft) wide.

CULTIVATION The same as *S. elegans* (*see* previous entry).

HARDINESS Half hardy/Z6–9

NOTES Salvias are part of the mint family and are the largest genus in this group. Attracts birds, bees and butterflies.

MAINTENANCE Moderate. Prune in winter or early spring when temperatures are cool and new growth is emerging. After flowering, keep shaped by tip-pinching.

Thymus vulgaris
THYME
FAMILY *Lamiaceae*

This commonly grown shrubby herb offers highly flavoured leaves and lilac flowers that are borne in small clusters. Grows to about 30cm (1ft).

CULTIVATION Grows best in a sunny position in light, well-drained soil. It works well as an edging plant or for a spreading growth over rocks.

HARDINESS Hardy/Z7

NOTES *T. serpyllum,* creeping thyme, reaches only 25cm (10in), a great choice for containers or a filler between paving stones. *T.* x *citriodorus* is a lemon-scented variety.

MAINTENANCE Easy.

BELOW Thymus serpyllum.

INDOOR PLANTS

For those who have downsized or have become too frail to work outdoors, growing indoor plants provides an invaluable opportunity for continuing to garden within your own four walls. These plants are dependent on you for regular care, and caring for natural living things promotes a rewarding sense of stewardship. Houseplants are known to reduce stress and improve psychological well-being and physical health, since many plants remove toxins, pollutants and carbon dioxide from our air. This list of plants should give you a head start in selecting the right plant for your environment and energy levels.

ABOVE *Begonias are easy and much-loved houseplants. They are equally prized for their flowers as for their showy leaves.*

Aechmea fasciata
BROMELIAD
FAMILY **Bromeliaceae**

Part of a distinct plant family, in the wild these plants are considered 'air plants' since they grow on trees and shrubs using their leaves as water and food absorbers. However, they are easy to grow indoors and will provide you with beautiful forms, foliage, and flowers that grow up to 60cm (2ft) tall and can last for 3 months. The 'tank bromeliad' forms a tight clumped rosette of sturdy leaves that encircle a small reservoir cup.
CULTIVATION Pot in shallow containers using an orchid potting mixture or one that provides good drainage. Keep some water in the reservoir cup at all times and make sure the potting medium is moist. They like bright light. Frequent mistings keeps the foliage clean and healthy.
NOTES The pineapple is one of the most familiar bromeliads. 'Silver Urn' is a very popular variety and a good beginner bromeliad with dark green leaves with silvery bands and a beautiful pink inflorescence.
MAINTENANCE Easy. Generally free of pest and disease problems.

Aglaonema
CHINESE EVERGREEN
FAMILY **Araceae**

This upright plant has subtly patterned greyish green, waxy, lance-shaped leaves that rise from a central growth. They may get to 90cm (3ft) tall and are grown for their handsome foliage as well as the spathe-shaped flower.
CULTIVATION Grow in a low light and avoid draughts or cold temperatures. They enjoy the same indoor temperature as you. For extra humidity, stand them on trays of damp pebbles. Water to keep soil moist, but between waterings let the top 2.5cm (1in) dry out.
NOTES *A. modestum* 'Silver Queen' has foliage that is silvery green with some dark green, or the reverse, mostly

LEFT Aglaonema modestum.

dark green with light green streaks.
MAINTENANCE Easy, but keep temperature above 12°C (55°F). Leaves may be toxic to pets and children so take care where you place it.

Begonia boweri
EYELASH BEGONIA
FAMILY **Begoniaceae**

Appreciated for its foliage, this gets its nickname 'eyelash begonia' from the hairs on the leaf margins. Grows to a height of 15–30cm (6–12in).
CULTIVATION These like filtered light and can tolerate shade. Give them a minimum night temperature of 15–18°C (60–65°F). They like a light, well-drained, soil-less or loam-based compost (soil mix). Keep the soil uniformly moist, but not wet. Fertilize once a month with a balanced fertilizer.
NOTES Propagate by dividing the rhizomes, or from leaf cuttings.
MAINTENANCE Easy.

Begonia rex
REX BEGONIA
FAMILY **Begoaniaceae**

This begonia species is the most striking with colourful patterns on the foliage. Tiny flowers on tall stems are overshadowed by lush leaves. Plants reach 30–45cm (12–18in) tall.
CULTIVATION Enjoys warm and moist conditions with indirect sun. Plant in loamy soil and keep soil dry in winter.

ABOVE Chlorophytum comosum.

NOTES They like a light, well-drained, soil-less or loam-based compost (potting mix).

MAINTENANCE Moderate. Mist daily.

Chlorophytum comosum
SPIDER PLANT
FAMILY **Liliaceae**

Spider plants just keep on giving. The foliage grows in clumps of soft drooping leaves, usually green or green and white, that have the appearance of long blades of grass. It reaches 15–20cm (6–8in) high and 15–30cm (6–12in) wide. Tiny white flowers are borne on long stalks, and plantlets are produced on attractive, hanging runners. Baby spider plants will normally appear frequently, but if you want to encourage more babies then keep the mother plant in a darkened room.

CULTIVATION It grows best in bright light but will survive with lower light levels. While best to keep it away from midday sun, it is tolerant of a variety of temperatures. When dangling babies start to form roots, they can be cut off and planted on their own.

NOTES Spider plants are believed to be among the most effective for removing toxins from the air.

MAINTENANCE Easy. Repotting may be necessary every couple of years. Brown tips are an indication of the soil being too dry and a feeding prompt.

Davallia fejeensis
RABBIT'S-FOOT FERN, SQUIRREL'S-FOOT FERN
FAMILY **Polypodiaceae**

This unusual fern has its delicate fronds rising from woolly-textured rhizomes – which are said to look like rabbits' feet. A perfect plant for a wire hanging basket since this container allows you to see both the furry feet and the delicate, airy and lacy fronds. Can reach 90cm (3ft)

CULTIVATION The rabbit's-foot fern likes to be near a bright window. Can tolerate cool temperatures without damage. Keep soil moist but not soggy. To propagate, separate a fuzzy rhizome with at least three fronds and plant in potting mixture. Loves humidity so mist daily and place on a tray of moist pebbles.

NOTES When repotting, plant rhizomes shallowly since they do not like to be covered with soil.

MAINTENANCE Moderate. Keep them well misted and moist.

Epipremnum aureum
POTHOS
FAMILY **Araceae**

Pothos will commonly trail beyond a distance of 3m (10ft). Leathery dark green leaves 5–10cm (2–4in) long are pointed and oval. Pruning them regularly keeps the plants full at the base.

CULTIVATION Pothos like to grow in a good light but can tolerate shade. Give them rich, loose, well-drained soil. Let the plant dry out between waterings. You can let them trail down or secure

RIGHT Epipremnum aureum.

them to a support or trellis. Each cutting can be rooted in water to create more plants.

NOTES There are many variegated and golden varieties available. Look for the golden 'Devil's Ivy' or the white and pale green flecked 'Marble Queen'.

MAINTENANCE Very easy. Sometimes the leaves need a dusting.

Fatsia japonica
JAPANESE ARALIA
FAMILY **Araliaceae (ginseng family)**

This dramatic plant has large glossy leaves up to 40cm (16in) wide. They are deeply lobed and slightly serrated. Flowers are white, held on a white stalk in small terminal clusters. Height ranges from 90–180cm (3–6ft). During the growing season, provide a monthly feeding of a complete organic fertilizer.

CULTIVATION Grows best in moist, acid, humus-rich soils. Likes part sun and can tolerate shade. Water when soil surface feels dry.

NOTES Can be grown outdoors during summers in temperate climates.

MAINTENANCE Easy, seldom bothered by pests or disease. If leaves turn yellow, supplement with iron.

ABOVE Phalaenopsis spp.

ABOVE Streptocarpus *x* hybrid.

ABOVE Saintpaulia ionantha.

Peperomia spp.
PEPEROMIA
FAMILY **Piperaceae**

A low-growing houseplant, the peperomia comes in diverse sizes (up to 25cm/10in), shapes and textures. The thick, fleshy, heart-shaped leaves often have attractive silvery variegations, and they produce unusual white or green flowers that resemble long, rounded or pointed sticks.

CULTIVATION These need to be shaded from the hot sun, but they like bright, indirect sunlight. Room temperatures of at least 12.5°C (55°F) will do, but they appreciate more warmth and good humidity. They do well in small or shallow pots.

NOTES The occasional pinching out of growing points will induce plants to produce more side-shoots and to become bushier. Houseplant favourites include P. 'Amigo Greensplit', which has leaves like bean pods, and the variegated succulent, *P. obtusifolia*.

MAINTENANCE Moderate. Water sparingly and always dry completely before watering, especially in the winter months.

Phalaenopsis spp.
MOTH ORCHID
FAMILY **Orchidaceae**

Moth orchids produce alternate wide, fleshy leaves, often marbled in silver with no visible stem. They are epiphytic, often growing on tree branches in the wild (though not parasitic), with aerial roots. The flower stalk is long and arching (up to 60cm/2ft tall) and bears up to 30 large flowers in white to purple shades. Each flower will last a month or more.

CULTIVATION Requires bright indirect light and high humidity. Use orchid compost, in a special orchid basket or transparent pot. When watering, drench it and let it dry out. Set plants on trays of gravel partly filled with water. During the warmer months mist them every day or two. In the autumn, cool night-time temperatures encourage flower spikes. Once these have developed, maintain a constant temperature, 20–21°C (68–70°F), since swings in heat can hurt blooms.

NOTES When the last flower fades, look at the spike for small, fleshy nodes and count out 3 from the base (ignore any that are dried out). Cut the spike 2.5cm (1in) above the third node.

MAINTENANCE Moderate. Fertilize twice a month with a weak fertilizer in the growing season, and water sparingly in winter. Check regularly for insect pests.

Pilea cadierei
ALUMINIUM PLANT
FAMILY **Urticaceae**

This fast-growing plant with watery stems gets it name from the silvery leaf markings on its pointed, oval leaves. Ideally suited for windowsills and tables, it can grow to 30cm (1ft).

CULTIVATION Does best in bright to filtered light. Keep the soil barely moist. Use an all-purpose potting soil.

MAINTENANCE Easy. If it becomes straggly, start new plants from cuttings or by dividing or detaching rosettes.

Plectranthus australis
SWEDISH IVY
FAMILY **Lamiaceae**

Not a true ivy, this plant is related to the mint family. Its leathery leaves are glossy green with crenate leaf edges. It is a fast-growing, trailing plant with spiky white flowers.

CULTIVATION Allow soil to dry slightly between waterings. Likes bright, indirect light. Pinch back to promote full growth.
NOTES Many types have a distinctive odour when touched.
MAINTENANCE Easy.

Saintpaulia ionantha
AFRICAN VIOLET
FAMILY **Gesneriaceae**

At the base of this flowering plant forms a rosette of green, velvet-like, round or pointed leaves from which emerge small, five-petalled flowers that come in many shapes and shades.
CULTIVATION Grow in medium light, ideally a bright, east window. Twelve hours or more light will improve flowering. Requires a moisture-retentive soil medium that is fast-draining. Water with room-tepid water from above or below, but avoid getting water on the leaves which causes spotting. Let it dry out between waterings.
NOTES It dislikes draughts and temperature changes, but if happy will flower for long periods.
MAINTENANCE Easy. Propagate from leaf cuttings or divisions. If mealybugs appear, dip a swab in rubbing alcohol and wipe off, repeating as necessary.

BELOW Schlumbergera x buckleyi.

Schlumbergera x *buckleyi*
CHRISTMAS CACTUS
FAMILY **Cactaceae**

Also called 'leaf cactus', this trailing cactus produces deep pink or red flowers in early winter. Can reach 60cm (2ft).
CULTIVATION Keep soil moist during the growing season and dry during dormancy. Can survive a low light, but you'll get more flowers in bright light.
NOTES Force your Christmas cactus to bloom in December (in the Northern Hemisphere) by keeping it in complete darkness for 12 hours a night, starting in mid-October, until buds appear.
MAINTENANCE Moderate. Feed every 2 weeks with balanced liquid fertilizer until blooms drop. Prune after blooming, if necessary.

Spathyphyluum wallisii
PEACE LILY
FAMILY **Araceae**

Favoured for its smooth, glossy, lance-shaped leaves, this is a great addition to a low-lit room. It is fun to watch a new leaf emerge as it unfolds from a sheathed stalk. In spring – and, if you are lucky, in the autumn – the spiky, cream-coloured flowers appear surrounded by white hoods (called spathes).
CULTIVATION Peace lilies like to be grown in medium or low light – direct sunlight will burn the foliage. Sensitive to dry air, they should be well-misted or placed on a tray of moist pebbles. Rarely grows higher than 65cm (26in).
NOTES To extend the blooming time, try to keep water off the flowers. Look for larger varieties, like 'Mauna Loa'.
MAINTENANCE Very easy. Considered one of the healthiest indoor plants.

Streptocarpus hybrids
STREPTOCARPUS
FAMILY **Gesneriaceae**

This robust bloomer has a rosette-forming base with coarse, crinkled, dark green, primrose-like leaves, 15–35cm

ABOVE Tolmiea menziesii.

(6–14in) long. Thin, tall flower stalks grow up from the base. Each plant bears between two and six pale-pink to dark-blue trumpet-shaped flowers. Often flowers stay all year round.
CULTIVATION Grow in bright light but not direct sunlight. They do well in warm room temperatures and need additional humidity in hotter environments. Water moderately, allowing the top half of the soil to dry out.
NOTES *S.* 'Constant Nymph' is a popular hybrid, with blue flowers.
MAINTENANCE Easy.

Tolmiea menziesii
PIGGY BACK PLANT
FAMILY **Saxifragaceae**

Has medium to dark green, hairy leaves, roughly heart-shaped with deeply lobed edges. The leaves are also deeply veined. Each leaf bears a live, young plant appearing in the axil where the leaf meets the short leaf stem. The plant can reach a height of nearly 30cm (1ft).
CULTIVATION Grow in bright light but not direct sunlight. Does well in warmer temperatures and needs additional humidity in hotter environments. Water moderately, allowing the top half of the soil to dry out.
MAINTENANCE Easy.

USEFUL ADDRESSES

SUPPLIERS

Australia

The Fruit Salad Tree Co.
T: (02) 6734 7204
www.fruitsaladtrees.com
Fruit trees with multiple fruits

Canada

M. K. Rittenhouse & Sons
T: 1-877-488-1914
www.rittenhouse.ca
Garden tools

Veseys
T: 1-800-363-7333 (toll-free)
customerservice@veseys.com
Seeds, bulbs and tools

UK

Black and Decker
T: 01753 567055
blackanddecker@mercieca.co.uk
www.blackanddecker.co.uk
Power tools and accessories

Bosch Lawn and Garden
T: 01449 742000
www.boschgarden.co.uk

Burgon and Ball
T: 01202 684141
www.burgonandball.com
Garden tools

C. K. Tools
T: 01758 704777
www.cki.uk.com

Crocus
www.crocus.co.uk
Plants and tools mail order

Darlac Ltd
T: 01753 547790
www.darlac.com
Garden tools

Dewit UK
T: 01865 552626
steve@town-garden.co.uk

Draper Tools Ltd
T: 023 8049 4333
www.drapertools.com
Garden and power tools

Eazitools Ltd
T: 01302 746077
www.eazitools.co.uk
Lightweight, strong, safe tools

Garden Images
T: 0845 130 4321
www.garden-images.co.uk
Gardening gloves and labels

Gardman
T: 01406 372222
www.gardman.co.uk
Garden products

Get Digging Ltd
www.get-digging.co.uk
Garden tools

GTech
0870 7944001
www.greytechnology.co.uk
Cordless trimmers and mowers

Handy Distribution
T: 029 2070 5295
www.b-tidy.co.uk/
Wheeled garden tidy

Harcostar Drums Ltd
T: 01663 764141
www.harcostar.co.uk
Slimline watering cans

Hozelock Ltd
T: 01844 291881
www.hozelock
Watering and pond equipment

Husqvana
www.husqvarna.com/uk to find a dealer near you
Power equipment

Magic Seeder Company Ltd
T: 01566 782064
www.magicseeder2.co.uk
Push button seedsower

Mower Magic Ltd
T: 0845 123 5844
www.mowermagic.co.uk
Garden machinery

Nucan Ltd
T: 01983 822588
www.nucan.co.uk
Controllable flow watering can

Parasene
T: 0121 508 6570
www.parasene.com
Weed wands

Peta (UK) Ltd
T: 01245 231118
www.peta-uk.com
Adaptable garden tools

Precision Seed Sower
www.mikecripps.co.uk
Seed-sowing equipment

Siesta Leisure Co.
T: 020 8683 4055
Harness for power equipment

Spear & Jackson
T: 0114 281 4242
www.spear-and-jackson.com
Hand tools

Sunrise Medical
T: 01384 446666
www.sunrisemedical.com
Wheelchair attachments

Tenax
01978 664667
www.tenax.co.uk
Seed-sowing equipment

Tynemount Ltd
T: 01488 648865
Rainstick watering device

Waterworks
waterworksnflk@aol.com
Outside tap easy-to-turn lever

A. Wright and Son
T: 0114 2722677
www.penknives-and-scissors.co.uk
Long-reach tools

Yeoman Garden Tools
www.yeomangarden.com
Trade only so refer to sites such as www.Green Fingers. com

USA

Accents in the Garden
www.accentsinthegarden.com
Garden accessories

Ames True Temper
T: 1 (800) 393 1846
www.ames.com
Wide range of garden tools

A. M. Leonard's Gardeners EDGE
T: 1 (888) 556 5676 (toll-free)
www.gardenersedge.com
Garden tools

Bigslider Utility Movers
T: 1 (713) 459 0660
info@bigslider.com
Inventive sliding utility movers

CobraHead LLC
T: 1 (866) 962 6272 (toll-free)
www.cobraheadllc.com
Cobrahead weeder

Dewitt
T: 1 (305) 888 1450
www.dewitt-tool.com
Garden cutting tools

EZ Access
T: 1 (800) 451 1903
www.ezaccess.com/ramps
Portable ramps

Felco
www.felcostore.com
Pruners, loppers and saws

Fiskars
T: 1 (866) 348 5661
www2.fiskars.com
Hand tools

Flexrake Corp
T: 1 (626) 443 4026 or (800) 266 4200; www.flexrake.com
Cleaning up tools

Gardening Supplies Guide
www.gardeningsuppliesguide.com/gardeningtools.html
Online hand and power tools

Gardening with Ease
T: 1 (800) 966 5119 (in USA)
T: 1 (603) 938 5116 (outside USA)
www.gardeningwithease.com
Ergonomically designed tools

Harmony Farm
T: 1 (707) 823 9125
www.harmonyfarm.com
Hori hori knife, irrigation systems and fertilizers

Motus
T: 1 (204) 489 8280
info@motus.ca; motus.ca
Ergonomic hand grips

Oswego Enterprises LLC
T: 1 (503) 697 1063
info@GrampasGardenware.com
www.grampasgardenware.com
Grampa's weeder

PotLifter Inc.
T: 1 (888) 644 4222
info@potlifter.com
www.potlifter.com
Potlifter to move heavy objects

Picnic Time Inc.
T: 1 (888) 742 6429 (toll-free)
www.picnictime.com
Carry baskets and garden stools

Radius Garden
T: 1 (734) 222 8044
www.radiusgarden.com

Red Pig Garden Tools
T: 1 (503) 663 9404
www.redpigtools.com
Trowels, weeders and cultivators

Seeds and Such Inc.
T: 1 (888) 321 9445 (toll-free)
nutwizard@hpcisp.com
www.seedsandsuch.com
Nut collection tool

U.S. Plastic Corp.
www.usplastic.com
Garden and storage products

Wellhaven
T: 1 (888) 564 1500
www.wellhaven.com
Gardening products

Winged Weeder
T: 1 (208) 523 0526
kirkfis@netscape.net
Winged weeder

International

Circlehoe (USA)
T: 1 (800) 735 4815
www.circlehoe.com
Weeder and cultivator

Circlehoe (Canada)
Rittenhouse & Sons
T: 1 (877) 488 1914
www.rittenhouse.ca

Circlehoe (Denmark)
Hortensia, ALROVEJ 54
Falling DK-8300, Odder

Dramm (Canada)
T: (905) 892 5644
canada@dramm.com

Dramm (USA)
T: 1 (920) 684 0227; toll-free
 1 (800) 258 0848;
garden@dramm.com
For international suppliers
 information@dramm.com
Watering and irrigation tools

Fiskars
eng-uk.fiskars.com (for UK)
www3.fiskars.com
 (international outlets)
Digging, cutting and lawn tools

Lee Valley Tools Ltd
USA: 1 (800) 267 8735 (toll-free)
Canada: 1 (800) 267 8761
 (toll-free)
Other: 1 (613) 596 0350
customerservice@leevalley.com
www.leevalley.com
Mail order and retail

Wolf Garten Tools (Germany)
info@Wolf-Garten.com
www.wolf-garten.com
International contacts
www.garden4less.co.uk
Distributes in the UK

HELPFUL ORGANIZATIONS

General

Center for Inclusive Design and Environmental Access (IDEA)
www.ap.buffalo.edu/sap/research/idea.asp
Research, education, design

Garden Forever
www.gardenforever.com
Links for those with disabilities, arthritis and allergies

Gardening for Good
www.gardening4good.org
www.gardenscape.on.ca/pages/linksenable.htm

Guelph Enabling Garden
www.enablinggarden.org

Horticultural Therapy and Therapeutic Recreation
www.horticulturaltherapy.info

Independent Living Centre NSW
www.ilcnsw.asn.au

National Center on Physical Activity and Disability
University of Illinois at Chicago
www.ncped.org
Resource material

Spinalistips
spinalistips@spinalis.se
Forum and advice for people with spinal cord injuries

Australia

The Australian Association of Occupational Therapists
www.otnsw.com.au/index.php

Australian Society for Growing Native Plants
http://asgap.org.au

Cultivate
Horticultural Therapy Soc. NSW
Telopea Centre, 250 Blaxland
Road, Ryde NSW 2112
T: 02 9448 6392

Independent Living NSW
www.ilcnsw.asn.au

Horticultural Therapy Association of Victoria Inc.
T: 61 3 9836 1128
contactus@htav.org.au
www.htav.org.au

UK

Able Products Ltd
Kilda Way, Perth PH1 3XS
T: 01738 639222
Supports disabled and older gardeners with reduced mobility

Gardening for Disabled Trust
www.gardeningfordisabledtrust.org.uk

Thrive
T: 0118 988 5688
www.thrive.org.uk
www.carryongardening.org.uk
Helps older and disabled people to continue gardening – courses, equipment lists, information service.

USA

The American Horticultural Therapy Association (AHTA)
Pennsylvania
T: 1 (484) 654 0357
www.ahta.org
Also at Denver, Colorado

American Society of Landscape Architects (ASLA)
4401 Connecticut Ave., NW
Washington, DC 2008
T: (202) 686-2752
Designers for accessible gardens

Alzheimer's Association
T: (800) 272 3900;
www.alz.org

Arthritis Foundation
T: (800) 283 7800
arthritisfoundation@arthritis.org

People-Plant Council
Department of Horticulture
Virginia Polytechnic Institute
www.hort.vt.edu.human/PPC.html
Newsletters and publications

GARDENS TO VISIT

Chicago Botanic Garden
Horticultural Therapy Services
1000 Lake Cook Road
Glencoe, Illinois 60022
www.chicagobotanic.org/therapy

Legacy Health Systems Therapy Gardens
Portland, Oregon
www.legacyhealth.org/documents/Gardens

Portland Memory Garden
SE 104th Ave & Powell Blvd
Portland, Oregon
www.portlandmemorygarden.org

Therapeutic Landscapes Network
www.healinglandscapes.org
Lists therapeutic gardens in the USA

INDEX

PLANT HARDINESS ZONES

Plant entries in the directory of this book have been given hardiness descriptions and zone numbers. Hardiness definitions are as follows:

Frost tender
A plant needing heated greenhouse protection through the winter in the local area. May be damaged by temperatures below 5°C (41°F).

Half hardy
A plant which cannot be grown outside during the colder months in the local area and needs greenhouse protection through the winter. Can withstand temperatures down to 0°C (32°F).

Frost hardy
A plant which, when outside, survives through milder winters in the local area, with additional protection. Withstands temperatures down to –5°C (23°F).

Fully hardy
A plant which, when planted outside, survives reliably through the winter in the local area. Can withstand temperatures down to –15°C (5°F).

There is widespread use of the zone number system to express the hardiness of many plant species and cultivars. The zonal system used, shown below, was developed by the Agricultural Research Service of the United States Department of Agriculture. According to this system, there are 11 zones in total, based on the average annual minimum temperature in a particular geographical zone.

Each plant's zone rating indicates the coldest zone in which a correctly planted subject can survive the winter. Where hardiness is borderline, the first number shows the marginal zone and the second the safer zone.

This is not a hard and fast system, but simply a rough indicator, as many factors other than temperature also play an important part where hardiness is concerned. These factors include altitude, wind exposure, proximity to water, soil type, the presence of snow or shade, night temperature, and the amount of water received by a plant. These kinds of factors can easily alter a plant's hardiness by as much as two zones. The presence of long-term snow cover in the winter especially can allow plants to survive in colder zones.

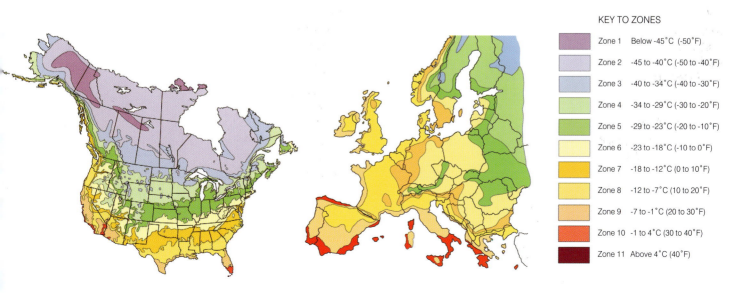

KEY TO ZONES

Zone 1	Below -45°C (-50°F)
Zone 2	-45 to -40°C (-50 to -40°F)
Zone 3	-40 to -34°C (-40 to -30°F)
Zone 4	-34 to -29°C (-30 to -20°F)
Zone 5	-29 to -23°C (-20 to -10°F)
Zone 6	-23 to -18°C (-10 to 0°F)
Zone 7	-18 to -12°C (0 to 10°F)
Zone 8	-12 to -7°C (10 to 20°F)
Zone 9	-7 to -1°C (20 to 30°F)
Zone 10	-1 to 4°C (30 to 40°F)
Zone 11	Above 4°C (40°F)

ACKNOWLEDGEMENTS

Many thanks to the companies and individuals who allowed us to take photographs in their gardens: Tony and Gillian Adams, Coxheath, Kent; Ann Adey, Normandy Community Therapy Gardens, near Guildford; Capel Manor College, Middlesex; Thrive Trunkwell Garden, near Reading, Berkshire; Elizabeth Morris and Mary Clegg, Dorset; Connie and Joy Coote, Foster House (Beach Studios), Kent; Pat and Maureen Sidders, Wittisham; Sue Martin, Brickwall Cottage Nursery, Frittenden; and Ann Frazier and Alice Turowski, Portland Oregon, USA.

Many thanks to the companies who generously provided equipment for photography or supplied us with images for reproduction (b = bottom, t = top, m = middle, l = left, r = right, c = centre, col = column): p58bl croc kneeler, Veseys; p58bm gardening stool, Picnictime; p59tl, tm, tr easy kneeler stool, Parasene; p59m Legend hedge shears, CK Tools; p60tr access ramp, EZ Access; p60br wooden ramp, Spinalist; p64 tough truck, Black & Decker; p65 mounted hose reel, Hozelock; p67tl long trowel, Draper; p67tr long-handled trowel, Spear & Jackson; p67 box top hand weeder, box middle children's shovel, box bottom pruning shears, all Ames/Truetemper; p68tl & tr easi-grip tools, Peta; p68 bottom 5 images all Radius Tools; p69tl & tr handle helper, Lee Valley Tools; p70tl backhandler spade, Veseys; p70tm & tr grip handles, Motus; p70 2 images bottom 3rd col t-clamp & arm support, Peta; p70br backsaver grip with rake, Veseys; p71tl, tm, tr easi-grip arm cuffs, Peta; p71bl & bm easy-grip handle, Peta; p72 all 5 multi-purpose tool & attachments, Wolf Garten; p77t spike aerator Ames/Truetemper; p77ml compost turner, Veseys; p77mr aerator with flanges, Rittenhouse; p81t & br backsaver auto spade, Veseys; p81b 2nd right garden spade, Eazitools; p81 3rd right edging spade, Spear & Jackson; p81 3rd left border spade, CK Tools; p81 2nd left folding shovel, Ames/Truetemper; p81bl long-handled shovel, Bellota; p82t ergonomic hand trowel; p82 2nd top hand trowel with gel grip, Ames/Truetemper; p82 3rd top hand trowel, Spear & Jackson; p82 2nd left border fork, CK Tools; p82 3rd left garden fork, Eazitools; p82 4th left long trowel, Draper; p82br post-hole digging bar, Ames/Truetemper; p84ml weeder cultivator, Ames/Truetemper; p84mm three-pronged cultivator, Ames/Truetemper; p84mr Dutch hoe, Spear & Jackson; p85tl, tr & br soil miller, Wolf Garten; p85 2 images bl hand cultivators, Ames/Truetemper; p85b, 2nd right single-wheel miller, Flexrake; p85b 3rd right garden cultivator, Ames/Truetemper; p86bl & above rootrainers seed trays, Sherwood (available via online companies); p89lt precision seed-sower, Mike Cripps; p89lm push-button seeder, Magic Seeder Company Ltd; p89lb proseeder, Tenax; p96bl bulb planter, Radius Tools; p96b 2nd right bulb planter, Ames/Truetemper; p96b 2nd left bulb planter, Dewit; p102bl pocket pruner, Lee Valley Tools; p102b 2nd left garden scissors, Darlac; p102b 3rd left garden scissors, Ames; p102b 4th left floral scissors, Ames/Truetemper; p103tm bypass pruning shears, Ames/Truetemper; p103tr bypass secateurs, Spear & Jackson; p103m 2nd from top bypass pruners, Lee Valley Tools; p103b cut-out easy reach pruners, Spear & Jackson; p103b easy reach pruner, Neill Tools; p104tl general-purpose pruner, CK Tools; p104tm anvil pruner, Ames/Truetemper; p104tr power anvil pruner, CK Tools; p104b & p105br anvil ratchet loppers, Spear & Jackson; p105t pruning

saw, CK Tools; p105 2nd top pruning saw, Lee Valley Tools; p105b far left compact shear, Fiskars; p105blm ratchet lopper, Darlac, p105b second right bypass loppers, Ames/Truetemper; p106tl hedge shears, Spear & Jackson; p106tm hedge shears, CK Tools; p106tr hedge shears, Ames/Truetemper; p106b 2nd left scissor shears, Spear & Jackson; p106br & bottom 2nd right hedge shears, CK Tools; p107 top 2 images & bottom 3rd from right edging knife, Spear & Jackson; p107bl & p107b 3rd left long-handled edging shears, Spear & Jackson; p107b 2nd left lawn shears, Ames/Truetemper; p107br top grass shears, Fiskars, p107br below grass shears, Ames/Truetemper; p108t pole pruner, Black & Decker; p108bl hedge trimmer, Spear & Jackson; p108bm & br hedge trimmer, Bosch; p109 Robomower, Husqvarna; p109b strimmer, Bosch; p114t multichange tool, Wolf Garten; p115tl hand weeder, Wolf Garten; p115tm weeding fork, CK Tools; p115tr hand weeder, Radius Tools; p115b 3rd from left push-pull weeder, Bellota; p115b 3rd right easy grip forked weeder, Peta; p115b 2nd right weeder, Radius Tools; p115br dandelion weeder, Ames/Truetemper; p116bl Hula Ho weeder, Flexrake; p116b 2nd left Grampa's weeder, Oswego Enterprises; p116b 3rd left crack weeder, Ames/Truetemper; p116 4th left ball weeder, Red Pig Tools; p116 5th left winged weeder, Winged Weeder; p116mr Hori Hori knife, Harmony Farm; p116 bml long-handled weeder, Cobrahead; p116bmr mini-circlehoe, Circlehoe; p116tr winged weeder, Burgon & Ball; p117bl pavement weeder, Dewit; p118bl & br Boronet weed puller, A. Wright and Son; p120br potlifter by Potlifter; p121tl & 2nd col 2nd down plant caddie, Rittenhouse; p121tm two-wheel wheelbarrow, Ames/Truetemper; p121r one-wheel wheelbarrow, Ames/Truetemper; p121bl garden bag, Picnictime; p121b 2nd left bees knees belt, Rittenhouse; p121b carry basket, Picnictime; p122tl folding cart, Ames/Truetemper; p122tm collapsible cart, Ames/Truetemper; p122tr leaf cart, Ames/Truetemper; p122 bottom 4 pictures folding hand truck, Draper; p123tl trolley, Black & Decker; p123tm potslider, Bigslider; p123tr easy reach pruner, Spear & Jackson; p123b tractor scoot, Ames/Truetemper; p124m watering cans, Dramm; p124b watering can, Nu-can; p125tm hose attachment, Hozelock; p125tr hose mount, Hozelock; p125b self-coiling hose, Draper; p126br watering wands, Dramm; p127tl hose guides www.crocus.co.uk; p127 bottom 2 hose reels, Ames/Truetemper; p130bl potato scoop, Burgon & Ball; p130b 2nd left lightweight snapper, Darlac; p130b 2nd right fruit harvester, Ames/Truetemper; p130br nut harvester, Ames/Truetemper; p131bl nut harvester, Seeds and Such; p131br fruit picker, Darlac; p132tl leaf rake, Yeoman; p132ml curved-head rake, Radius Tools; p132br B-tidy, Handy Distribution; p134t secateur sharpener, Neill Tools; p134lb blade sharpener,

Lee Valley Tools; p134rt diamond sharpeners, Darlac; p134rb blade sharpener, Burgon & Ball; p135tl geckohose, Veseys; p164t citrus fruit salad tree, The Fruit Salad Tree Company.

Many thanks to the models who kindly gave us their time: Tony and Gillian Adams; Jean Braban; Sue and Geoff Bylett; Bob Cooke; Connie and John Coote; Marie Cornish; David Dedrick; Heather Earl; Harry and Greta Freeman; Edward and Judith Grigg; Dorothy Hope; Brian Jenna; Keith Jenner; Sandy Marshall; Alan Martin; Leila and Peter Mellor; Fred Paine; Allen and Daphne Pincott; Hilda and Stuart Pratt; Mr and Mrs Rose; Pat and Maureen Sidders; Jim Smith; Neil and Mona Warwick; Frank Wenham; Sylvia Winwood; Michael Wood; Peter and Barbara who put up the raspberry agriframe; Sylvia, Erica, Alan and Daphne from The Canterbury Oast Trust, Woodchurch, Kent; Ann, Marilyn, Bernard and Leslie from the Wednesday group at Capel Manor, Middlesex; Keith, Michael and Jean from St Michael's Hospice, St Leonards-on-Sea, East Sussex; and an extra special thanks to Sue Martin who helped throughout the shoot.

The publishers would also like to thank the following agencies and individuals for permission to reproduce their images: Alamy: p8t A Room with Views, p19tr Blickwinkel, p44b John Glover, p60tl Allan Bergmann Jensen, p217b CuboImages srl, p221tr CuboImages srl; Adrian Burke: p6b; Patty Cassidy: p96 middle col, p176b; Felicity Forster: p154b & p155; Gap Photos: p13bm Ron Evans, p19b Matt Anker, p31t Graham Strong, p34t Lynn Keddie, p34br Gerald Majumdar, p38br S & O, p39br Friedrich Strauss, p41bl Jonathan Buckley, p55br Leigh Clapp, p56tm Linda Burgess, p58t Gap Photos, p102t Dave Bevan, p127tr Gap Photos, p135tr Elke Borkowski, p164bl Friedrich Strauss, p165b Lynn Keddie, p168t Jonathan Buckley, p208b Victoria Firmston, p211m BBC Magazines Ltd, p215b Jonathan Buckley, p218t Pernilla Bergdahl, p219b Dave Zubraski, p220t Howard Rice, p223b Jenny Lilly, p224b Dave Bevan, p225b J. S. Sira, p227t John Glover, p228t J. S. Sira, p228b Carole Drake, p229t John Glover, p230tl Martin Hughes-Jones, p232t Howard Rice, p232b Geoff Kidd, p235tr Maxine Adcock, p237b Pernilla Bergdahl, p238m Jonathan Buckley, p240b FhF Greenmedia, p241b Paul Debois, p243t John Glover, p246t Fiona McLeod, p248l Friedrich Strauss, p248m Maddie Thornhill, p249b John Glover; Garden Picture Library: p16bl Jason Ingram, p40bl Anne Green, p135b Friedrich Strauss, p159 Georgia Glynn Smith, p247t Andrew Lord; Garden World Images: p135tl Jacque Dracup, p209b Gilles Delacroix, p221tl Jenny Lilly, p231 Gilles Delacroix; Robert Highton: p126tr; istock: p15, p32, p39cl, p39 centre 2nd right, p39bl, p55t, p112bl, p112br, p142tl, p157t & br, p210t; Claire Rae: 138br; Lynn Morton p27t.